Twentieth-Ce
Europe

Twentieth-Century Europe

A Brief History

SECOND EDITION

Michael D. Richards,
Sweet Briar College
and
Paul R. Waibel,
Belhaven College

Harlan Davidson, Inc.
Wheeling, Illinois 60090-6000

Visit us on the World Wide Web at www.harlandavidson.com.

Library of Congress Cataloging-in-Publication Data

Richards, Michael D.
  Twentieth-century Europe : a brief history / Michael D. Richards and Paul R. Waibel.— 2nd ed.
     p. cm.
  Includes bibliographical references and index.
  ISBN-10: 0-88295-235-8 (alk. paper)
  ISBN-13: 978-0-88295-235-2 (alk. paper)
  1. Europe—History—20th century. I. Waibel, Paul R. II. Title.
  D424.R517 2006
  940.5—dc22
                          2005006426

Cover photograph: A woman waves EU and Czech flags in support of the Czech Republic's European Union membership, June 14, 2003. (AP Photo/CTK, Michal Krumphanzl).

Manufactured in the United States of America
13 12 11 10 09   2 3 4 5 6 VP

Contents

v

Preface

Like its predecessors, *Twentieth-Century Europe: A Brief History*, Second Edition, is intended to meet the need for a concise yet comprehensive survey of the significant themes of European history during a century of both achievement and barbarism. Although the text is short enough to permit additional outside readings, it will nevertheless serve the reader as a reliable introduction to European civilization during the twentieth century.

The authors attempt to engage the reader in several ways. We aim for a clear writing style, and one that encourages the reader to keep turning the page. Our approach is chronological. We divide the century into four parts, two before the outbreak of World War II, and two after the war begins. Each part is introduced by an "Overview" summarizing the main themes of the period covered. Each part is then divided into three chapters.

We have carefully selected and placed maps, tables, and illustrations throughout the text to aid the reader's comprehension. The maps show national boundaries at key points during the century. We have avoided cluttering them with superfluous detail. In addition, we have compiled tables either to clarify certain events (such as the German inflation of 1923) or to provide an overview of specific themes (for example, key events in the exploration of space). We have placed photographs, some from our own collections, within all the chapters to help focus the reader's interest.

Each chapter begins with a brief chronology and ends with a list of "Suggested Books and Films." While far from exhaustive, the lists will provide the student or general reader with material that is interesting and dependable. We have also included a brief essay on additional sources available for the study of European history. A list of abbreviations and acronyms and an index round out the resources available in the text.

The original book written by Michael D. Richards, *Europe, 1900–1980: A Brief History*, served as a model for the first edition of this text. That first edition, however, was in its own right a careful and thorough reconsideration of Europe's experience in the twentieth century. The second edition contains one completely new chapter (Chapter 11) and one substantially revised chapter (Chapter 12). All the other chapters have been carefully reviewed to reflect current scholarship.

We have each taught thousands of students over careers spanning more than thirty years apiece and in that time have accumulated debts to teachers, friends, and former students that can never be repaid. This book is to some extent a product of many years of conversations about European history inside and outside the classroom. We owe major debts of gratitude to our editor and publisher, Mr. Andrew J. Davidson, and to our clever and conscientious copy editor, Ms. Lucy Herz. Their encouragement and expertise have been invaluable. Finally, we are grateful for the support and encouragement of our families. Mr. Richards wishes to thank John Richards; David, Jeanne, and Will Richards; Arie, Rebecca, and John C. Richards; and also Nancy Dutton Potter. Mr. Waibel wishes to thank Darlene, Elizabeth Joy, and Natalie Grace Waibel. We sincerely hope readers will find this book both informative and enjoyable.

Michael D. Richards
Paul R. Waibel

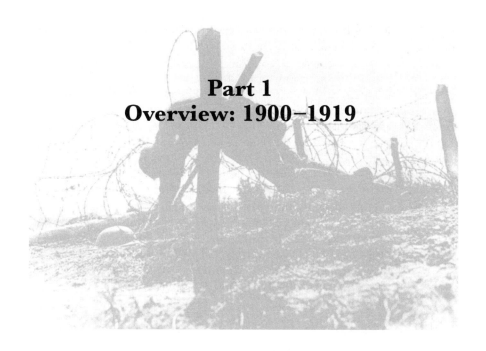

Part 1
Overview: 1900–1919

THE TWO DECADES FROM THE DAWN of the twentieth century to the end of the First World War formed the era during which European civilization peaked. It was also the period in which the very foundations of European civilization began to crack beneath the weight of inner contradictions and new challenges.

In 1900 Europeans could have said, somewhat paradoxically, that Europe was the world and the world was Europe's. For the first time in history a world civilization existed, and that civilization was European. By 1914 "Europeans" controlled 84 percent of the world's land surface. Only Japan, which since 1871 had been pursuing a self-conscious policy of westernization, was accepted as a "civilized," although non-Western, nation.

The Europeans' sense of superiority seemed confirmed by history. The Scientific Revolution, Enlightenment, and Industrial Revolution gave to the West a scientific and technological advantage over the non-Western world. By the end of the nineteenth century the lion's share of the world's wealth flowed into the Western nations.

In Europe itself, the remnants of the old aristocracy still occupied thrones and, in some countries like Russia, Germany, and Austria-Hungary, still possessed real or potential power. But the period from the end of the Napoleonic wars to the outbreak of the First World War, the Great War, in 1914, was the golden age of the middle class, or bourgeoisie. They were the

1

self-confident children of modernity, the Enlightenment tradition. Their ideology was classical liberalism, both political and economic. Their social status and, in some countries like Great Britain and France, their political power, derived from their growing wealth.

This Europe of Strauss waltzes and middle-class outings captured in impressionist paintings was being transformed just as it was reaching its fulfillment. Forces that had their origins in the nineteenth century were about to topple centuries-old dynasties and with them their archaic nobility. Likewise the middle class, the real pillar of the existing order, was under serious attack. The middle class was being challenged politically and economically by the emergence of a working class organized in increasingly powerful labor unions and political parties.

The Great War changed the course of European history. What began as a localized crisis resulting from the assassination of the heir to the Austro-Hungarian empire, rapidly escalated into a world war. All participants felt they were fighting a defensive war to save their homeland from an aggressor. All felt that the war, when it came, would be a brief one of motion, over in time for them to be home for Christmas. All were disappointed. The enthusiasm that greeted the outbreak of war in August 1914 soon changed to morbid resignation.

Since no one expected the war that began in 1914, none of the participants was prepared. By 1916, as the war at the front turned into a war of attrition in which each side tried to bleed the enemy to death, governments began to organize their home fronts. Governments assumed a role in their economies and in the private lives of their people unknown before the war. Scarce economic resources vital to the war effort were carefully rationed, as were consumer goods. Government-sponsored propaganda, together with censorship, were employed to mobilize "human resources" for more than just military service. Civil liberties often received only a polite wink, as the need to combat the spirit of defeatism grew.

Nineteen seventeen was a momentous year. In February, the German High Command persuaded the Kaiser to authorize a resumption of unrestricted submarine warfare. What was meant to bring about the defeat of Great Britain resulted in the United States coming into the war in April, thus assuring Germany's eventual defeat. In March, revolution broke out in Russia, where the Russian soldiers had voted against the war, as Lenin said, with their feet. But the Provisional Government of well-meaning liberals failed to govern effectively. In November, the Bolsheviks seized power in Russia, thus setting the stage for one of the dominant themes in twentieth-century European history.

The appearance of fresh American troops in large numbers tipped the scales in favor of the Allies on the Western Front. Allied armies broke through the Siegfried Line in July 1918. The Central Powers began to collapse. Revolution broke out in Germany. On November 9, the Kaiser abdicated and went into exile in Holland. Two days later, on November 11, Germany signed an armistice. The guns of August were finally silenced. The task of peacemaking lay ahead.

Germany had signed the armistice expecting to participate in the peace conference. It was not to be. The victors who gathered in Paris to draft a treaty that would be a fitting conclusion to the war fought to end all wars were divided between new world idealists and old world realists. What came out of the peace conference was a "victors' peace" that was to poison the future and make a second world war almost a certainty, if not a necessity.

Chronology

1899–1902	Boer War
1901	Death of Queen Victoria
1904–1905	Russo-Japanese War
1905	Revolution in Russia
	Tsar Nicholas II issues the October Manifesto
1906	Algeciras Conference
	Great Britain launches *H.M.S. Dreadnought*
1908	Austria-Hungary annexes Bosnia and Herzogovina
1914	Assassination of Franz Ferdinand

1
Before the Deluge:
Europe, 1900–1914

AT 6:30 P.M. ON JANUARY 22, 1901, Queen Victoria died at Cowes on the Isle of Wight. Although her son Edward, the Prince of Wales, was present, she died in the arms of her favorite grandson, Wilhelm II. The German Kaiser had rushed from Berlin to be at her side. Deeply moved that the Kaiser conducted himself with such stately dignity at the Queen's funeral, the new king, his "Uncle Bertie," made him a British field marshal.

Victoria (1819–1901) was more than the queen of an empire upon which the sun never set. Many throughout the world viewed her as the beloved sovereign, at least symbolically, of the civilized world. Even those peoples who were not regarded as "civilized" by Europeans revered her. Four hundred million people spread over twelve million square miles of land were her subjects. Leaders from around the world paid homage to her memory. Even in the United States flags flew at half-mast and newspaper editorials eulogized the late queen and the age to which she gave her name.

There was something very reassuring about Queen Victoria's funeral. Royalty and government leaders from all over Europe, including her grandson the Kaiser and his cousin Nicholas II, Tsar of Russia, gathered to say farewell. To have been present, or even to view the film footage of the funeral, was to be caught up in the solemn splendor of such a gathering of the world's political leadership. The observer might be pardoned for equating the pomp with power, and concluding that the future was safe and secure. But such a feeling would have been only an illusion. The fabric of European civilization was already tearing at the seams and coming unraveled.

Europe and the World

Europeans before the Great War divided the world into "civilized" and "uncivilized peoples," much as we today speak of "developed" and "developing" nations. Europeans were better housed, better fed, and better

5

clothed than people anywhere else in the world. They no longer lived in fear of unseen forces. Scientific knowledge had given them mastery over nature, showering upon them a cornucopia of material blessings. They also governed themselves, while virtually all of the non-Western world was subject to the more advanced Europeans.

Europe's monopoly over useful knowledge was largely a by-product of its critical world view. It in turn was the result of a synthesis of two traditions in European history, classical civilization and Judeo-Christianity. Both demythicized nature, treating natural phenomena as an objective reality subject to natural laws. Also, both traditions placed great value upon the individual and the role of human reason. The resulting disparity between the European nations and the non-Western world was evident in statistics on birth, death, infant mortality, and literacy rates, as well as the rapid growth of European industry. No matter what standard of comparison was used, European civilization had surged ahead, appearing to leave the rest of the world with its ancient civilizations far below on the evolutionary ladder.

Nowhere was the apparent superiority of European civilization more pronounced or consequential than in the area of military technology. It was superior military technology that enabled Europe to subdue the world in the period from the opening up of Africa in the mid-1870s to 1900. Civilizations more ancient than Europe's succumbed to the rapid fire of the machine gun.

The superiority of European arms and the Europeans' sense of moral ascendancy is well illustrated by the Battle of Omdurman in the Sudan in 1898. Sudanese tribesmen charged repeatedly a British force under the command of Major General (later Lord) Kitchener (1850–1916) armed with machine guns. When the battle was over, eleven thousand Muslims lay dead, while only twenty-eight British soldiers had been killed. Despite the smug arrogance of imperialists, to a certain degree Europe's sense of moral superiority was justified. Europe's moral values, fundamentally religious in origin, were taken over and secularized by the eighteenth-century intellectuals. Emerging from the Enlightenment as inalienable human rights, these values were summarized by John Locke and Thomas Jefferson as the individual's right to life, liberty, and property (or happiness), the foundation of classical liberalism. In practice, during the nineteenth century their enjoyment was often qualified by considerations of property and/or sexual identity.

By 1900 the "relics of barbarism," such as slavery, infanticide, blood sports, and torture, were expunged from the European nations. Even women, who were still denied the vote and full equality with men in employment and education, possessed the same human rights as every other human being. And where human rights clashed with cultural or religious practice, human rights were deemed superior. European women were not subjected to such barbarous practices as genital mutilation or *suttee*, the burning of a Hindu widow on her husband's funeral pyre. Nor were they condemned to a lifetime of illiteracy and unquestioned submission to the arbitrary will of father or husband. This message of universal and inalienable human rights went wherever the might of European imperialism was felt. For some the humanitarian impulse was as much a motivation for European imperialism as geopolitical considerations.

The civilizing mission was only one of the motives for European imperialism. In fact, many have suggested it was more a justification, or excuse, for European domination and exploitation of the non-Western world. Economic considerations were prominent, especially among policymakers influenced by neo-mercantilist arguments. They felt colonies were a vital economic resource. Expanding industrial growth in Europe itself meant that colonies would provide safe markets for finished goods, as well as safe reserves of vital raw materials. In reality, as some historians have pointed out, the cost of colonies often surpassed any economic benefit they provided for the mother country. More important was what colonies meant for national prestige and national rivalry among the European great powers.

To be regarded as a great power in 1900 necessitated possessing an empire. And the greatest power in the world during the nineteenth century, Great Britain, possessed the most impressive empire. Those who wished to challenge, or at least qualify, Great Britain's preeminent status either already possessed large colonial empires or, like the United States and Germany, were busily constructing new ones. Even Japan, always quick to adopt those aspects of Western civilization that appeared to be reasons for, or signs of, national strength and independence, was rapidly becoming a major imperial power in the Pacific. By 1900, there was an obvious correlation between national rivalry among the European great powers and their roles in the competition for empire. Both in turn were linked to the economic status of the individual great powers and the growing perception of the role of sea power in determining great-power status.

The European Great Powers

On the surface, at least, the European great powers in 1900 were the same powers regarded as such in 1815. They were the traditional five, including Great Britain, France, Russia, Austria-Hungary (the Habsburg Monarchy), and Germany (formerly Prussia). Italy was considered by many in 1900 to be a great power, but, as the events of the Great War were to demonstrate, this was more a clever ruse on Italy's part than an accurate assessment of its resources. In reality, there were only three great powers, since both Russia and Austria-Hungary lagged behind in those areas vital to maintaining great-power status into the twentieth century. Both had resisted the modernist ideas that came out of the Enlightenment, especially liberalism. There were some signs of industrialization and urbanization in the Austrian portion of the Habsburg lands and in Russia around St. Petersburg and Moscow, in Russian Poland, and the Donbas in the south. Still, both remained predominantly agrarian states of a few fabulously wealthy landlords and a multitude of poverty-stricken peasants.

Austria-Hungary

The Dual Monarchy, as Austria-Hungary was often called, maintained a cumbersome form of government with separate parliaments for Austria and Hungary. Common to both halves of the empire were ministries for war, finance, and foreign affairs. Uniting the vast multinational realm was the emperor, Franz Joseph (1830–1916), who had come to the throne in 1848, and who would stubbornly resist death until November 21, 1916. Like Queen Victoria, Franz Joseph was the much beloved symbol of a great historic tradition. The House of Habsburg was the oldest and most prestigious dynasty in Europe. But unlike Queen Victoria, Franz Joseph was committed to, and lived in, a world that no longer really existed.

If Austria-Hungary was held together by soldiers, bureaucrats, parades, and a living symbol of past glory, it was being torn apart by nationalism. Poles, Czechs, Slovaks, Serbs, Croatians, and Ruthenians were only the more numerous of the minorities who inhabited the Habsburg lands. Following defeat in the Austro-Prussian War (1866), Franz Joseph avoided dissolution of the empire by appeasing the Magyars. The result was the Dual Monarchy. By 1900, the Czechs were pressing for a further reorganization.

One solution to the problem of trying to appease so many minority populations was a triple monarchy with the organization of an autonomous Yugoslav (South Slav) state from portions of Austria and Hungary. Another was a federal state composed of a number of largely autonomous units. The greatest obstacle to any of the various solutions proposed was Magyar intransigence. Magyar elites dominated Hungarian politics and opposed any reorganization of the empire. Many, during the period before the Great War, felt that only the aging emperor himself held the empire together.

Russia

Russia had much in common with Austria-Hungary. Russia's status as a great power in 1900 rested upon its immense size and the fact that it had defeated the great Napoleon in 1812. Like Austria-Hungary, Russia was an old-fashioned agrarian state. The Romanovs, who ruled Russia since 1613, devoted their energies to the maintenance of autocratic rule. The current Tsar, Nicholas II (1868–1918), upon ascending the throne in 1894, promised: "I shall preserve the principle of autocracy as firmly and un-deviatingly as did my father."[1] The ideas of the Enlightenment, especially any thought of liberal political reform, were dismissed by Nicholas II as simplistic nonsense. Handsome, intelligent, but weak-willed and easily dominated by those around him, his one goal in life was to leave to his son and heir a Russia unchanged. He was not well suited to rule Russia in the troubled years before the Great War.

The century began badly in Russia with an economic recession, strikes, peasant disorders, and acts of terrorism. The government's difficulties increased after Russia became involved in war with Japan in 1904. Repeatedly defeated by the Japanese, the Russian government faced a rising tide of discontent at home among workers, peasants, intellectuals, and members of minority nationality groups. The Revolution of 1905 was triggered by "Bloody Sunday" in January of that year. It involved a peaceful procession to the Winter Palace in St. Petersburg, organized by a Russian Orthodox priest, to present a petition by workers to the Tsar. As the peaceful crowd marched to the Winter Palace respectfully singing "God Save the Tsar," they were fired on by troops and dispersed with a great loss of life. The event touched off waves of strikes and disturbances that led to the Tsar's issuing the October Manifesto (1905).

The October Manifesto, the document establishing the *Duma* or parliament, was seen by many as the beginning of a new era in Russian history. The revolutionary forces split. Most moderates and liberals were hopeful that a true parliamentary system would evolve. A party of moderates, the Octoberists, was founded on that hope. The major group of liberals, the Kadets, was more skeptical of the government, but it, too, hoped for the best. Some of the socialists, however, especially the Marxist revolutionaries, wanted to continue the revolution.

Liberal and moderate hopes were soon dashed. As the government regained confidence in 1906, it worked to limit the powers of the Duma and to repress any remaining signs of the revolution. In June 1907, the electoral

1 Quoted in C. L. Sulzberger, *The Fall of the Eagles* (New York: Crown Publishers, 1977), 173.

laws were changed to disfranchise many workers and those persons from non-Russian parts of the empire. The various revolutionary groups were either destroyed or forced underground.

Piotr Stolypin (1862–1911), the minister of the interior between 1906 and 1911, carried through an important series of measures that allowed a peasant to claim his land from the village commune as a unified, independent holding. The idea behind the measure was that the peasants would be more conservative politically if they had property of their own. Furthermore, if they farmed as independent farmers free of the restrictions of the commune, or *mir,* they would be more productive.

Some historians, in assessing Russia in 1914, point to the changes that the Stolypin land reforms were making, the spontaneous revival of the industrial economy, and the continued existence of institutions of parliamentary government, to justify an optimism about the solidity of the empire had it not then been wrecked by war. Others, however, emphasize continuing problems in the countryside with low productivity and over-population, the precarious and generally fruitless existence of the Duma, the chasm between educated society and the government, and the hostility between urban workers and society to buttress their case that collapse of the empire was inevitable. They also point to the lack of political leadership in Russia after the assassination of Stolypin in 1911. As with Austria-Hungary, the future did not appear bright for Russia.

Germany

Germany after 1900 was the dominant power on the continent and Great Britain's leading rival in the world. On the eve of war, Germany produced nearly a third more pig iron and twice as much steel as Great Britain, and only slightly less coal. Having industrialized much later than Great Britain, German industry was able to take advantage of new sources of power and new techniques. Hence, its electrical and chemical industries flourished. German industry produced far more than could be consumed within the Reich. After 1880, Germany rapidly increased its share of world trade. By the outbreak of war in 1914, Germany's merchant marine was the second largest in the world behind Great Britain's.

Germany's surge to world-power status was not due only to its industrial development. Germany led the world in scientific development, and, although no longer simply the land of "poets and philosophers," it still held a commanding lead in intellectual and cultural affairs. Its educational system from elementary schools through graduate universities was the model for, and envy of, all other developed countries. The number of German university students in 1911 was nearly twice the number of students enrolled in universities in any other of the European great powers.

In other areas too, Germany appeared to be the most progressive nation in the world. Under Otto von Bismarck's leadership as the first chancellor (1871–1890) of the German Reich, Germany was the first nation to develop a system of social insurance. Designed to win the support of the working class, which it failed to do, the system provided for accident and sickness insurance, old-age pensions, and unemployment benefits. English workers would have to wait until 1906–1914, and American workers until Franklin Roosevelt's New Deal (1933–1939), to receive such benefits.

But Germany was far from being a liberal democratic country in the same way Great Britain and France were. Political liberalism was defeated in Germany in the revolutions of 1848. After that, German liberals expended their energies on developing economic liberalism. The task of achieving national unity was carried out by conservatives with the enthusiastic support of the masses. Consequently, Germany emerged from the nineteenth century as one of the world's great industrial powers, but with a governmental system that can best be described as a "pseudoconstitutional absolutism."

The German crown prince Wilhelm stands over a tiger he shot in a big game hunting trip to Ceylon, c. 1912, a fitting symbol of European dominance in the world before the Great War. Photograph appears in *From My Hunting Day-Book* by Crown Prince Wilhelm.

Outwardly, Germany appeared to be a liberal constitutional monarchy. But this was only an illusion based upon the fact that the *Reichstag*, or parliament, was elected on the basis of universal manhood suffrage of all citizens over twenty-five. In fact, the Reichstag possessed little real power other than to refuse to pass the federal budget. Past experience in the Prussian parliament (1862–1866), however, left liberals with the conviction that this one "real" power was best left untested in the Reichstag.

The German Reich was in fact a federal union of individual German states in which real power was divided between Prussia, the largest state, and the *Bundesrat*, or federal parliament. Sovereignty was vested by the constitution in the Bundesrat and presided over by the Reich chancellor who was appointed by, and accountable to, the Kaiser (the King of Prussia). The delegates were appointed by the individual state governments, and voted en bloc as directed by their governments. All really significant measures required approval by Prussia. Any attempt to amend the constitution could be defeated by fourteen votes in the Bundesrat. And Prussia possessed seventeen votes.

The period from 1890 until Germany's defeat in 1918 is referred to as the "Wilhelmian era," for it was the Kaiser who determined the course of events in Germany. In foreign policy, Wilhelm II (1859–1941) charted a "new course," meant to achieve for Germany a commanding role in world affairs, or as he put it, a "place in the sun." Wilhelm II's new world policy, or *Weltpolitik*, brought Germany into conflict with France and Great Britain, especially the latter.

The "new course" meant colonies, and colonies meant a great navy capable of a commanding presence throughout the world. For Germany, the greatest military power in Europe, to build a fleet capable of challenging British naval supremacy was a direct challenge to Great Britain. It was to prove a dangerous, and ultimately disastrous, course. As in Austria-Hungary and Russia, in Germany the emperor possessed real power. Whatever the constitutional trappings, Wilhelm II ruled Germany. What made the situation dangerous for world peace was the fact that, unlike Austria-Hungary and Russia, Germany possessed the economic power and national unity to make the Kaiser's wildest dreams possible. Without responsible leadership, the German Reich was a real threat to the peace of Europe.

In the minds of many, responsible leadership was precisely what Germany lacked in the years before 1914. Special interest groups achieved positions of influence in Germany. The Bülow tariff of 1902, a protective tariff, was brought about by the cooperation of industrialists from the Rhineland and Junker landowners from East Prussia. The combination of rye and steel was powerful in Germany. Similarly, the Navy League, composed of merchants, businessmen, and the military, supported and

Kaiser Wilhelm II (1859–1941), Germany's supreme warlord in the Great War. Courtesy German Information Center.

encouraged the Kaiser's naval construction. And the general staff of the army increasingly usurped the government's prerogatives in voicing opinions or making commitments.

In the 1912 elections both the Social Democratic Party (SPD) and Catholic Center party made strong showings. If they had banded together with the Progressive Party, a majority on the left and left-center might have been created to press for a revision of the political system. Such a coalition was unthinkable, however, and Germany continued into 1914 without leadership except for that provided by nationalists and militarists.

France

France, like Germany, was an industrialized nation, although on the eve of the Great War it lagged far behind Germany, Great Britain, and the United States. Unlike its competitors, France was a nation of small businessmen, small farmers, and small manufacturers, a nation of petit bourgeoisie rather than giant industrialists. More than half of the French still made their living from agriculture.

Of the great powers, France was the most democratic. Like Great Britain, it had a parliamentary system, but in France the upper house, or Senate, was elected. Also, unlike in Great Britain with its two large political parties, in France politics found expression in numerous small parties. The proliferation of parties meant that every government was a coalition, often only briefly in office. Between 1890 and 1914, a period of only twenty-four years, France had forty-three different governments and twenty-six different premiers. At the turn of the century French politics and French society were plagued by a sharp polarization between Left and Right. In part this was historic. The Left saw themselves as the heirs of an anticlerical, democratic revolutionary tradition reaching back to 1789. The Right were conservatives, those who, from their base within the church and army, called for more order, while blaming France's decline in power on too much democracy. In short, it can be said that the Third Republic, a republic born of France's defeat in the Franco-Prussian War of 1870–1871, was divided between those who favored a republican form of government and those who desired a restoration of monarchy but were unable to determine the "rightful" monarch.

The divisions within French society intensified as a result of the Dreyfus Affair between 1894 and 1906. In 1894, Captain Alfred Dreyfus (1859–1935) was accused of selling military secrets to the Germans. Tried and convicted, Dreyfus was sentenced to life imprisonment in the infamous penal colony on Devil's Island. Believing Dreyfus was falsely charged, a group of noted politicians and intellectuals waged a public campaign for his release. Until his final exoneration in 1906, France was bitterly divided by an often violent controversy that involved anti-Semitic, anticlerical, and antirepublican issues.

Between 1906 and 1911, a period in which the Radicals (a left-center party devoted to the preservation of the French Republic and to the advancement of the interests of the "little man" in French society) were dominant, two developments unfurled. One was the emergence of a radical right movement centered on the opinions espoused in the newspaper *Action Française* and the writings of Charles Maurras (1868–1952) and Leon Daudet (1867–1942). *Action Française* favored a return to strong government at home and a highly nationalistic and aggressive policy abroad. Its views were shared by many who were not royalists but still found the Third Republic lacking. At the same time that a sizable opposition arose on the right, labor militancy increased on the left. Strikes among vineyard workers took place in 1907 and again in 1911. A major strike by postal workers occurred in 1909 followed by a strike of railroad workers in 1910. The premier, Aristide Briand (1862–1932), a former socialist, called out the troops. The railroad workers pressed for a general strike but the movement collapsed. The criticisms and demands of neither the left nor the right had been met; they had only been sidestepped. France in 1914 possessed a workable system of government provided not too many demands were placed on it.

Great Britain

In contrast to the other European great powers, Great Britain at the turn of the century appeared to be the shining example of Western Civilization in its golden age. Great Britain possessed the world's largest empire and the world's largest navy to protect it. Although its rate of economic growth was slipping behind that of Germany and the United States, especially in the key industries of steel, iron, and coal, nevertheless, Great Britain was at the center of world trade, with vast, highly profitable foreign investments. London remained the financial capital of the world.

In contrast to the appearance of political and social fragmentation in France, Great Britain possessed a stable, two-party parliamentary system. The trend in Great Britain through the nineteenth century had been in the direction of steady, if at times slow, social and political reform. Beginning with the Great Reform Bill of 1832, and including the Reform Bill of 1867 and the Franchise Bill of 1884, Parliament had gradually extended the suffrage until virtually every adult male could vote. By 1900, it appeared that Great Britain, of all of the European great powers, would make a smooth transition to democracy.

It was the Liberal Party, which came to power in 1906 and remained in power until after the Great War, that actually presided over the transition from aristocratic conservatism to popular democracy and the first signs of a future welfare state. In 1909 David Lloyd George (1863–1945), the chancellor of the exchequer and leader of the radicals within the Liberal Party, presented a budget that proposed a revision of the tax system so as to place the burden for financing the new social legislation upon the wealthiest classes. It was a radical new departure that foreshadowed the future British welfare state. The proposed budget led, not unexpectedly, to a showdown between the two houses of Parliament. The outcome severely curtailed the power of the House of Lords to veto legislation passed by the House of Commons, making the House of Commons unequivocally the center of political affairs in Britain.

The Liberals remained in power between 1906 and 1914 partly through agreements with the Labour Party and the Irish delegation to Parliament. By 1914 these agreements were fast becoming liabilities. The Labour Party was increasingly dissatisfied with its alliance with the Liberals, despite the gains made. Even more important, working-class militancy grew enormously from 1911 to 1914. A series of strikes in 1911 and 1912 reflected the influence of the idea that change would come only through direct action. In the spring of 1914 a "triple industrial alliance"of transport workers, railwaymen, and miners was formed. Beyond the control of the moderate union officials or the Labour Party, it was watched nervously in the summer of 1914.

That same spring, the question of home rule for Ireland, promised to the Irish delegation in return for their support, came before the House for the third time and passed. Ireland was to receive home rule with no separate provision for northern Ireland (Ulster). Volunteer armies in northern and southern Ireland were already in existence. Many in the British army had indicated that they would not act to enforce home rule. Civil war seemed a possibility. A militant suffragist movement completed the forces, making for what has been described as "domestic anarchy" in 1914. That summer Britain faced its worst crisis in decades.

United States of America

In the period before the Great War, the United States of America was emerging as a major power in world affairs. Its population stood at 76 million in 1900. An additional 13 million immigrants, including 1 million Jews, were added prior to 1914, mostly from central and southern Europe. The immigrants provided an energetic and willing labor force for the burgeoning northeastern industrial complex that was rapidly becoming the most productive in the world. Between 1900 and 1914 manufacturing replaced agriculture as the nation's chief source of wealth. The great captains of American industry and finance, like J. Pierpont Morgan (1837–1913), Andrew Carnegie (1835–1919), and John D. Rockefeller (1839–1937), were every bit as worthy of note as any of Europe's "robber barons." Blessed with abundant natural resources, a democratic yet business-friendly environment, and a vision of America's destiny, the United States was becoming the world's greatest industrial power.

America's rising status was not due solely to its industrial growth. The same spirit of nationalism that drove Europe's great powers was propelling the United States to establish its place in the sun. The belief in "Manifest Destiny" that drove America's expansion across the continent from the Atlantic to the Pacific oceans was thrusting the United States onto the world stage during the late-nineteenth and early-twentieth centuries. Albert J. Beveridge (1862–1927), the expansionist senator from Indiana proclaimed:

> Fate has written our policy for us. . . . The trade of the world must and shall be ours. . . . We will cover the ocean with our merchant marine. We will build a navy to the measure of our greatness. . . .[2]

The great apostle of sea power, Alfred Thayer Mahan (1840–1914), was an American. After reading Mahan's magnum opus, *The Influence of Sea Power on History* (1890), Kaiser Wilhelm invited Mahan to lunch aboard his yacht, the *Hohenzollern*, then ordered that copies of the book be placed aboard every ship in the German navy. The Japanese adopted *The Influence of Sea Power on History* as a textbook in their military and naval academies.

---

2 Quoted in Barbara W. Tuchman, *The Proud Tower, A Portrait of the World Before the War: 1890–1914* (New York: Macmillan, 1966), 154.

In 1890, America's navy was little more than a collection of "washtubs," as one congressman put it. But that soon changed.

Theodore Roosevelt (1858–1919), the flamboyant Progressive politician, became one of Mahan's disciples. "TR," or "Teddy," as he was affectionately known, had himself written a book on *The Naval War of 1812* (1882). When he became president in 1901, following the assassination of President William McKinley (1843–1901), TR took every opportunity to make America's presence felt in world affairs. In 1905, Roosevelt offered to mediate between Russia and Japan and hosted the peace conference at Portsmouth, New Hampshire, that ended the Russo-Japanese War. In the following year, Roosevelt was instrumental in persuading his admirer, the Kaiser, to agree to an international conference at Algeciras, to relieve tensions over the Moroccan crisis. In 1907, he sent the new American navy on a cruise around the world, just to show the flag. It was standard TR theatrics, a bit of bluster perhaps, but with a serious purpose.

A booming industrial plant and a great navy were two signs of great-power status, or at least the aspiration to such status. Another sign was the acquisition of a colonial empire. Here too, the United States was taking action that earned it membership in the ranks of the world's imperialist powers at the beginning of the twentieth century.

The Hawaiian Islands were formally annexed to the United States in July 1898. One month later, the Spanish-American War ended, with the United States gaining portions of the old Spanish Empire in the Caribbean and the Pacific. Puerto Rico, Guam, and the Philippines became American possessions, while the island of Cuba became, in essence, an American protectorate. In 1899, America's demand that China be open to commercial exploitation by all (the so-called "Open Door Policy") was accepted by those with interests in China. The United States asserted a kind of informal sovereignty over the Western Hemisphere. With the Roosevelt Corollary (1904) to the Monroe Doctrine, the United States asserted the right to intervene at will in the matters of any Latin-American state. When Columbia refused an offer of 10 million dollars for America's right to build a canal through Panama, the United States encouraged the Panamanians to revolt, gaining independence from Columbia. Like Cuba, Panama then became a virtual protectorate of the United States to whom it "leased" the Canal Zone.

The United States was emerging as a great power before the Great War but was not yet a member of the club. In 1917, it would enter the war to decide its outcome in favor of the Allies, but afterwards would retreat into isolation. Not until the second great war, World War II, would America reenter world affairs. During the Cold War that followed World War II, the United States would be the dominant power in the west. By the end of the century, it would emerge as the dominant power in the world, with no apparent challenger on the horizon.

The Class Structure

The class structure of Europe before the Great War was still a pyramid, with a handful of very wealthy at the apex and a great multitude of poor at the base. The ruling aristocracy at the turn of the century was a union of the old landed wealth and the new industrial wealth. Titled, land-owning families with pedigrees that stretched back for centuries formed marriage alliances of convenience with the wealthy new plutocrats of commerce and industry. This new elite shared common patterns of education and consumption, and similar economic and political views. Generally, the greater the industrialization of a nation, the closer was the upper middle class tied to the government. Peers of the realm and the giants of industry and commerce (the "robber barons") often had the same values, the same political interests, and the same condescending attitude towards the propertyless classes at the base of the pyramid.

The Working Class

Most of those at the base of the pyramid were better off in 1900 than previously. At least this was true for those living in the industrialized nations of Great Britain, France, Belgium, and Germany. For them, the quality of life was improving. Not only had real wages risen, but purchasing power had almost doubled in the decade before 1914. Even so, poverty was a reality for most Europeans, even for those in the most prosperous nations.

Out of a population of 44.5 million in Great Britain before the war, 15.5 million earned less than £50 a year. This at a time when the "poverty line" was estimated to be £55 a year for a family of five.[3] One study of London households in 1899 revealed that almost one-third of the inhabitants of the world's richest city lived in poverty. Poverty was even more pervasive in the less industrialized areas of eastern and southern Europe. Life expectancy in the Balkans and in Spain remained at less than thirty-five in 1900.[4]

Politically, the laboring classes were attracted to ideologies that, in contrast to liberalism, emphasized equality of reward over equality of opportunity. The two most attractive political ideologies were anarchism and Social Democracy (i.e., Marxism). Anarchism sought the violent overthrow of all existing order and the establishment of a stateless, voluntary order in

3 Tuchman, *The Proud Tower*, 27.
4 Cited in William Carr, *A History of Germany, 1815–1945*, 2nd ed. (New York: St. Martin's Press, 1979), 157.

its place. Anarchism was most appealing to the urban and rural unemployed in the more backward regions of eastern and southern Europe.

More important than anarchism was the appeal of Social Democracy for the working class in the more industrialized nations of northern and western Europe. Grounded in Marxism, Social Democracy was undergoing a transformation by 1900. Known as "revisionism" in Germany, the emphasis was shifting away from revolution to evolution. Also, like the Fabian socialists that influenced the Labour Party in Great Britain, the revisionist Social Democrats in Germany looked more and more to a future welfare state as their goal, rather than the classless utopia of Marx's dreams.

The German Social Democratic Party (SPD) was the strongest in Europe. Publicly, it staunchly defended Marxist orthodoxy on the need for revolutionary overthrow of bourgeois society and the state. At the same time, many within the party worked for limited improvements by legislative action. This was undoubtedly the goal of the German trade union movement. Although acceptance of the industrial system was never made explicit by the SPD or the trade unions, there were numerous indications that it was tacitly accepted by large numbers within both groups.

The SPD and the German working class have been characterized as existing in a state of "negative integration" with German society in the early part of the twentieth century. Mutual hostility and suspicion prevailed; integration was only partial in that the SPD and the working class did not (and often were not allowed to) participate fully and positively in all aspects of German life. Yet the SPD was set firmly in the framework of German society and German workers participated in national life in many ways. Examples might include the veneration of the Kaiser or working-class fascination with the growth of Germany as a world power.

In general, the working class in Europe reacted to changing circumstances less according to national characteristics than according to the stage of industrialization reached in a particular area. Where experience was lacking, hostility and friction were vented in radical and often violent protest. Where experience with industrial life reached back over two or three generations, a durable if not always satisfying relationship between working class and industrial order emerged. For workers in Britain, France, Belgium, and Germany, the industrial system was becoming increasingly acceptable, even if expectations always seemed to race ahead of fulfillment.

The Middle Classes

In later decades, the middle classes were to view the era before 1914 largely as a golden age, *les bon vieux temps,* "the good old days." In retrospect it seemed that there had never been a better time for the well-to-do than in the two decades before the war. A prosperous middle-class family with an annual income of $10 thousand could employ a staff of ten full-time servants for only one-quarter of that income. One measure of middle-class standing was the ability to employ one full-time maid.

Economic opportunities abounded, political influence was increasing, and even social prominence was on the rise. The changing economic structure offered few opportunities for individuals or families to own and control their own enterprises, but this was compensated for by an expansion of positions within management and the civil service. Wider educational opportunities also made it possible for many to enter the professions or the upper reaches of government bureaucracies. Possibilities, especially in western Europe, of achieving a comfortable income and a commensurate status were good.

The middle class was not a unified group. The views of one group of businessmen often conflicted with those of professionals or other business groups. The middle class was, nonetheless, a formidable political power in states where parliamentary government was well established. Politics was increasingly the preserve of professionals, both elected and unelected, and the middle class supplied more and more of these people. At the same time, the middle class furnished the leadership of most major European political parties. This was true even of some socialist parties, where renegade members of the middle class formulated most of the policies and interpreted doctrine for the rank-and-file. Governments were increasingly sympathetic to middle-class views, as demonstrated by the trend toward protective tariffs and other legislation favorable to business.

The middle class was beginning to set the tone for all of society. The activities of the aristocracy and particularly the royal families of Europe were still of great interest to many Europeans, but, more and more, standards were set by a new elite drawn from both the middle class and the aristocracy. The upper class with its vast wealth became an important source of patronage for the arts and had a significant influence on fashion and style.

The lower middle class, like the middle class, was not a unified group. One component, the independent lower middle class of shopkeepers, merchants, and artisans, had long been a part of the European scene. It had emphasized familiar middle-class ideals of family, property, and respectability. A second component, largely dependent, was a product of recent structural changes in the economy. The expansion of distribution and sales, together with the increased complexity of organization, required vast numbers of clerks, salespeople, and technicians. Governments also began to require larger and larger numbers of clerical and technical personnel.

Both elements of the lower middle class had in common a sense that in terms of status and behavior they were distinct from the working class. As regards income, the lower middle class no longer earned a great deal more than the working class. Lower-middle-class people spent their money differently, however, either buying or saving mainly for items connected with social status, such as a piano; the working class tended to spend on immediate pleasures. The intense consciousness of status was reflected not only in the behavior but also in the politics of the lower middle class, which was usually conservative, antisocialist, and sometimes also anti-Semitic. In politics the lower middle class favored parties such as the Radical Party in France or the Christian Social Party in Austria, parties that catered to the "little man" and stressed the importance of order, property, and attachment to the nation.

Like the middle class, the lower middle class enjoyed the good times of the era before 1914 including prosperity, status, and political power. Living in close proximity to the lower classes, the lower middle class tended to take the good times less for granted than the middle class and to be more anxious about any developments that might threaten their position in society.

The Coming of the War

The long-term causes of the war included the economic and imperial rivalry between the great powers and the armaments race, especially the naval race between Germany and Great Britain. The holding of two peace conferences at The Hague in 1899 and 1907 belied the fact that the participants were arming for war. Many of the tensions between the great powers resulted from the loss of a balance of power in Europe following the Franco-Prussian War and unification of Germany in 1871.

A system of defensive alliances substituted for the balance-of-power principle as the mechanism for maintenance of peace in Europe after 1871. The alliance system was largely the work of German chancellor Otto von Bismarck. According to Bismarck's reasoning, France was the major threat to peace because of its defeat in the Franco-Prussian War and its desire to avenge that affront to French national honor. It became Bismarck's goal in foreign policy to isolate France. Referring to the traditional five great powers of Europe, Bismarck said: "The key was always to be in a majority of three in any dispute among the five great European powers."[5]

---

5 Quoted in *The Great War and the Shaping of the 20th Century, Episode One: Explosion* (Burbank, CA: PBS Home Video, 1996).

The first and most enduring of Bismarck's alliances was the Dual Alliance between Germany and Austria-Hungary concluded in 1879. The Dual Alliance provided that one partner would aid the other in the event that either was attacked by Russia. The Triple Alliance, concluded in 1882 between Germany, Austria-Hungary, and Italy, bound the three to act together in the event that either Germany or Italy was attacked by France. To allay Russian fears of a hostile Austro-German alliance, Bismarck signed the Reinsurance Treaty with Russia in 1887. It provided for one partner assuming a policy of benevolent neutrality, if the other partner were attacked. Thus France was left isolated, while Germany was allied with the other great powers on the continent. Peace was maintained, that is, until Bismarck's retirement in 1890, when the alliance system began to unravel.

Now Wilhelm II's "new course" in foreign policy, which aimed at elevating Germany to world-power status, was a direct challenge to Great Britain's position as the world's leading power. The threat of a great German navy that would rival Britain's control of the seas, together with a growing feeling of diplomatic isolation resulting from the Boer War in South Africa (1899–1902), led the British to abandon "splendid isolation" and seek allies. In 1902, Britain concluded the Anglo-Japanese Alliance, followed in 1904 and 1907 by two informal "understandings," or "ententes," that resolved outstanding imperial disputes with France and Russia, respectively. Autocratic Russia was already in a formal defensive alliance with democratic France since December 1894. Russia, one might justly say, was pushed into the waiting arms of France by Wilhelm's decision not to renew the Reinsurance Treaty in 1890. The alliances between France, Russia, and Britain, when considered together, comprised what became known as the Triple Entente. By 1907, Europe was divided into two increasingly hostile camps, the Triple Alliance and the Triple Entente.

The existence of a potentially dangerous new power alignment in Europe was evident at the Algeciras Conference in January 1906, the last time the European great powers would meet together in congress before the outbreak of the Great War. Germany provoked a crisis over Morocco in north Africa, desiring to drive a wedge between France and Britain, support the Sultan of Morocco in his bid to resist French imperialism, and make a public demonstration of Germany's claim to world-power status. Germany was outmaneuvered on all three. In the end, Britain and France stood together against Germany and were joined by Germany's ally in the Triple Alliance, Italy. Bismarck's alliance system was now undone. Germany, now supported only by Austria-Hungary, was isolated, as France had been in 1890. Rather than demonstrating Germany's world-power status, its vulnerability was exposed.

Soon the Balkans emerged as the new "hot spot" in Europe just as the continent was polarizing into two hostile camps. In 1908, Austria-Hungary annexed Bosnia and Herzegovina, which it had been administering since 1878 on behalf of Turkey. Austria's action, supported by Germany, inflamed Serbian nationalism. The Serbs had hoped to create a Great Serbia in the Balkans, and they regarded Bosnia, with its large Serbian population as a necessary part of an independent state. Serbian nationalism was encouraged by the Russians, who, following their defeat in the Russo-Japanese War (1904–1905) turned their attention once again to their opportunity in the Balkans with the increasing disintegration of Turkish power there. The Balkans was becoming the focus of European great power diplomacy.

The Great War started over an incident in the Balkans, as predicted decades before by Otto von Bismarck. The Balkans, noted Bismarck, was an area the whole of which was not worth "the healthy bones of a single Pomeranian musketeer."[6] The incident that served as the impetus for war was the assassination of Archduke Franz Ferdinand, heir to the throne of Austria-Hungary, by a Serb. But it was not for the Archduke that the guns of August were unleashed, for upon hearing of the death of his nephew, of whose marriage he disapproved, the aging emperor expressed relief—it was, he believed, divine judgment.

If Austria had acted promptly to punish Serbia for its part in the assassination, the rest of the world would no doubt have accepted its decision. But Austria hesitated. Austrian prestige demanded some military action against Serbia, but prudence, or perhaps fear, demanded that Germany's backing be secured first. The delay allowed time for Russia to conclude that Russian prestige could not allow Austria to crush Serbia. Similar crises had occurred in the past but were resolved by diplomacy. In the final analysis, what transformed the July crisis into the cause célèbre for the Great War was a failure of diplomacy.

On July 5, Austria obtained assurance of German support for whatever action it chose to take against Serbia. Germany believed that the so-called "blank check" was justified in part, because it feared for its own position in Europe should Austria decline as a power. Germany did, however, expect Austria to act while world opinion was still favorable. But Austria delayed further, first to win over Count Istvan Tisza (1861–1918), prime minister of Hungary, and then to investigate Serbia's actual role in the assassination. In the meantime, Russia's position had begun to harden, and it warned Austria that it would not tolerate the humiliation of Serbia.

6 Quoted in William Carr, *A History of Germany, 1815–1945*, 2nd ed. (New York: St. Martin's Press, 1979), 157.

Austria ignored the warning and presented an ultimatum to Serbia on July 23. Serbia accepted all but one term which, by allowing the Austrians to take part in the Serbian investigation of the assassination plot, would have infringed on its sovereignty. Serbia's reply was seen by all the powers, Germany and Austria included, as remarkably conciliatory. Yet Austria, went ahead with mobilization and a declaration of war on July 28. Germany was beginning to have second thoughts by this time but did not effectively apply pressure to halt Austrian preparations for war

Also on July 28, the Russians ordered a partial mobilization and then, for technical reasons, on July 30 ordered full mobilization. Otherwise, it was felt, Russia would have no chance of influencing Austria. Russian mobilization made it imperative that Germany put the Schlieffen Plan into effect. Since this plan called for Germany to deal with France first, then quickly turn back to the east, each day that the Russians had to mobilize before the Germans launched their drive to the west further jeopardized the success of the plan. After Russia's mobilization, it was all a matter of railroad timetables. Germany attacked France, violating Belgian neutrality in the process. Britain came into the war to aid the French and to defend the principle of neutrality. Of all the great powers, only Italy remained, for the time being, out of the conflict.

Some of the very elements that had made Europe master of the world worked in the Great War to destroy it. Industrial productivity and the capacity to mobilize troops and money made possible the carnage few Europeans could have anticipated before 1914. The five years of war and revolution damaged the fabric of European life beyond repair. The contradictions of the prewar period, more or less successfully repressed at the time, emerged to challenge old certainties. It was the end of one era and the beginning of another, and darker, one.

Suggested Books and Films

Oron J. Hale, *The Great Illusion, 1900–1914* (1971); Edmond Taylor, *The Fall of the Dynasties: The Collapse of the Old Order, 1905–1922* (1963); and Barbara W. Tuchman, *The Proud Tower: A Portrait of the World Before the War, 1890–1914* (1966). Very readable overviews of the period before the Great War.

Mollie Hardwick, *The World of Upstairs, Downstairs* (1976). A lively illustrated social history of Britain from the turn of the century to the Great Depression based upon the popular BBC series.

Adam Hochschild, *King Leopold's Ghost: A Study of Greed, Terror, and Heroism in Colonial Africa* (1998). A well-written, much-praised case study of the dark side of European imperialism in Africa and the Belgian king whose plantation in the Congo triggered the "scramble of Africa."

James Joll, *The Origins of the First World War* (1984); Laurence Lafore, *The Long Fuse: An Interpretation of the Origins World War I* (1971); Annika Mombauer, *The Origins of the First World War: Controversies and Consensus* (2002); and Barbara W. Tuchman, *The Guns of August* (1962). Exellent studies of the causes and early fighting of the Great War.

Roland Robinson and John Gallagher, with Alice Denny, *Africa and the Victorians* (1981). A study of the strategic motivation behind European imperialism.

A. J. P. Taylor, *The Struggle for Mastery in Europe, 1848–1919* (1954). Still the best scholarly study of the diplomatic background to the war.

The Guns of August, 1993, MCA/Universal Home Video that surveys the war using contemporary film footage.

Montparnasse Revisited: The Brilliant Years—1900–1914, 1993, Momevision. A look at the artistic life of Paris before the war.

Nicholas & Alexandra, 1971, Hollywood drama about tsarist Russia.

Upstairs, Downstairs, 2002, A&E Home Video. Widely acclaimed BBC series on the British upper class at the turn of the century.

Chronology

2
The Great War, 1914–1917

THE WAR THAT THE DIPLOMATS failed to prevent in July 1914 was not the war the generals were prepared to fight. During that fateful month, they had assured their reluctant monarchs that the conflict would be a brief and glorious little war, not unlike the wars of German unification, where the rapid deployment of troops on open battlefields decided the day. Indeed, the military strategies that the generals were schooled in differed little from those of the wars of Napoleon a hundred years earlier. But a century of technological "progress"—railroads, telegraphs and telephones, airplanes, submarines, machine guns, tanks, poison gas, flame throwers, and a host of other wonders of modern civilization—shortly transformed a little war in the Balkans into the Great War, the First World War.

The blustery saber-rattling monarchs of those ancient and soon-to-be vanquished empires of Germany, Austria-Hungary, and Russia tried to avert war in the final hours before the guns began firing. There was a rapid exchange of notes between Wilhelm II and his cousin, Nicholas II. Nicholas pleaded with Wilhelm to restrain Austria, for he was being "overwhelmed by pressure" and would soon "be forced to take extreme measures" leading to war.

Neither was the Kaiser, Germany's supreme warlord, in command of events. As the German chancellor Theobald von Bethmann-Hollweg (1856–1921) related to the Prussian Council of Ministers on July 30, despite the peaceful intentions of everyone concerned, events progressed under their own momentum. If anyone was in control of the direction of those events as the crisis deepened, it was the generals. But they, themselves, were captive to plans for mobilization and war that they felt unable to vary or tinker with in even the most minute detail.

The Failure of the Schlieffen Plan

The fateful role played by the war plans was particularly evident in the case of Germany. The German plan for war, known as the Schlieffen Plan after

27

General Alfred von Schlieffen (1833–1913), Chief of the German General Staff from 1891 to 1905, presupposed a two-front war with France and Russia. It was a bold plan that called for the rapid movement of German forces through neutral Belgium to the north and west of Paris, in a sweeping arc that would encircle and crush the French armies. Once this had been accomplished, German forces would turn back to the Eastern Front in time to deal with the Russian armies, which would just then be completing mobilization, according to German calculations. Within six weeks the war would be over and Germany's position as a world power secured. The Schlieffen Plan was a daring gamble that came close to succeeding, but it failed.

While the Schlieffen Plan looked good on paper, a number of miscalculations and unforeseen exigencies interfered with its successful execution. On July 31, Germany refused a British demand that Belgium neutrality, guaranteed by international treaty since 1839, be respected. Three days later Belgium rejected a German demand for free passage across its territory. By the afternoon of August 3, German troops were pouring into Belgium. On August 4, Germany declared war on Belgium, referring to the 1839 treaty as "a scrap of paper."Although no match for the swiftly advancing Germans, the Belgians put up a valiant fight, slowing the German advance and costing the German army time critically needed if the Schlieffen Plan were to succeed.

Belgian resistance was not factored into the Schlieffen Plan. Neither was the speed with which the Russians threw an army into East Prussia on August 17. To meet the Russian threat, and believing the war against France already won, General Helmuth von Moltke (1848–1916) detached two corps from his vital right wing and sent them east. It was a fatal error, which, together with other corps detached to hold the Belgians at Antwerp, seriously weakened the German army's right wing, upon which the Schlieffen Plan depended for its success. On August 30, with the Schlieffen Plan days behind schedule, Moltke began to have doubts. He turned his right flank south, while still east of Paris. This maneuver opened the door for the French commander-in-chief, Joseph Joffre (1852–1931), to launch a counterattack against the German left flank along the Marne River.

The First Battle of the Marne, September 5–9, remembered as the "Miracle of the Marne," saved France from defeat by halting the German advance. Meanwhile in the East, the Russian advance had been halted at the Battles of Tannenberg Forest (August 30) and Masurian Lakes (September 15). General von Moltke resigned in disgrace. General Aleksandr Samsonov (1859–1914), the Russian commander at the Battle of Tannenberg, attempted to redeem his honor by committing suicide. Field Marshal Paul von Hindenburg (1847–1934) and General Erich Ludendorff, (1865–1937)

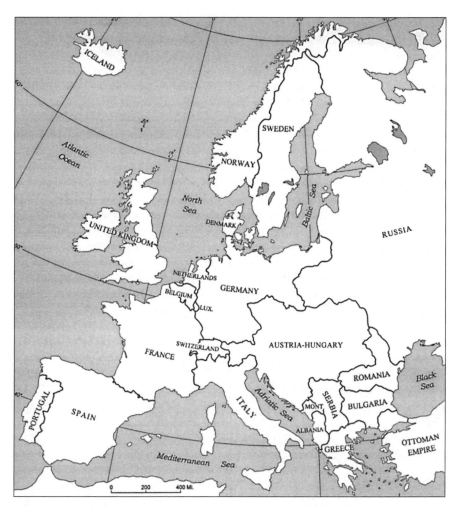

Europe in 1914

the victors of Tannenberg, emerged heroes and, as the war progressed, became virtual military dictators of Germany.

Many volumes have been written by historians trying to explain both the cause of (and who was to blame for) the outbreak of the Great War and the reasons for the failure of the Schlieffen Plan. With respect to the former, it is true, as the German historian Fritz Fischer has alleged, that Germany ambitiously pursued world-power status. It is also true, as the English historian A. J. P. Taylor has demonstrated, that the German plan for mobilization was tantamount to a declaration of war, since mobilization was to be completed inside France and Belgium. When all the arguments and counterarguments have been considered, however, David Lloyd George's comment that the European great powers simply slithered over the brink into a war no one desired remains the best explanation. Diplomacy had failed. In a similar vein, the historical consensus today is that the Schlieffen Plan was a desperate gamble that under the best of circumstances was not likely to succeed.

What followed the defeat of the Schlieffen Plan in the West was the so-called "race to the sea." The opposing armies tried to outflank each other, as they steadily moved north to the English Channel. By December 25, the soldiers, who went into battle with expectations of being home for Christmas, stood opposite each other in a line of trenches that stretched from the English Channel in the north to Switzerland in the south, a distance of about four hundred miles. There followed nearly four years of stalemate, wherein the line of trenches remained virtually unchanged despite the expenditure of millions of casualties in futile attempts to break through the lines and turn the stalemate into a war of motion the generals could understand. This "troglodyte world" of trench warfare would later strain the imaginations of artists, writers, and poets, as they tried to depict it for those who had not experienced it firsthand.

Trench Warfare

The Great War was like no other war before it, although there were some hints of what this first industrial war might entail. The American Civil War (1861–1865), the Boer War (1899–1902), and the Russo-Japanese War (1904–1905) each foreshadowed in some way what "industrialized warfare" would mean. Even "Queen Victoria's little wars" in the colonial world should have provided some insight. The effectiveness of rapid-firing machine guns at, for example, the Battle of Omdurman in the Sudan (1898) demonstrated the obsoleteness of massed cavalry or infantry charges in modern warfare. But these lessons were lost on the generals who planned the battles of the Great War. Unlike the campaigns of Julius Caesar or the great Napoleon, the more recent battles were not in the textbooks studied at Europe's prestigious military academies. In response to the machine guns, the soldiers went underground.

Siegfried Sassoon (1886–1967), a British infantry officer and war poet, once commented that "when all is said and done the war was mainly a matter of holes and ditches." And these holes and ditches were enormously complicated. For example, the French system, with a frontage of about 270 miles, contained approximately 6,250 miles of trenches

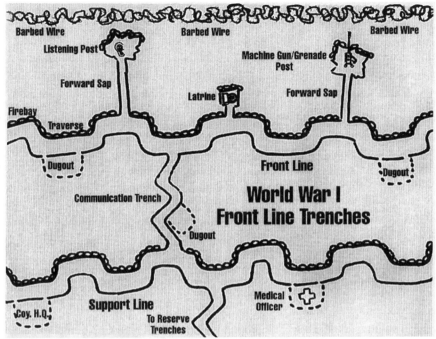

Barbed Wire
Listening Post
Forward Sap
Firebay
Traverse
Barbed Wire
Machine Gun/Grenade Post
Latrine
Forward Sap
Barbed Wire

Dugout
Communication Trench
Dugout
Front Line
Dugout

World War I Front Line Trenches

Coy. H.Q.
Support Line
To Reserve Trenches
Medical Officer

Along the Western Front from the English Channel to the Swiss border was an elaborate complex of zigzagging trenches in parallel lines. Courtesy Dayton Castleman.

of one sort or another. Trenches usually were arranged in three roughly parallel lines: first was the front-line trench; then several hundred yards behind this was the support trench; and finally, another few hundred yards behind the second line of trenches ran the reserve trench. In addition to the three parallel lines of trenches, the firing trenches from which attacks were launched and enemy attacks repulsed, there were various trenches running perpendicular to the firing trenches. Behind the front there were communication trenches along which came ammunition, reinforcements, and food. Running out from the front line into No Man's Land were "saps," shallow ditches leading to forward observation and listening posts, grenade-throwing and machine-gun posts. Dimensions of firing trenches varied, but they would almost always be deeper than a man was tall, with, on the enemy side, a parapet of earth or sandbags rising another two or three feet off the ground. Trenches were built in a zigzag fashion to minimize damage from shelling and to make it difficult for an attacking enemy to clear a trench. In the sides of the trenches were one- or two-man holes, "funk-holes," and deeper dugouts. There was something of a national style in trenches: German trenches tended to be deeper, drier, and more elaborate than British or French systems; the British systems seemed the most provisional and least carefully worked out.

With the digging of the trenches the war of motion, the war the generals understood, ended. Throughout the war the generals on both sides hoped to break the stalemate on the Western Front and turn the war into a war of motion once again. The strategy for the great breakthrough was the same on both sides. Large numbers of troops were massed at some spot along the front. Artillery bombarded the enemy trenches unceasingly (for seven days and nights at the Battle of the Somme) to "soften up" the enemy's position. Then, the artillery fell silent, and the command was given for the infantry to "go over the top" and across the No Man's Land of 100 to 500 yards before meeting the first line of the enemy's trenches. Trudging through a barren waste of barbed wire, shell holes, and rotting bodies from previous failed assaults, the advancing infantrymen were cut down by enemy machine guns. Perhaps the first line of trenches would be taken, but eventually the assault failed, and the advancing columns, or what was left of them, fell back to their own trenches to await counterattack. And so it continued, without significantly altering the line of opposing trenches.

The sights and sounds of trench warfare were enough to change forever those who experienced it. The sight of mass mutilation was everywhere. Ernst Jünger (1895–1998), a novelist who won Germany's highest decoration, described a scene near the front at the Somme after enemy artillery made a direct hit on a house where German soldiers were quartered:

> We grabbed the limbs sticking out of the rubble and pulled the corpses out. One was missing its head, and the neck sat on the torso like a large bloody fungus. On another shattered bones protruded from the stump on an arm, and the uniform was sodden with blood from a huge chest wound. On a third the innards flowed forth from a body that had been slit open. As we were pulling this one out, a splintered board that had stuck in the terrible wound gave resistance, making gruesome sounds.[1]

An Englishman whose dugout was hit with a shell took a photograph of his dead comrade lying next to him, his body "laid open from the shoulders to the haunches like a quartered carcass in a butcher's window."[2] Such scenes were not easily forgotten when the war was over.

Between assaults, life in the trenches was an incessant struggle against boredom, extremes of weather, and the pitiless assault of the vermin that

1 Quoted in Modris Eksteins, *Rites of Spring: The Great War and the Birth of the Modern Age*, (New York: Anchor Books, 1990), 152.
2 Ibid.

infested the trenches. At Flanders rains transformed the battlefield into a quagmire of mud into which a fallen soldier could disappear from sight and drown. Winter along the Western Front could be so cold that wine froze in November, and rations turned into chunks of ice. To such discomforts were added the ever present battle against vermin attracted by the stench of the trenches and the men and corpses that occupied them.

Some of the pests, such as flies, fleas, and mosquitoes were a nuisance that the battle-hardened warrior could get used to, but the lice and the rats were different. Lice laid their eggs in the soldiers' clothing and multiplied with terrifying speed. Nothing helped. Hot baths and washing clothing, when possible, brought only temporary relief. Soldiers on both sides took consolation in the belief that the lice afflicting the enemy were larger.

Rats were everywhere, attracted by the rotting corpses in the trenches. Soldiers reported rats as large as cats or small dogs. The battle against the rats, fought with spades, clubs, or whatever was readily at hand, was an unceasing one. For some, "rat-hunting" became an obsession, vented during the interludes between assaults. The only relief from the rats and other vermin came as a result of a gas attack, which temporarily cleared the trenches of vermin. But, like the enemy across No Man's Land, the rats and the lice returned.

The enthusiasm that greeted the call to arms in July–August 1914 died in the trenches. The trenches bred a sense of alienation and estrangement from civilian life and values that endured long after the war. The life the soldiers lived before the war seemed distant and unrecoverable. Life in the trenches had to be experienced to be understood. If the civilians back home could somehow see it, wrote Wilfred Owen (1893–1918), one of England's greatest poets, who died one week before the Armistice, then

> My friend, you would not tell with such high zest,
> To children ardent for some desperate glory,
> The old Lie: Dulce et decorum est
> Pro patria mori.[3]

The Course of the War: 1915

Though the Schlieffen Plan had failed, the Germans were in a strong position at the beginning of 1915. They had gained control of Belgium and the industrialized northern regions of France. General Erich von Falkenhayn (1861–1922) assumed command from the failed Moltke. Falkenhayn launched a major offensive against the British in April at Ypres. The battle,

---

3 "It is sweet and becoming to die for one's country," a quotation from the Roman poet, Horace.

known as the Second Battle of Ypres (April 22–May 24), is primarily remembered for the first poison gas attack of the war. Taking advantage of favorable winds, the Germans released the gas from canisters in their own trenches. (The British first used gas at the Third Battle of Artois in September–October 1915.) The surprise gas attack opened a large gap in the British lines, but the Germans were not prepared to take full advantage of it. They broke off the attack in late May. After the failure at Ypres, the Germans assumed a defensive posture on the Western Front, while attempting to defeat the Russians in the East and rescue their beleaguered ally, Austria-Hungary.

Austria, who many believed had started the war, was on the verge of collapse by the end of May 1915. A Russian offensive in 1914 had captured Galicia and threatened Hungary. Italy, having defected from the Triple Alliance in 1914 by declaring neutrality, succumbed to Allied bribes and declared war on Austria-Hungary on May 23, 1915. (It did not declare war on Germany until August 28, 1916.) Also, Austria's conscripts from among its polyglot empire's minorities were deserting in large numbers. To save the situation, the Germans launched a major offensive on the Eastern Front. The Russians fell back, abandoning not only Galicia, but Poland also. The Germans, however, were unable to achieve their objective of trapping the Russian armies.

Millions of soldiers died on the Western Front along the "Path of Glory." Here a British soldier lies among the barbed wire in November 1918. Courtesy Library of Congress.

If victory eluded the Germans in 1915, so too did it elude the Allies. The Italians entered the war militarily unprepared. As the war dragged on, they proved to be more of a burden than an asset to the Allies. In an effort to relieve pressure on the Western Front, an Anglo-French force attempted to capture the Dardanelles, a plan masterminded by David Lloyd George and Winston Churchill (1874–1965). The poorly planned and bungled landing at Gallipoli on April 25 proved a disaster. Churchill resigned his cabinet post. Lloyd George was appointed Minister of Munitions.

Direction of Allied war efforts in the West remained in French hands during 1915. Joffre, no longer believing that one great victory would end the war, hit upon a plan to bleed the enemy to death, what the French called the "war of attrition." The phrase later took on a surrealistic life beginning with the Battle of Verdun in February 1916. Meanwhile, Joffre launched a series of offensives beginning in May. By the end of the year, despite great losses, the Allies had gained nothing. The front remained virtually unchanged from where it had been at the beginning of the year.

There was fighting in the Middle East as well, where the Ottoman Empire fought as an ally of Germany and Austria. The British, with the help of forces from India, Australia, and New Zealand, were able to protect the Suez Canal and oil installations. In return, they worked to encourage Arab nationalism against the Ottoman Empire. They and the French laid the basis for much of the present dilemma in the Middle East by making contradictory promises to Arab nationalists and to Zionist organizations seeking a national Jewish homeland.

Sausage Machine: 1916

The common soldier, we are told by the British novelist and poet Robert Graves, spoke of the front as the "sausage machine," because "it was fed with live men, churned out corpses, and remained firmly screwed in place."[4] A sausage machine was an appropriate image for the major battles fought along the Western Front during 1916. Each side began the year believing that the elusive great breakthrough could be achieved by massing enormous quantities of men and firepower along a limited sector of the front.

The Germans set the example at the Battle of Verdun. Verdun was of no strategic importance to either side, but General Falkenhayn believed, correctly, that the French would defend it doggedly. Falkenhayn reasoned that if the Germans could kill five French soldiers for every two Germans the French killed, it was possible to bleed the French white at Verdun.

The battle opened on February 21, with a German artillery bombardment that rained two million shells down on Verdun and its ring of forts.

4 "What Was That War Like, Sir?" *Observer,* London, November 9, 1950.

General Henri-Philippe Pétain (1856–1951) was sent in to take command of the defense of the fortress. "They shall not pass" was the motto Pétain used. Falkenhayn forgot his original intentions and became as obsessed with capturing Verdun as Pétain was with saving it. When the bloodletting was halted on December 16, half a million men had perished in the sausage machine. Nearly one-half were Germans. Total casualties (killed and wounded) were reckoned at 400,000 for the French and over 350,000 for the Germans. Clearly, Falkenhayn had miscalculated. It was the longest battle of the war.

In an effort to relieve pressure on Verdun and to end the war, the Allies planned a major three-pronged offensive for the summer of 1916. The British were to attack along the Somme. The Italians were to attack Austria along the Isonzo River, and the Russians were to launch a major offensive into both Poland and Galicia.

The Russian offensive opened on June 4, but after some initial success, the Russian steamroller ran out of steam and stalled without having achieved its objectives. The Italians attacked the Austrians on August 6 with their usual results. Despite heavy casualties, they were able to capture only the town of Gorizia. Meanwhile on July 1, the British began the bloodiest battle of the war along the Somme.

The site chosen by the British command was heavily fortified by the Germans and of no strategic importance. An impressive arsenal of heavy and light artillery, tanks, and airplanes was assembled along a twenty-three-mile front. The British had one gun for every twenty yards. The French had twice as many guns. The British began the battle on June 24 with a seven- day-and-night bombardment of the German trenches. Four million rounds were fired by the British guns on the first day. Sir Douglas Haig (1861–1928), commander of the Allied forces, expected the artillery bombardment to win the battle before the infantry, and possibly even cavalry, would move in to "mop up" whatever resistance remained.

The Allied artillery barrage failed to do its job. It did not, for example, cut the barbed wire as expected. The German machine gun crews went underground and waited. When the British and French infantry went "over the top," on July 1, the Germans emerged from their dugouts and manned the machine guns. The slaughter that ensued was made all the more certain by orders that the advancing infantrymen attack in formation carrying sixty-six pounds of equipment. The result was the highest casualty rate in the history of modern warfare. The British alone suffered 60,000 casualties, including 40 percent of their officer corps, on the first day of the battle. Not one yard had been gained. When the battle ended on November 18, the British had sacrificed over 400,000 men and the French over 200,000. German casualties stood at about 450,000.

The inconclusiveness of the campaigns of 1916, including the only major naval battle of the war, the Battle of Jutland in May, led to changes in the German and French commands, but not the British. Falkenhayn was replaced by the team of Hindenburg-Ludendorff. On the French side, Joffre was replaced by General Robert Nivelle (1856–1924), whose inept leadership brought on the massacre of French soldiers at the Second Battle of the Aisne in April 1917, and the subsequent mutiny of some fifty-four divisions.

Away from the front, the Austrian Emperor Franz Joseph died on November 21, 1916, after sixty-eight years on the throne. His successor and grandnephew, Karl I, began looking for a way out of the war. Perhaps more auspicious for the future was the reelection of Woodrow Wilson (1856–1924) as president of the still neutral United States. Nineteen-sixteen had been a bloodbath during which human lives had been reduced to a matter of statistics, just like any other material resource. The civilians on the home front, too, were beginning to feel the stress of prolonged industrialized war.

The Home Front

Unless there is a decisive victory early in the war, a modern industrial war will be decided on the home front. In a prolonged war, the advantage lies with the side that is best able to organize its economic and human resources. Otherwise, the heroism of the soldiers at the front is in vain. This was one of the lessons the leaders of 1914 should have learned from, for example, the American Civil War, but did not. None of the belligerents was prepared for a prolonged war. By the end of 1915, each government was taking steps in order to wage "total war." As a result, the role of government in regulating economic life and manipulating public opinion reached heights from which it has never fully descended.

Germany was the first to mobilize its economic resources. As early as 1914, Walther Rathenau (1867–1922), one of the nation's leading industrialists, began to organize each branch of production so that raw materials were allocated to producers who were the most efficient and involved with work of the highest priority. Rathenau also pushed efforts to develop substitute products and to manufacture some items synthetically. His *Kriegsrohstoffabteilung* (KRA or War Raw Materials Administration) became a model for state organization and regulation of the economy. It was not until the end of 1916, however, that a comprehensive attempt was made to mobilize the human resources of Germany through the Auxiliary Service Law, which placed all males between the ages of seventeen and sixty at the disposal of the war effort.

Germany's eastern ally was less successful at organizing the home front. In Austria-Hungary, the two halves of the empire competed with each other for food, effectively thwarting any attempt to set up a unitary agency, such as Germany's KRA or Britain's Ministry of Munitions. As the war deepened, the inherent ethnic conflicts within the empire crippled efforts at organizing either the economy or public opinion. Indeed, urged on by Allied propaganda, the various nationalities and ethnic groups did what they could to undermine the war effort.

If the outlook in Austria-Hungary was grim, it was virtually hopeless in Russia. No belligerent suffered more from a failure of leadership than Russia, which did the least of any of the warring nations to mobilize the home front. The Tsar and his officials greeted with suspicious hostility all efforts at cooperation between the government and citizenry to bring together resources and solve the problems of supply and distribution plaguing the Russian war effort. Everywhere Russian officials saw civilian attempts to help as efforts to bring in reform and revolutionary change by the back door, thereby undermining the autocracy. Constitutional change was more feared than military defeat.

The British and French faced fewer problems than the three empires in the east, but still had to struggle to improvise means for conducting war on an unprecedented scale. Rumors of a shortage of shells led to a broadening of the Liberal cabinet in Britain into a nonpartisan regime in May 1915. Following this, in July 1915, a Ministry of Munitions was created, headed by David Lloyd George. He quickly turned the ministry into the British equivalent of Germany's KRA, controlling the allocation of resources and men and the level of profits from the manufacture of arms. Through control of the munitions industry, Lloyd George was increasingly involved in the regulation of the entire economy.

In France the government (i.e., the military) had extensive authority to commandeer resources in time of war, a tradition going back to the Revolution. France, like Britain, benefitted from the Royal Navy's blockade of Germany. Both allies could draw upon imperial resources, as well as those of the United States. Everywhere, the increased role of big government in the regulation of the economy was one of the most important legacies of the Great War.

In the atmosphere of total war, civilians, no less than soldiers, were an important resource that had to be mobilized. Each nation introduced conscription, not only to assure adequate fighting forces but to ensure that skilled workers remained in the factories. The war benefitted the working classes. Not only did unemployment vanish, but the increasing importance of the labor force, together with its loyalty, led to an increased acceptance of trade unions and collective bargaining.

The demand for soldiers opened up opportunities for women at home. Women stepped in to fill the slots left in the factories by men sent to the front. In Britain alone, approximately 1.5 million women obtained jobs previously not open to them, or in which they had only nominal representation. As with labor, the role played by women in the war effort helped to advance women's efforts for equality. It was much harder after the war for society to resist, for example, the demand for women's suffrage.

On the negative side of the ledger, civil liberties suffered as opposition to the war mounted. As enthusiasm for the war slackened, war propaganda was employed in an attempt to shore it up. Atrocity stories about the enemy, often false or exaggerated, helped to transform the war into a moral crusade for justice.

Opposition to the war on moral or other grounds was viewed as treasonous. In England, the Defense of the Realm Act (1914) permitted the arrest of dissenters as traitors and the censorship of newspapers or even their outright suspension. In France, after Georges Clemenceau (1841–1929) became virtual dictator in November 1917, civil liberties were suppressed. Newspaper editors were drafted for publishing negative reports on the war, or, in at least one case, executed for treason.

Decision, 1917–1918

When 1917 opened all of the belligerents were at the point of exhaustion. For each side, 1917 was unquestionably the low point in the war. Yet the scales were not clearly tipped in either's favor. As the momentous events of 1917 unfolded, it seemed possible for either side to snatch victory from the jaws of defeat. What was to eventually assure an Allied victory was the entry of the United States into the war on April 6, 1917, as an "Associated Power" on the side of the Allies.

American entry into the war, although perhaps likely when viewed with the benefit of hindsight, was not a foregone conclusion in January 1917. In December 1916, President Wilson asked the belligerents to state their war aims in an attempt to bring about a negotiated peace. It is astonishing to recall that after more than two years of bloodletting neither side had actually formulated any specific aims. In December 1916 neither side felt the need to be conciliatory, and hence the demands of each amounted to nothing short of complete victory. On January 24, just over two weeks after Wilson stated his Fourteen Points as a basis for negotiations, Germany and Austria-Hungary declined a joint American-British peace proposal. Wilson was rebuffed.

On January 17, 1917, British naval intelligence intercepted a telegram from the German foreign minister, Arthur Zimmermann (1864–1940), to the German envoy in Mexico, suggesting a possible alliance between Germany and Mexico. American public opinion was incensed. What was to force Wilson's hand, however, was the German decision of January 31 to resume unrestricted submarine warfare.

The German attempt to starve Britain—long dependent upon its world trade—into submission by sinking, without warning, all ships on their way to Britain, was a desperate gamble. When the Kaiser pointed out that such a move would surely bring the United States into the war against Germany, he was assured that not a single American soldier would set foot on the continent before England surrendered. It was a fatal miscalculation.

Believing that the German crimes against American lives on the high seas were of such a nature that they could only be addressed by the United States becoming a belligerent, Wilson asked Congress for a declaration of war. On April 6, 1917, Congress complied with Wilson's request. With the vast human and material resources of the United States available to the Allies, it appeared only a matter of time before the Central Powers would be defeated. But the outcome was not yet certain.

American entry into the war was made more plausible by events unfolding in Russa during early 1917. Between March 8 and 14,[5] a revolution broke out that toppled the autocratic tsarist regime (see Chapter 3). A Provisional Government was established by former deputies of the Duma as a first step toward the creation of a liberal-democratic government. This initial phase of what would prove to be a two-part Russian Revolution had two immediate influences: the end of the autocratic rule of the Tsar and the promise of a consitutional government in Russia helped move American opinion in favor of intervention in the war. It was simply easier for Americans to enter a war ". . . to make the world safe for democracy," if they would be fighting alonside a constitutional rather than tsarist Russia.

A second immediate influence of the March revolution in Russia was to energize the German command with new hope, perhaps the last hope, for a German victory in the war. If Germany could bring the war with Russia to an end and transfer significant numbers of troops from the Eastern Front to the Western Front, it was possible to achieve victory before American troops began to arrive in Europe. The decision of the new Provisional Government of Russia to defy popular demand and remain in the war caused further deterioration of the Russian home front and a second revolution on November 7, led by the Bolsheviks. The Bolshevik Revolution brought to power a communist government committed to an immediate end to the war. Russia requested an armistice on December 5

---

5 Russians were still using the Julian calendar in 1917, which was thirteen days behind the Gregorian calendar used in the West. Hence, the events are often referred to as the "February" and "October" revolutions.

and began negotiations on March 5, 1918. Germany was victorious on the Eastern Front. But the outcome of the Great War itself was yet to be decided on the Western Front.

In a final desperate effort to achieve victory on the Western Front, Germany launched the last major offensive of the war on March 21. Ludendorff threw everything he had left into the offensive. The Allies were taken by surprise. The Germans broke through, finally turning the war into a war of motion. By May 31, the Germans were once again on the Marne River, within forty miles of Paris. As in 1914, the French government made preparations to leave the capital. Time, however, was running out for the Germans.

On July 18, buttressed by nine fresh American divisions, the Allies counterattacked. A surprise British assault on August 8, assisted by 450 tanks, gained five miles in half a day, as the German lines began to crack. It was "the black day" of the German army, according to Ludendorff. On September 4, the Germans retreated to the Siegfried Line, a defensive line from Lens to Rheims. With military defeat imminent, and in an effort to prevent a "revolution from below" as occurred in Russia, Ludendorff and Hin-denburg informed the Kaiser on September 29 that an immediate armistice was necessary.

The Kaiser was stunned by the news of impending defeat. After admitting that he could not work miracles, he appointed his cousin, the liberal Prince Max von Baden (1867–1929), chancellor. On the following day, the Prince asked Wilson for an armistice as preliminary to a peace conference to negotiate a settlement on the basis of Wilson's Fourteen Points.

With Germany's allies already suing for peace, and with a mutiny among the sailors at Kiel, the Kaiser yielded to advice from Hindenburg and abdicated on November 9. At the request of the British royal family, he was granted exile in the Netherlands. Two days later, at 5 A.M., a German delegation signed the armistice. In accordance with the terms of the armistice, the fighting stopped at 11 A.M. on November 11, 1918. At last, it was "all quiet on the Western Front."

Suggested Books and Films

Humphrey Cobb, *Paths of Glory* (1935); Ernst Jünger, *Storm of Steel* (various editions); and Erich Maria Remarque, *All Quiet on the Western Front* (1929). Three passionate fictional accounts of the war experience.

Modris Eksteins, *Rites of Spring: The Great War and the Birth of the Modern Age* (1989). The experience of trench warfare and how it altered the psychology of Europe.

Fritz Fischer, *Germany's Aims in the First World War* (1967). Controversial account of Germany's role in the Great War.

Allister Horne, *The Price of Glory* (1967). Especially good account of the Battle of Verdun.

Michael Howard, *The First World War* (2003). A quick survey of the Great War by a distinguished British historian.

Eric J. Leed, *No Man's Land: Combat and Identity in World War I* (1979). Scholarly look at the impact of trench warfare.

Hew Strachan, *The First World War* (2004). A one-volume edition of Strachan's three-volume study. Highly recommended.

A. J. P. Taylor, *A History of the First World War* (1966). A very good brief survey of the war.

John Williams, *The Other Battleground* (1972). War on the home front in England, France, and Germany.

Paths of Glory, 1957, a classic movie.

All Quiet on the Western Front, 1930, also a classic movie.

All Quiet on the Western Front, 1979, a made-for-television movie.

"The Great War and the Shaping of the 20th Century," 1996. An eight-part PBS television special.

Chronology

3
Revolution and Peacemaking, 1917–1919

THE EUROPE, INDEED THE WORLD, that welcomed the armistice in November 1918 was very different from the Europe that enthusiastically greeted the outbreak of war in August 1914. The "old order" had fallen, but no one was quite sure what the "new order" would be like. At its outset, the war was an old-fashioned affair of kings, emperors, and statesmen defending dynastic and/or national honor against the aggressor. By 1916, it had become a war for territorial expansion. In 1917, the Russian Revolution and the entry of the United States transformed the Great War into an ideological struggle, a crusade for a new world order. Two different visions of the future were, at least initially, personified by the American president, Woodrow Wilson, and V. I. Lenin (Vladimir Ilyich Ulyanov, 1870–1924), the Bolshevik leader of the new Russia. Each proposed a new world order entirely different from what Europeans had known before the war. Each vision, in its own way, held out the hope that the Great War might not have been waged in vain.

Wilson's vision took shape partly in response to Lenin's call for an immediate peace of justice without victors or vanquished. Wilson, who as late as 1916 campaigned for reelection on his record as an isolationist, began to speak of a new democratic international order based upon the abstract "universal principles of right and justice." Before a joint session of Congress in January 1918, he outlined in his "Fourteen Points," the principles on which a just peace settlement must be negotiated. They included "open covenants openly arrived at," the principle of national selfdetermination, and a "general association of nations" in order to assure the political independence and territorial integrity of each nation. In the ensuing months, as the peace conference unfolded, Wilson's "general association of nations," the League of Nations, became his chief goal, the essential basis of his new world order.

Lenin and Wilson had much in common, although they were in fact very different. Both were products of Enlightenment thought. Both believed in the innate goodness of man. Hence, they were both humanitarians, but

Lenin mobilized the raw energy of the masses to bring the Bolsheviks to power in the second Russian revolution. Courtesy Bildarchiv d. ÖNB, Wien.

with a difference. Wilson's belief that man is by nature good, possessing certain inalienable natural rights, led him to become a liberal-democrat, for whom the loss of American lives to U-Boat attacks was a crime which justified American intervention in the Great War. Lenin's humanitarianism was more abstract. He had great compassion for humanity in general, but as a Marxist he viewed individuals as expendable cogs in the wheels of history. And although Lenin defended orthodox Marxism as objective truth, he did not adhere, as Marx did, to historical determinism. Lenin was, much like Hitler, a voluntarist, for whom will power (the will of the leader) was the decisive factor determining the flow of history.

Wilson's vision appealed mainly to middle-class liberals, who wished to replace the old world of aristocratic privilege and secret diplomacy with a new international order of democratic nation-states cooperating in a League of Nations. This was a free, democratic, but not a classless, world order. None of Wilson's Fourteen Points dealt with Lenin's most pressing concern: the need for a new social order. In Lenin's view, imminent world revolution, for which the Russian Revolution was a catalyst, would sweep away both nation-states and classes to liberate mankind from the corruptive influence of past historical development. Although Lenin's program appealed to millions, it was feared by millions more. His ideas were feared because behind them lay the fact of the Russian Revolution and the forces that it had unleashed. No one, Bolshevik or bourgeois democrat, quite knew what might develop from the events of 1917 in Russia.

Revolution in Russia

The Russian Revolution of 1917 was actually two revolutions. The first occurred in March (February, according to the Julian calendar then in use in Russia) and resulted in the creation of a liberal Provisional Government. The Provisional Government was organized by former deputies of the Duma, suspended by the Tsar in September. The second, or Bolshevik Revolution, occurred in November (or October) and was carried out by the Bolsheviks, a radical Marxist faction within the Soviet of Workers' and Sailors' Deputies, or *Petrograd Soviet*. The Petrograd Soviet came into existence on the very same day as the Provisional Government. From its beginning, the Petrograd Soviet functioned as a shadow government, issuing decrees of its own and countermanding decrees of the Provisional Government.

That there was a revolution in Russia at all was due to the failure of the Tsar's government to deal adequately with the demands of the war. This in turn was the result of a number of factors. Russia was the most effectively blockaded of the belligerents. At the same time, it was unable to exploit its vast natural resources due to its general economic backwardness and the government's unwillingness to organize the economy and society for a total war effort. In short, it was an abdication of authority by the Tsar's government that led to the creation of the Provisional Government and the Petrograd Soviet. Why the Provisional Government failed, why there was a second revolution in November, is one of the great historical questions of 1917.

But the reason the Provisional Government failed is not as simple as sometimes believed. It is true that the Provisional Government forgot the first duty of any government: to govern. But there were both ideological and practical reasons why the Provisional Government did not act decisively. It was a coalition of liberals who were committed to defending civil liberties, but did not feel they had the right to make any fundamental changes in Russian society until a constitutional assembly had been elected and met to draft a constitution. They believed that the fundamental issues of how to interpret the inalienable rights of the individual and define the limits of governmental authority must be decided by a duly elected constituent assembly. Until then, the Provisional Government saw itself as just that, "provisional," the transitory caretaker of national sovereignty.

This overly legalistic approach, more than anything else, crippled and doomed the Provisional Government. Faced with growing economic problems and the pressures of continuing an increasingly unpopular war, it was unable to provide the firm leadership that the Russian masses were desperate for in 1917.

The expectations of the people were a major challenge faced by the Provisional Government. Tsarism had ended and "democracy" was now established, or being established, but "democracy" meant something different to each group within Russian society. It was not possible for the Provisional Government to address these expectations, given its legalistic interpretation of its provisional status. Rather than address the demands of the masses, it made the fatal decision to continue the war, and even launched a new, major offensive in July.

It was the decision to continue the war that doomed the Provisional Government. In part, this was a matter of honor. Russia had obligations to fulfill with its allies. There were also more selfish reasons for continuing the war. Some members of the government hoped to gain indemnities and the various territories promised Russia in secret treaties made during the war. Whatever the reasons, the Provisional Government failed to see the necessity of extricating Russia from the war, a hard reality that Lenin forced the Bolsheviks to accept in 1918.

It was the arrival of Lenin in Petrograd in mid-April that altered the course of the revolution. Lenin was living in exile in Switzerland when the February Revolution occurred. It was the German military who facilitated Lenin's return to Russia as a "secret weapon" in the war with Russia. In a speech given shortly after his arrival in Petrograd, Lenin established the Bolshevik position—immediate peace, a transfer of governmental authority to the soviets, and a nationalization of land. Lenin argued that the second stage of the revolution, the proletarian revolution, was at hand, and it was the task of the Bolsheviks to take the lead.

The Bolsheviks grew rapidly in the spring and early summer of 1917, in an atmosphere of increasing anarchy. At the same time the Provisional Government was losing the limited power that it once had. Aleksandr Kerensky (1881–1970), minister of war after May 19, attempted to rally the troops for a new offensive that began on July 1. After some initial success, a German counterattack all but destroyed the Russian army as an effective fighting force. The Russian troops began deserting in large numbers. As Lenin correctly observed: "The army voted for peace with its feet."

The failure of the July offensive was disastrous for the Provisional Government. The cabinet resigned. A new government was formed with Aleksandr Kerensky as prime minister succeeding the liberal Prince Georgi

Lvov (1861–1925). Growing chaos caused fear among some liberal and conservative army officers, businessmen, and political leaders who feared that Russia was drifting towards civil war. This liberal-conservative coalition found a champion in the colorful Cossack general Lavr Kornilov (1870–1918), Kerensky's new commander-in-chief.

Fearing that his commander-in-chief was plotting a coup, Kerensky dismissed Kornilov on September 8. Kornilov refused to obey and ordered army units to begin marching on Petrograd. Swift action by the Petrograd Soviet, however, robbed Kornilov of the support of the troops. The soldiers simply deserted as they approached Petrograd. The Kornilov "coup," if indeed it was ever meant to be such, fizzled out. The Provisional Government was saved, but by the action of the Petrograd Soviet, not itself.

What existed in Russia in September 1917 was a kind of organized anarchy. No single organization could really speak for all the people. A process of fermentation was at work within the armed forces, among the peasantry and the workers, and within various national and ethnic groups. The aspirations of these many different groups could not be adequately expressed in conventional political terms, as Kerensky was trying to do by patiently preparing for the election of a Constituent Assembly. The energies of the masses had been unleashed by the destruction of the traditional authorities. No government could succeed unless it tapped those energies or, at the least, managed to ride their currents.

From his hideout in Finland, where he fled in mid-July when the Provisional Government cracked down on the Bolsheviks, Lenin sought to direct the raw energy of the masses to the goal of seizing power. He saw the possibility of combining the anarchistic rebelliousness of the masses with the revolutionary efforts of the vanguard of the proletariat, the party. In September, he wrote to the Central Committee of the Bolshevik faction to announce that "the Bolsheviks must seize power at this very moment."

Lenin's proposal met with opposition from some of his closest associates, who argued that the time was not right. The differences were resolved at a secret meeting of the Central Committee attended by Lenin on the night of October 23. Lenin prevailed. The Central Committee agreed to prepare for a coup. Since Lenin wished to remain in hiding, leadership of the coup was given to Leon Trotsky (Lev Davydovich Bronstein, 1879–1940).

The seizure of power by the Bolsheviks took place on November 7 (October 25), 1917. Actually "seizure of power" is too glorious a phrase to convey the reality of the confused situation in Petrograd. It would be more accurate to say that once the Provisional Government failed in its attempt to destroy the Bolsheviks and the Military Revolutionary Committee, power was dumped into the lap of the Bolshevik faction. Trotsky's preparations made it appear that power had been seized in the name of the Soviet movement. Not all members of the Second Congress of Soviets, meeting at that time in Petrograd, accepted that notion; but the delegates who remained at the meeting, although a minority, voted to accept a Bolshevik government. For the time being, it was also accepted in Moscow and other important cities. Perhaps more important, it was accepted in most areas at the front. In the provinces, distant from central authority in any case, a watchful attitude was adopted. At the same time, centers of resistance sprang up, but the Bolsheviks managed to retain power without great difficulty in the last months of 1917.

The situation became much graver in 1918. The revolutionary government faced several difficult situations. First, it had to contend with the Constituent Assembly, elected in November after the revolution. The Bolsheviks were badly outnumbered, notably by the Socialist Revolutionaries who had received strong peasant support. At the initial meeting of the Constituent Assembly in January 1918, delegates began immediately to criticize the government sharply. The government responded by dispersing the assembly at the end of the first day; there was not even enough organized support for parliamentary rule to counter this move.

The second problem could not be dealt with so easily. It involved ending the war with Germany. Trotsky led the Russian delegation in negotiations with Germany and Austria beginning in December. He was not able to moderate the harsh demands laid down by the German general staff. Lenin, as he had so often in the past, used his powers of persuasion and his prestige to get the Bolsheviks to agree to accept the German terms. With great reluctance, Russia signed the Treaty of Brest-Litovsk on March 3, 1918, abandoning Poland, Lithuania, the Ukraine, the Baltic provinces, Finland, and Transcaucasia. Russia lost major portions of its industrial capacity and food-raising capabilities but gained time in which to attend to internal problems without the demands of war impinging. It was a substantial but necessary sacrifice. Otherwise, it is difficult to imagine how the government could have survived the three years of civil war that followed.

As Russia left the war its former allies felt that they had been betrayed. Even more important, they feared Russia's revolutionary example and began to offer aid to the various counterrevolutionary forces in the Russian civil war, the third and last of the difficulties facing the Bolsheviks in 1918. The Allies also contemplated direct intervention, such as the possibility of mounting a crusade against Bolshevism. The threat of revolutionary infection from Russia remained on the minds of leaders of the Allied governments in the last months of the war and during the efforts to reach a peace settlement as well.

Revolution in Germany

The revolution in Germany was, like the Russian Revolution, actually two revolutions, or attempted revolutions. Forces on the left attempted a "revolution from below," but were checkmated by forces on the right, who attempted a "revolution from above." The result was the establishment of an "accidental" republic that lacked popular support. The traditional elites of the army, judiciary, bureaucracy, church, and wealthy landowners and industrialists remained entrenched and hostile towards the republic. During the republic's brief existence the forces of extreme right and left struggled to achieve their respective revolutionary goals until the final victory of the extreme right in January 1933.

The main challenge facing Ludendorff and the High Command in October 1918, once it became clear that the war was lost, was how to save the old order. Guilt for the defeat had to be spread as broadly as possible, without including the military leadership. The solution was to create a broadly based civilian government of center-left parties that would be burdened with the task of asking for an armistice and making the necessary peace. Hence, Prince Max von Baden was appointed chancellor; ministers became responsible to the Reichstag; the Prussian three-class voting system was abolished; and the Kaiser lost much of his control of the armed forces. Germany became a constitutional monarchy, but not a republic. All of this was to create a responsible civilian government capable of accepting the burden (or blame) of defeat, while at the same time preventing a possible Bolshevik-style revolution from below.

Germany seemed ripe for a revolution from below in November 1918. On November 3, the sailors at the Kiel naval base mutinied. It was a spark that ignited revolutions across Germany. On November 8, Kurt Eisner (1867–1919), an Independent Socialist,[1] established a Constituent Workers', Soldiers', and Peasants' Council in Munich, and proclaimed a Republic of Bavaria. Revolt also broke out in Berlin on November 8. On the following day, Prince Max von Baden announced both the Kaiser's abdication (which the Kaiser had not yet agreed to) and his own resignation. As he resigned, he transferred his powers to Friedrich Ebert (1871–1925), leader of the Majority Social Democrats. The transfer of power gave an aura of legitimacy to Ebert's government, although Prince Max had no

---

1 The Independent Socialists split off from the Majority Socialists (SPD, or Social Democratic Party of Germany) in 1915 to protest the SPD's continued support of the war. In 1917, the Independent Socialists formed the USPD, or Independent Social Democratic Party of Germany. The *Spartakusbund* and KPD (Communist Party of Germany) evolved out of the USPD.

actual constitutional authority to do so. The "Ebert Cabinet," which called itself the "Council of Peoples' Deputies," derived its authority from the Workers' and Soldiers' Councils of Berlin and from the two parties on the left, the SPD, and the USPD.

The moderate socialists in the SPD and USPD were willing to accept government responsibility because they, as well as the trade union leaders and a majority of the people they represented, feared a revolution from below as much as did the traditional elites. Initially, their intent was to preserve a constitutional monarchy. The abdication of the Kaiser and the proclamation of a republic by Philipp Scheidemann (1865–1939), deputy leader of the SPD, on November 9, was not a part of the original plan. Once it was a fact, however, Ebert and his supporters felt the immediate need was to establish order first, then elect a constituent assembly that would draft a constitution, which in turn would determine the nature and extent of reform.

Ebert was very upset when he first learned that his deputy had proclaimed a republic. What Scheidemann had done was something of an instinctive reaction to a momentary crisis. He was having lunch, eating a bowl of potato soup, at the Reichstag on November 9, when he was informed that Karl Liebknecht (1871–1919), a radical leader of the *Spartakus-bund*, was about to proclaim a Soviet Republic from the balcony of the imperial palace. Scheidemann went to the window and made a brief speech to the crowd outside, which he concluded with, "Long live the new! Long live the German Republic!" Hence, Germany became a democratic republic because the alternative, a Soviet Republic, was simply too frightful.

Much ink has been spilt by historians trying to explain why the Social Democrats, a party whose historical roots and party program were Marxist, did not initiate fundamental changes in Germany once they had governmental responsibility. The reasons given are varied. Certainly, one reason is that a radical revolution lacked a mass base of support. Also, the radicals in Germany faced strong opposition from the conservative traditional elites. The army, if defeated on the battlefront, was still a formidable force in internal affairs. The bureaucracy was still functioning efficiently. Even though the old government had collapsed, most of the other institutions in Germany were still sound and committed to preventing any real change in German society. Finally, the more radical forces found little sympathy for their demands among the Majority Socialists.

Any chance that the Majority Social Democrats would lead a "real" revolution in Germany was short-circuited by the so-called Ebert-Groener Pact on November 9, and the Stinnes-Legien Agreement on November 15. In the former, General Wilhelm Groener (1867–1939), Ludendorff's successor, offered the Ebert government the support and protection of the army in exchange for Ebert's promise to "suppress Bolshevism," that is, to suppress the soldiers' councils and recognize the authority of the officer corps.

The Stinnes-Legien Agreement was an agreement between employers and trade union leaders concluded on November 15. The employers agreed to recognize the unions as the only legitimate representatives of labor, abolish company unions, hire returning soldiers, and implement codeter-mination in all firms employing at least fifty workers. In return, the trade unions agreed not to push for any changes in the existing property structure of Germany.

Many have argued since November 1918 that the real "stab in the back" occurred in November, when the Majority Social Democrats allegedly were taken captive by the forces on the right. Caught between a revolution from above and a revolution from below, they opted for the former. Whatever the truth, the leftist uprisings during 1919 were swiftly put down by the army and the *Freikorps*, paramilitary associations of former soldiers. A USPD-led revolt in Berlin in January 1919 was crushed. Rosa Luxemburg (1871–1919) and Karl Liebknecht, leaders of the Spartakusbund, were murdered by the Freikorps. Further uprisings in February and March in Berlin, Munich, and other areas and a brief Soviet Republic proclaimed in Bavaria in April were all likewise suppressed. The German Revolution, unlike the revolution in Russia, stopped halfway.

Elsewhere in central Europe, defeat in war, the disintegration of the old governments, and the powerful example of 1917 in Russia created potential revolutionary situations. In Austria there were disorders throughout 1919, but no revolutionary accomplishments. In Hungary the revolution in October 1918 had created a government of socialists and communists, but in March 1919 that government became a communist dictatorship under Béla Kun (1886–1936). Communist Hungary did not last long. Romanian troops invaded in April. At the same time a counterrevolution began and by August 1, Béla Kun fled the country.

Despite setbacks, by the end of 1919 the fate of world revolution was still undetermined. Revolutionaries were still optimistic but, as it developed, much of their optimism was unfounded. Success in Russia had been based on two factors, the utter collapse of the old regime and widespread rebellion among the lower classes in the city and especially in the countryside. Neither factor led to success in Germany, where the empire collapsed but the institutions and traditional elites undergirding it remained. There was no German equivalent to the Russian peasantry on which the small, isolated radical groups could base their activity. In central Europe a large peasantry existed, but it was fragmented by ethnic and national differences and kept under control by great landowners, the aristocracy, and the military who, sometimes with difficulty (as in Hungary), managed to dominate politics after the Great War in every central European state except Czechoslovakia. The only successful revolution outside Russia in the immediate postwar period was in Turkey, where army officers and nationalists rallied in 1919 and 1920 to prevent the victorious Allied powers from imposing peace terms on their nation.

Revolution, if relatively unsuccessful by 1919, still had an enormous impact on postwar Europe. As in the United States, in Europe there was considerable and often irrational fear of a Bolshevik menace. A good deal of energy and time were spent at the Paris Peace Conference working out methods by which the Russian Revolution might be quarantined or possibly destroyed. An informal counterrevolutionary movement developed that led to dictatorships, initially in eastern and southeastern Europe, then in Italy and the Iberian peninsula, and finally in Germany.

Peacemaking, 1919

In the midst of this disorder and turmoil, when the threat of revolution looked a good deal more imposing than it did by the end of 1920, the victorious powers began meeting in Paris, not simply to end the Great War but also to reconstruct the world. One cannot avoid the temptation to compare the Paris Peace Conference with the Vienna Congress (1814–1815) that concluded the Napoleonic Wars. Both came at the conclusion of major Europe-wide conflicts, and both attempted to set right the map of Europe and draft a peace that would last indefinitely. However, the Vienna Congress seems to have succeeded, whereas the Paris Peace Conference failed. Apart from the brief wars of German unification, there was general peace in Europe for one hundred years following the Vienna Congress. The Paris Peace settlement lasted only twenty troubled years before Europe, and the world, was plunged into a second, and even more devastating war.

The Europe of 1919 was very different from the Europe of 1814–1815. The diplomats who went to Vienna represented monarchies and were answerable only to their sovereigns. Hence, they enjoyed a freedom of action not allowed the diplomats of 1919, who represented liberal-democratic governments, which in turn were answerable to the people. Ideology was enlisted as a weapon during the Great War to mobilize whole nations. This was true only of France in the Napoleonic Wars. Furthermore, the peacemakers at Vienna met at the end of a revolutionary cycle and at the beginning of a century of modern ideology. The peacemakers at Paris were meeting at a time when Europe was erupting with turmoil and revolution fed by the new "isms" that had emerged during the intervening century.

The Vienna Congress was guided in its decision making by a set of principles: balance of power, legitimacy, and compensation. Every decision was weighed against the guiding principles. Hence, there was an agreed-upon basis for peace. Not so at Paris.

The only guiding principle at Paris in 1919 was the desire of the victors to contain their differences of opinion and present a united front to the defeated powers. There was no agreed-upon basis for peace. Thus every decision was a political compromise among the victors. Wilson's Fourteen Points, which the Germans expected to be the basis of a negotiated peace, were shunted aside as a victors' peace emerged.

The Versailles Treaty with Germany was the work of the "Big Four" (France, Great Britain, Italy, and the United States), actually the "Big Three," following Italy's noncooperation after being denied the territorial compensation it demanded for its participation in the war. France, represented by Georges Clemenceau, wanted a treaty that would assure French

The "Big Four" enjoy a cordial chat at the Paris Peace Conference, 1919, (left to right) British Prime Minister David Lloyd George, Italian Premier Vittorio Orlando, French Premier Georges Clemenceau, and American President Woodrow Wilson. U.S. Army Signal Corps photograph. Reproduced courtesy of the George C. Marshall Research Library, Lexington, Virginia.

national security and require Germany to pay for war damages. France's desire for a harsh treaty was somewhat mitigated by a willingness to compromise in order to achieve assurances of American cooperation in postwar Europe. David Lloyd George, Britain's representative, was compelled by the results of the December 1918 elections to side with Clemenceau, and thus support harsher peace terms than he personally felt were justified.

The role of Woodrow Wilson, who personally represented the United States, has been analyzed in great detail by historians. His idealism clashed with the realism of his European counterparts, especially Clemenceau. The extent to which his unwillingness to make the treaty a bipartisan political issue at home resulted in the U.S. Senate's, and the people's, ultimate rejection of it, also has been examined at length. What remains true is Wilson's sincere commitment to a just peace as a basis for building a new world order. He believed that the League of Nations was the essential cornerstone of that new order, but its existence required the postwar cooperation of the victors. To see the League become a reality, Wilson was forced to compromise, often at Germany's expense. Compromise was possible, since he believed that whatever defects the treaty contained could be repaired in later years by international cooperation through the League.

Perhaps the most glaring defect of the peace conference was the failure to include Russia (now the Soviet Union) and Germany, especially the latter. Russia was not represented both because the Bolsheviks, if in fact they were the legitimate government, were little interested in what seemed to them a meaningless farce, and also because of the fear that the Bolshevik revolution caused among the "civilized" nations gathered at Paris. They feared, as the British historian A. J. P. Taylor has pointed out, that Soviet Russia represented a "genuine element of social change," that threatened to spread: hence, the need to at least quarantine, or if possible snuff out, Bolshevism.

That Germany was not allowed to join the conference was a serious flaw. As the treaty took shape, however, it became clear that the result must be a victors' peace. The demand that Germany pay the costs of the war necessitated an admission of guilt by Germany. Thus the infamous Article 231, or "war-guilt clause," was included in the treaty. To accept the burden of reparations, the amount of which was left unspecified in the treaty, was an injustice. But to accept responsibility for a war for which the Germans felt they were not to blame, was a burden that could only be imposed. It could not be willingly accepted. Had Germany participated in the peace conference, as France did the Vienna Congress, it would have meant a deadlock at the conference and deepening political crisis at home for the diplomats of the victorious Allies.

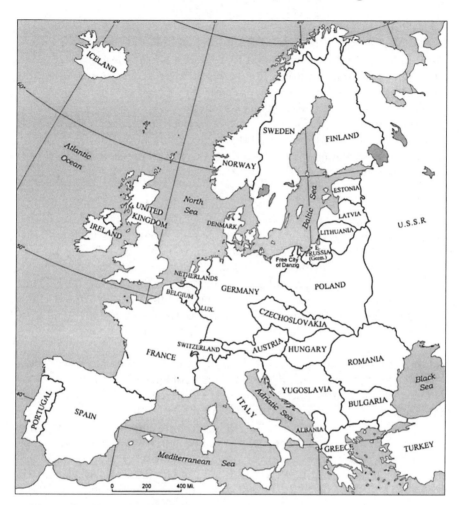

Europe Between the Wars

Germany was weakened by the Versailles Treaty, although not fatally as the French had initially wanted. It lost little territory in the west. Alsace-Lorraine was returned to France. A part of Schleswig was ceded to Denmark after a plebiscite (or popular vote). A few border communities were transferred to Belgium (but restored to Germany in 1926). The coal mines of the Saar were placed under French control for fifteen years after which a plebiscite would determine the national status of the area. The Rhineland remained a part of Germany, despite extensive French efforts, but the area west of the Rhine and a strip fifty kilometers to the east were "demilitarized." Allied troops were to occupy the west bank for fifteen years. In the east, Germany lost a good deal more territory. A large part of Posen, West and East Prussia were ceded to Poland. Danzig was declared a free city within the Polish customs union. Memel was ceded to the Allies and later taken over by Lithuania. Upper Silesia's fate was to be determined by plebiscite. Germany also lost its colonies.

As a military power, Germany was much reduced in size. It was allowed an army of no more than 100,000 men with limitations on the types of weapons that they might have. Its navy was reduced in size and was forbidden to have submarines. Furthermore, Germany was not allowed to have an air force.

The Treaty of Versailles was regarded by most Germans as extremely unfair and harsh. They had, of course, forgotten their own treatymaking efforts at Brest-Litovsk. The "war-guilt clause," reparations, unilateral disarmament, the loss of territory in Europe and colonies outside Europe—all furnished texts for German nationalists in the next decade.

Had the Treaty of Versailles been the only product of the Paris Peace Conference, Europe might have maintained political stability in the 1920s and 1930s. There were, however, four additional treaties and the League of Nations Covenant. The failure of several of these agreements, combined with the limited success of the Treaty of Versailles, created an extremely volatile situation in the 1930s. Of the four treaties, two can be disregarded: the Treaty of Sèvres with Turkey never went into effect; the Treaty of Neuilly with Bulgaria had no important repercussions. The other two, the Treaty of St. Germain with Austria and Trianon with Hungary, created problems that were never fully resolved between the two world wars. Instead, two different problems were created. First, Austria and Hungary, before the war semiautonomous parts of the Habsburg empire and each dominant in its own sphere, became small, relatively weak states. Austria particularly was an anomaly, a landlocked state of over 6 million, of whom 2 million lived in Vienna. The state was lopsided in every imaginable way, but especially economically. Unfortunately, Austria was not allowed to join with Germany for fear that this would unduly strengthen the latter.

The other problem involved the creation of a series of new or reconstituted states in central and eastern Europe and conflicting claims over territory and population. The idea of national self-determination was extremely difficult to apply in this area with any fairness. Czechoslovakia, for example, included areas in which the majority of the population was German or Polish; these areas had been included for strategic reasons, as was the Sudetenland with its majority of Germans, or for historic reasons, as was Teschen with its Polish majority. Poland included areas with German majorities. Romania and Yugoslavia had large concentrations of Magyars. Numerous other examples could be cited of the impossibility of a simple, completely fair division of territory according to the principle of national self-determination.

The irony of the settlement in eastern Europe is that the frontiers established by the treaties and the quarrels arising from them had torn apart what had been an important economic unit. Factories were now in one state, their sources of raw materials in a second, and their traditional markets in a third. This contributed to the weakness and instability of the area and nullified any possibility that the states of eastern Europe could serve as a proper counterbalance to either a resurgent Germany or the strengthening Soviet Union.

The League of Nations

The Paris Peace Settlement, as mentioned, failed to provide a lasting peace. With the benefit of hindsight we can see that its failure was due in part to an inability to recognize, or perhaps an unwillingness to accept, the new realities of 1919. By the end of the war the economic and financial center of the world had shifted from Europe to the United States. The *Pax Britannica* ended with the Great War, but no one, least of all Great Britain, wanted to admit it. Neither was the United States ready to assume the new responsibilities being thrust upon it.

Wilson fought hard to have the League of Nations made a part of each of the treaties that together comprised the Paris Peace Settlement. The European Allies saw in the League a means by which to involve the United States in postwar Europe. In order to secure French support for the League and to soften France's demands for a harsh and punitive treaty with Germany, Wilson agreed to a defensive alliance with Great Britain and France. But the U.S. Senate refused to ratify the Versailles Treaty without alterations to protect United States' sovereignty, changes Wilson refused to accept. Therefore, the United States rejected the treaty, and with it both membership in the League of Nations and the defensive alliance.

Blame for America's failure to ratify the treaty or join the League has often been laid at the feet of Wilson. There can be no doubt that Wilson, at the time suffering the aftereffects of a major stroke, completely mishandled the whole affair back home. But much of the blame must be assigned to the American public. Many Americans felt that participation in the war in Europe had been a mistake. The war over, most Americans wanted to return to a policy of isolationism (except when it came to collecting war debts), or as the popular slogan of the time put it, "back to normalcy."

The United States turned its back on Europe, but to say that in so doing it doomed the peace is too severe. The problems arising from the imperfect treaties might have been minimized, or entirely avoided, had the League of Nations Covenant been successfully implemented. The Covenant, or constitution, contained an adequate machinery for maintaining peace in the world. It made provisions for an International Court of Justice, submission of disputes to arbitration or to the Council or Assembly of the League, and even the use of force to resolve disputes.

Apart from America's refusal to participate, the League was made ineffective by the absence of both Germany (which did join in 1926), and the Soviet Union (which joined in 1934, shortly after Germany had left). There were other pertinent factors, also. In the formative period Britain and France, each having a different idea of how the League should be run, canceled each other out. Later in the early thirties, the League failed some crucial tests (e.g., the Italian invasion of Ethiopia), perhaps because the issues involved were not seen as central to European politics.

Given the ineffectiveness of the League, all that was left to maintain the peace was a return to the old-fashioned principle of the balance of power. But that was not possible so long as Soviet Russia remained ostracized and Germany was held down by the Versailles Treaty. One of the neglected realities of the 1920s was the fact that Germany was still potentially the most powerful nation on the continent. All it needed was to get out from under the restrictions of the treaty.

Europe and the world faced an uncertain future in the spring of 1919, as Germany, bowing before the inevitable, signed the Versailles Treaty. Both Europe and its relationship to the world had changed, but much of this was ignored. Scattered groups and individuals recognized the changes. Their voices were sometimes heard in the first troubled years of the twenties, but they were soon overwhelmed by the refusal of the majority to acknowledge the full extent of change in Europe.

Perhaps the best contemporary assessment of the peace comes from the French poet Romain Rolland (1866–1944), who ended his wartime journal on June 23, 1919, with the comment: "Sad Peace! Laughable interlude between the massacres of peoples!"

Suggested Books and Films

Thomas A. Bailey, *Woodrow Wilson and the Lost Peace* (1963). Looks at the compromises Wilson had to make at Paris and how he lost the peace at home.

Sheila Fitzpatrick, *The Russian Revolution, 1917–1932*, 2d rev. ed. (2001). An excellent brief survey.

Margaret Macmillian, *Paris 1919: Six Months that Changed the World* (2003). The best study of the Paris Peace Conference now available.

Harold Nicolson, *Peacemaking, 1919* (new ed., 1945). A classic and very human appraisal of the conference by a member of the British delegation.

Richard Pipes, *The Russian Revolution* (1991). A thorough and very readable survey of the revolution.

John Reed, *Ten Days That Shook the World* (1919). A personal account of the Russian Revolution by a pro-Bolshevik American reporter who witnessed it.

A. J. Ryder, *The German Revolution of 1918* (1967).

Alan Sharp, *The Versailles Settlement: Peacemaking in Paris, 1919* (1991). A well-written brief history of the peace conference.

Richard M. Watt, *The Kings Depart* (1973). A very readable account of the peace conference and the revolution in Germany.

Reds, 1981. Tells the story of John Reed and the Russian Revolution.

Dr. Zhivago, 1965. Romantic fictional account of the Russian Revolution.

Part 2
Overview: 1919–1939

THE TWENTY YEARS FROM 1919 TO 1939 form a crucial period in the history of Europe. Those who began the period under the assumption that the world would once again be like it was before 1914 had to face the reality that the Europe of 1919 was very different from prewar Europe. The ancient empires of Germany, Russia, Austria-Hungary, and Turkey had vanished. In their places were newly proclaimed republics struggling to survive in a hostile environment. Everywhere communist parties emerged to champion a third alternative to both the old order and the new liberal idealism advocated by Woodrow Wilson and his supporters.

Among the former great powers there were signs of serious troubles ahead. Great Britain, the world's superpower in 1914, was suffering from the economic impact of the war and would never fully recover. France, one of the victors, remained politically confused and fragmented. Germany, the key to European recovery, was a republic without republicans. Burdened by the terms of the Versailles Treaty and dependent upon antirepublican forces for its survival, the future looked grim for the Weimar Republic. Italy, also a victor in the Great War, suffered from an injured national pride, and, like the rest of Europe, was troubled by economic and social problems. Italy was the first of the former great powers to succumb to the lure of fascism. In Soviet Russia a new style of authoritarian government was taking shape that would present a serious challenge to the historic values of Western civilization until the last decade of the century.

In addition to the political and economic disruptions of the prewar order there was disillusionment and intellectual uncertainty that called into question the very foundations of European civilization. A generation that experienced four years of trench warfare and the great battles of the Western Front found it hard to believe anymore in a rational order to the universe. If people are reasonable and by nature good, as the Enlightenment thinkers alleged, then how did the Great War happen? Was it a failure of diplomacy, or a chance event in a universe of random chaos? Novel theories were emerging to explain the human predicament, and modern prophets were waiting in the wings, as Friedrich Nietzsche predicted, to offer fresh myths for the birth of a new order.

Yet by 1925, there were hopeful signs for the future. The Dawes Plan in 1924 dealt with the reparations issue in such a way as to stimulate economic recovery in Germany and throughout western Europe. The Locarno treaties signed in 1925 seemed to herald an era of rapprochement between Germany and France. A "spirit of Locarno" was in the air as many Europeans began to believe that a lasting peace was, after all, possible. Prosperity and optimism suffered a fatal blow, however, as the Great Depression, originating in the United States, hit Europe in the early 1930s.

Much was changed by the Depression. It discredited liberalism, both political and economic, especially for the middle class, historically the mainstay of the liberal order. The failure of the liberal-democratic governments to deal effectively with the unemployment and accompanying miseries caused by the Depression created doubts among the working class. They, like the middle class, began to look for alternatives to liberalism, increasingly viewed as a failed idea from the past.

Most European countries contended also with political crises intimately connected with the economic difficulties. The Weimar Republic fell apart in the early 1930s, creating conditions which made it possible for Adolf Hitler and the Nazi Party to come to power. Hitler, like Joseph Stalin (1879–1953) in the Soviet Union, constructed a new authoritarian dictatorship in Germany that was the very antithesis of liberalism. Unlike the traditional conservative dictatorships that sought merely to defend the status quo, the new authoritarian dictatorships sought a wholly new ideological order based upon a "born again" believer citizen-subject.

The major issue of the late 1930s was the threat of war and how this threat might best be met. The League of Nations proved to be useless in this regard. Britain and France failed to meet Nazi Germany's challenges, even when the Soviet Union seemed to be offering its support, until after the destruction of Czechoslovakia at the Munich Conference in 1938. When Hitler early in 1939 broke promises he had made in Munich, the stage was set for the Polish crisis and the beginning of the Second World War in September 1939.

Changes in all areas of life had been extraordinarily rapid and pervasive in the period. Europe remained the center of world civilization during the interwar period, but there were already signs that Europe's problems could not be solved without the intervention of the United States in European affairs. But America was not yet willing to assume the responsibilities that its economic resources and potential military strength would eventually force upon it. That development would have to wait until the outcome of a second great war. As Europe entered World War II, many could not help but feel that it would not survive a second major conflict without drastic alteration. What most did not realize was the extent to which life had already changed.

Chronology

1859	Charles Darwin defines human beings as thinking animals
1882	Frederich Nietzsche's "God is dead" philosophy cuts humanity adrift in a meaningless universe
1917	Albert Einstein's Theory of Relativity
1918–1922	Oswald Spengler predicts the death of western civilization in *Decline of the West*
1922	T. S. Eliot portrays postwar European culture as a waste land
1930	Sigmund Freud and José Ortega y Gasset see civilization as an artificial creation

4
Aftershocks of the Great War

THE GREAT WAR WAS PERHAPS the most traumatic event in Europe's history since the fall of the Roman Empire in the West. The twentieth century is often termed the "Age of Anxiety" because it was a century of change that left the future of European civilization in doubt. But the Great War did not cause the Age of Anxiety. It only acted as a catalyst for trends that were already well established before 1914.

Intellectually, philosophers and theologians, as well as natural and social scientists, were already questioning the presuppositions (or axioms) that undergirded Western civilization. Artists, writers, poets and musicians, in short, the creators and guardians of culture, were already reflecting the new assumptions. The emergence of the "masses" into political life (e.g., growth of liberal democracy) and the development of a "mass culture" (e.g., organized sports, vaudeville) as distinct from "high culture" was already well advanced before 1914. Likewise, the economic forces that would undermine the dominant position of the middle class were well established before the Great War.

Intellectual Trends

According to the Enlightenment tradition, autonomous reason could discover the natural laws that governed society as well as nature. Assuming that humans were by nature good (although perhaps corrupted by history), the eighteenth-century intellectuals believed that by the application of reason humans could build a better world, perhaps even a utopia. Theories put forth by the leading philosophes (e.g., John Locke's environmentalism in *Essay Concerning Human Understanding* [1689]) created a faith in progress and a sense of optimism about the future. Setting themselves free from all accepted authority (especially Christianity), they created a vision of a future humanity guided by the light of reason. History had meaning. It was going somewhere. The individual was meaningful, for the individual

67

was a thinking, reasoning creature, and thereby the master of his or her own fate and of history.

During the decades before the Great War a second scientific revolution and a new set of intellectuals brought forth new theories and scientific discoveries that called into question whether the individual human being was, after all, a reasoning, rational being in an orderly, meaningful universe, or rather an irrational animal adrift in a universe of random chaos. For many thinking individuals, the experience of the Great War made more urgent the need to find new answers to the most basic questions of ultimate meaning. The Great War merely accelerated the movement away from the fundamental assumptions of the Enlightenment tradition.

A Second Scientific Revolution

The popular acceptance of Charles Darwin's (1809–1882) theory of the evolutionary origins of life as presented in *Origin of the Species* (1859) and the *Descent of Man* (1871) was a key development. The theory of the evolutionary origin of life was as ancient as the Greek philosopher Anaximander (610–ca. 547 B.C.) of Miletus, who first suggested it in the sixth century B.C. Darwin benefitted from the acceptance of Charles Lyell's (1797–1875) principle of uniformitarianism (*Principles of Geology* [1830–1833]), by which the earth was thought to be millions of years old. Lyell's theory provided the immense time span required by Darwin's theory, if it was to have any credibility.

Although Darwin did not directly attack Christianity, the implications of his theory called into question the truth of biblical revelation, and hence Christianity. Also, according to Darwin, humans were no longer a special creation, but just a higher form of animal life, albeit thinking animals. And history still had meaning, for, as understood from the assumptions of the Enlightenment tradition, evolution implied progress toward some goal, whatever that might be. Life may have begun as a chance event in some primeval slime, but by Darwin's day evolution of life had progressed to the stage of a reasoning biped (e.g., Darwin).

The human being as a reasoning animal, however, was soon under attack, as was the validity of scientific reasoning. The German philosopher Friedrich Nietzsche (1844–1900) more than any other thinker of the nineteenth century saw clearly where autonomous reason was leading. He argued that the discoveries of modern science and philosophical reasoning had led to the conclusion that the "myth" of God was no longer tenable, that is, "God is dead." Since the Judeo-Christian understanding of God was the essential basis of Western civilization, his absence cut humans adrift in a universe without meaning (see, e.g., the parable of the madman in *The Gay Science* [1882]). The Enlightenment's rejection of Christianity while

No one better symbolized the changing views of reality during the twentieth century than Albert Einstein. Courtesy AP/Wide World

trying to retain Christian ethics was a hoax. There were no absolute values. The universe is not governed by rational principles. Humans, said Nietzsche, were driven by dark instinctual drives, not motivated by reason.

Other intellectuals like Henri Bergson (1859–1941) and Georges Sorel (1847–1922) also questioned the validity of scientific reasoning as a guide to truth (positivism) and claimed that humans were irrational by nature. None, however, was more influential than Sigmund Freud (1856–1939), the founder of psychoanalysis. Although Freud clung to the Enlightenment's belief that reason and scientific inquiry made civilization possible, his conclusion that humans are motivated by primitive, irrational drives hidden deep in the subconscious tended to undermine the Enlightenment's image of humanity. Also, Freud rejected both the Christian belief that evil was essentially a moral problem and the Enlightenment's assumption that it was an environmental problem. Rather, Freud believed that evil was rooted in human nature. For him, there was no utopia in the future. Faith in progress and optimism about the future no longer had a basis. Human beings as the thinking (reasoning) higher animals of Darwin's vision, like human beings created in the image of God, were now obsolete.

What threw the Enlightenment tradition into total disarray was the revolution in physics from the 1890s to the 1920s. The discoveries of

Max Planck (1858–1947), Niels Bohr (1885–1962), Werner Heisenberg (1901–1876), and especially Albert Einstein (1879–1955) challenged, and for many effectively overthrew, the Newtonian view (classical physics) of the universe upon which the Enlightenment tradition rested. Classical physics taught that the universe was a three-dimensional, objective reality, whose properties could be measured from an absolute reference point. The new physics taught that there was no objective reality. Space and time did not exist independent of the observer. There is no fixed (absolute) reference point anywhere in the universe. "There is no absolute knowledge. . . . All information is imperfect."[1]

The Enlightenment's view of the individual as an autonomous being making rational choices in a meaningful universe was gone, and with it optimism about the future of Western civilization. The individual was now cut adrift in a cold, mysterious universe without any coherent answer to the question "Who am I?" At best, the individual was a random chance "happening," thrown up by an impersonal universe, whose ultimate reality was only the molecules of which he or she was composed.

Table 4.1 Select List of Fifty Significant Books of the Century[2]

1900	Sigmund Freud, *The Interpretation of Dreams*
1902	V. I. Lenin, *What Is To Be Done?*
1912	Wassily Kandinsky, *Concerning the Spiritual In Art*
1916	Vilfredo Pareto, *The Mind of Society*
1917	Albert Einstein, *Relativity: The Special and General Theory*
1918–22	Oswald Spengler, *Decline of the West*
1919	Karl Barth, *The Epistle to the Romans*
1919	H. G. Wells, *The Outline of History*
1921	Karl Jung, *The Psychological Types*
1925	G. K. Chesterton, *The Everlasting Man*
1925–27	Adolf Hitler, *Mein Kampf*
1926	Joseph Stalin, *Problems of Leninism*
1927	Martin Heidegger, *Being and Time*
1929	Ernst Jünger, *Storm of Steel*
1930	Sigmund Freud, *Civilization and Its Discontents*
1930	José Ortega y Gasset, *The Revolt of the Masses*
1932	Joseph Stalin, *Foundations of Leninism*

1 Jacob Bronowski, *The Ascent of Man* (Boston, 1973), p. 353.
2 We have selected only works of nonfiction by European writers.

1932	Leon Trotsky, *The History of the Russian Revolution*
1932	Karl Barth, *Church Dogmatics*
1934–54	Arnold Toynbee, *A Study of History*
1936	John Maynard Keynes, *The General Theory of Employment, Interest, and Money*
1937	Dietrich Bonhoeffer, *The Cost of Discipleship*
1941	Erich Fromm, *Escape From Freedom*
1943	Christopher Dawson, *The Judgment of Nations*
1943	C. S. Lewis, *The Abolition of Man*
1943	Jean-Paul Sartre, *Being and Nothingness*
1944	Friedrich Hayek, *The Road to Serfdom*
1944	Jacques Maritain, *Christianity and Democracy*
1945	Karl Popper, *The Open Society and Its Enemies*
1946	Ernst Cassirer, *The Myth of the State*
1946	Jean-Paul Sartre, *Existentialism as a Humanism*
1947	Primo Levi, *If This Is A Man*
1948	Winston Churchill, *The Second World War*
1949	Simone de Beauvoir, *The Second Sex*
1948–51	Antonio Gramsci, *Prison Notebooks*
1949	Dietrich Bonhoeffer, *Ethics*
1953	Czeslaw Milosz, *The Captive Mind*
1955	Claude Lévi-Strauss, *Tristes Tropiques*
1957	Milovan Djilas, *The New Class: An Analysis of the Communist System*
1958	Hannah Arendt, *The Origins of Totalitarianism*
1959	C. P. Snow, *The Two Cultures, and the Scientific Revolution*
1961	Michel Foucault, *Madness and Civilization*
1964	Jacques Ellul, *The Technological Society*
1966	E. P. Thompson, *The Making of the English Working Class*
1968	Erich Fromm, *The Revolution of Hope*
1969	Isaiah Berlin, *Four Essays on Liberty*
1974–76	Aleksandr Solzhenitzyn, *The Gulag Archipelago*
1978	Jacques Ellul, *Betrayal of the West*
1987	Mikhail Gorbachev, *Perestroika*
1990	Vaclav Havel, *Living in Truth*

Postwar Despair

The new view of reality destroyed the foundational premise of classical liberalism and democracy, as well as humanitarianism. The experiences of the Great War together with the economic crises and social dislocations that followed, and in part resulted from it, further deepened the dark shadow over the future. Those who had experienced the "sausage machine" of trench warfare might well agree with the view that Western civilization was dying.

No one better expressed the postwar mood than the German school teacher and philosopher Oswald Spengler (1880–1936). Spengler's *Decline of the West* (1918–1922) was the most famous postwar prophecy of impending doom. Spengler viewed Western civilization as a living organism which, like any living organism, must pass through the stages of life from birth to death. The signs of degeneration were everywhere, said Spengler. Western civilization was on its deathbed, and its demise was unavoidable.

Spengler's ideas were very popular, especially in Germany, where they were often discussed and cited. Those on the extreme right exploited them by claiming to construct a new order upon the ruins of a dead civilization. Nietzsche had prophesied the rise of supermen (*übermenschen*), who would create new myths to take the place of God, who had been murdered by the advance of civilization. In a sense, Hitler can be understood as one such "superman," and the Nazi racial state as one such myth. Likewise, Lenin, Stalin, and the Soviet Union may be understood as fulfillments of Nietsche's prophecy.

Other writers used the theme of apocalypse to emphasize the possibility of renovating European civilization and a new Dark Age. This approach culminated in two remarkable books that appeared at the end of the 1920s: Sigmund Freud's *Civilization and Its Discontents* (1930) and José Ortega y Gasset's (1883–1955) *The Revolt of the Masses* (1930). Both men emphasized that civilization was an artificial product of human effort, maintained only by work and sacrifice. Freud, in line with his research before the Great War, stressed the idea that civilization was based on the repression of natural instincts, so that one paid a psychic price for living in a civilized society. However, from his vantage point at the end of the 1920s, Freud saw the failure to maintain civilization exacting an even higher cost in the long run: the destruction of all human values.

The new Bolshevik order in Russia also benefitted from the despair of the postwar years. There too a Nietzschian prophecy was apparently being fulfilled. The new socialist individual and a new Marxist doctrine of progress to a future utopia on earth were attractive to many, especially leftist intellectuals, who sought to escape despair by a leap of faith. Many took the pilgrimage to the Soviet Union during the 1930s. Some, like the American journalist Lincoln Steffens (1866–1936), returned convinced that they had been to the future, and that it worked. Others, like the British journalist Malcolm Muggeridge (1903–1990), came back thoroughly disillusioned. The Soviet Union was not an answer to despair, but rather a symptom of postwar demoralization.

Many intellectuals, artists, and writers of various sorts during the 1930s took one side or the other in the great ideological struggle between fascism and communism. The "Auden Generation," for example, which included the poets W. H. Auden (1907–1973) and C. Day Lewis (1904–1972), important continental writers such as André Malraux (1901–1976), Ignazio Silone (1900–1978), and Arthur Koestler (1905–1983), and artists such as Max Beckmann (1884–1950) and Max Ernst (1891–1976) lent their talents in one fashion or another to the defense of democracy and the criticism of fascism. The support offered fascism by intellectuals and artists was less substantial. Scattered examples, such as the playwright Gerhart Hauptmann (1862–1946) in Germany or the novelist Louis-Ferdinand Céline (1894–1961) in France, come to mind. By and large, however, commitment by artists and intellectuals meant a defense of democracy (and often a defense of the socialist democracy of the Soviet Union) and a condemnation of fascism.

The experiences of the Great War also helped promote the careers of the utopian demagogues of the 1930s and 1940s in other ways. Not only were the new discoveries of science and the new philosophical theories beyond the comprehension of the masses, so too was the carnage of the war. The social and economic dislocations resulting from the collapse of the old order drove large numbers of people to seek answers. It was easy for the new demagogues to direct the resentment of the masses to an identifiable enemy, be it the Jews, capitalists, communists, or simply the establishment. Somewhere some personified evil force was to blame for the chaos from which it benefitted.

It was also possible to preach the mass extermination of the enemy race or class. The Great War had cheapened life. It left behind images of mass death previously unknown. If millions of lives could be sacrificed to gain a few yards of churned-up earth, did it not make more sense to sacrifice millions of lives to create a classless or racially pure utopia? The Holocaust of Nazi Germany and the "Gulag" of Soviet Russia were to some extent conceivable because of the images left by the Great War.

Culture

The new world view that took shape even before the Great War was given expression by the artists, writers, poets, and musicians. The new emerging world view assumed that there is no *Truth*, not even in science. Instead of *Truth*, there are only *truths*. Instead of order, there is only chaos. Instead of value for humans and history, there is no value (although the post–World War II existentialists would say that the individual can give his or her life and history value through action). The new world view was a fragmented view of reality. Great art is the merger of technique with world view. The purveyors of culture after the Great War developed a technique of fragmentation to fit the new world view.

In art, the transition began with the impressionist painters in the 1870s. In the name of "realism," they rebelled against the practice of portraying the world around them in camera-like realism. The impressionists (e.g., Claude Monet [1840–1926], Pierre Auguste Renoir [1841–1919], Camille Pissarro [1830–1903], Alfred Sisley [1839–1899], and Edgar Degas [1834–1917]) emphasized the play of light as they perceived it. In so doing, they abandoned objective reality (portraying the world around them) for a subjective response to the real world. The question was now what was "real," the object, or the artist's mental "impression" of it?

The impressionists were succeeded by a group known as the post-impressionists. They sought reality in the recesses of the mind. Reality was now the observer's (i.e., individual artist's) mental reflections upon the sensory images coming into the mind as light waves. Among the leading postimpressionists were Paul Cézanne (1839–1906), Vincent Van Gogh (1853–1890), Paul Gauguin (1848–1903), and Georges Seurat (1859–1891). By 1910, postimpressionism yielded to abstract art.

The abstract artists totally abandoned reality. No longer did the artists see as their task simply painting the objective world around them. As with the new physics, there was no fixed reality. Reality was what the artist said it was. A painting was not a portrait or even an impression of reality. Rather, it "created" reality. Also, there could no longer be an objective standard by which to judge what was good art or bad art. Art had become a vehicle for the new world view.

As in any age, only a relatively small segment of the population was aware of the changing intellectual and artistic understanding of reality, or wrestled with the implications of an acceptance of the new view of humans as irrational animals in an impersonal, morally neutral universe. The masses only slowly absorbed the new world view, and then only passively and in cursory form through the mass media (e.g., radio, motion pictures, etc.). They would borrow "sound bites" from the new physics or psychology and speak of "relativity" or the "unconscious," much as in an earlier period they spoke of "survival of the fittest" or "natural selection," without any real understanding of the meaning or implications of these "buzz words." The average individual does not sit down and try to systematically understand what is his world view, or the presuppositions underlying it. Still, everyone has a world view and acts according to it, as much as artists, philosophers, or politicians do.

The message of the artistic movements of the interwar years was one of anarchy, even nihilism. In responding to the disillusionment of war, the dadaists rejected all order and reason. Whatever reality there was, was created in the individual's mind in response to the fragmented images created by the artist. Surrealism, which flowed out of dadaism, sought reality in the unconscious, beyond the reach of reason. Both were responses to the apparent chaos of the time, but without any hint of an answer.

In the skilled hands of artists like Otto Dix (1891–1969), George Grosz (1893–1959), Pablo Picasso (1881–1973), Max Beckmann, Käthe Kollwitz (1867–1945), and others, the new fragmented technique was employed to make paintings powerful statements against the insanity of war and the decadence of postwar society and politics.

The message that passed through the artist's brush onto the canvas also passed through the poet's or novelist's pen onto the page, and thence into the mind of the reader. James Joyce (1882–1941) used the literary technique known as "stream-of-consciousness" in *Ulysses* (1922) to portray a single day in the lives of middle-class Dubliners. In both the title and the style of *The Waste Land* (1922), T. S. Eliot (1888–1965) used a fragmented form of poetry to convey a fragmented message:

> *Le Prince d'Aquitaine à la tour abolie.*
> These fragments I have shored against my ruins
> Why then Ile fit you.
> Hieronymo's mad againe.
> Datta. Dayadhvam. Damyata.
>   Shantih shantih shantih.

Joyce and Eliot were among the avant-garde. Interwar literature aimed at mass consumption consisted largely of realistic novels and accepted poetic styles. The same was true of music and the new art form, the cinema.

Jazz was a peculiarly American contribution to both popular and high culture between the wars. It first appeared as a distinct form of music in New Orleans around the turn of the century, where it was "composed" and performed without written music by African-American street musicians who had no formal training in music. From New Orleans it spread to Chicago and Harlem. After the war, the "Jazz Age"3 was born, as white jazz bands began to appear across America and in Europe. Jazz music found a home in Paris, one of the two centers of European culture during the 1920s. There, and later in Berlin, the other locus of cultural life in the 1920s, Josephine Baker (1906–1975), an African American from St. Louis, delighted audiences dancing the charleston wearing only a string of bananas around her waist, as she sang jazz favorites. Berlin, where life was a cabaret, was a Mecca for those from all over Europe seeking a decadent lifestyle that included jazz, nightclubs, drugs, liquor, prostitution, and homosexuality.

Berlin was also the center of the motion picture industry prior to the Nazis' ascent to power. Not all of the films produced were meant only for entertainment. In Weimar Germany film became a serious art form. Pictures like *The Cabinet of Dr. Caligari* (1920), *The Golem* (1920), and others merged technique and message to produce works of expressionist art. Perhaps the best known, and perhaps the most significant, film produced in Weimar Germany was *The Blue Angel* (1930), starring Marlene Dietrich (1901–1992). Some critics have seen in it an allegory of the triumph of the new (and decadent) Germany over the old. Through their music and atmosphere, *The Blue Angel* and Bertolt Brecht's (1898–1956) stage play, *The Threepenny Opera,* captured the mood of Weimar Germany's cultural life. *The Threepenny Opera* premiered at the Schiffbauerdamm Theatre in Berlin, with a musical score influenced by jazz and composed by Kurt Weill (1900–1950).

It was in the 1920s, and especially the last half of the 1920s, that one could begin to speak of a "popular culture" as distinct from "high culture." Of course, popular culture had its roots in the last half of the nineteenth century. But it was in the 1920s that it developed into what we know today. Originally the property of the working classes and class oriented, popular culture had become by the late 1920s largely a matter of entertainment, recreation, fashions, and fads which, for a short period of time, might bind people from different social backgrounds together and blur the still significant differences that existed.

Whether good or bad, popular culture in the affluent and vital late 1920s developed most of the attributes familiar in today's society. Entertainment became increasingly commercialized and built on changing fashions. New songs, new dance steps, and new movie stars followed one another in an accelerating pace. The growth of spectator sports was only one example of the trend toward passive involvement in culture. In all areas of entertainment, the lowest common denominator was sought in order to attract as wide an audience as possible.

The masses were the passive consumers of culture during the interwar years. The disintegration of the Enlightenment tradition and its conse-

3 The first talking motion picture was *The Jazz Singer,* starring Al Jolson (1927).

Bertolt Brecht's best-known play, *The Threepenny Opera*, is often seen today as a romance rather than as a serious, Marxist-inspired social criticism. Film still courtesy Filmmusem Berlin–DeutscheKinemathek Photoarchiv.

quences, which preoccupied the scientists and philosophers and found anguished expression in the creative works of the artists and poets, did not immediately affect the masses. It was not until after the Second World War that the assumptions of the new world view (in the form of, e.g., existentialism) would filter down to the masses through the mass media. Catalyzed again by war and economic dislocations, they would find violent expression during the 1960s and 1970s, before giving way in the last quarter of the century to an individual quest for personal peace and affluence, one troubled still by a vague feeling of anxiety.

The Social Impact

Even in the best-run war efforts, there was much dislocation and suffering among civilians, but one of the most important ways in which the Great War changed social relations was to reduce the importance of class or status. The emphasis from the beginning had been on the cooperation of all layers of society in the war effort. Each country had its equivalent of the French *union sacrée* or the German *Burgfrieden*. Governments erased many distinctions through rationing and other efforts to make the burdens of war equitable. Governments also erased distinctions by the first efforts toward the standardization of life, an example of which were the form postcards that civilians received from the front: on the card were only a few standard messages from which the soldier could choose. In a more positive manner, the comprehensive mobilization of each population during the war created a sense of participation in the affairs of the nation and a sense of individual self-respect that many had not felt before. Many were thrust into new responsibilities and discovered in themselves abilities and aspirations that had previously lain dormant. One such person was Rosina Whyatt, a household servant before the war, who went to work in a munitions plant and after the war became a labor organizer. Many felt that after the war they could not accept a return to the old society and that, in any case, they had earned a reward for their sacrifices. These feelings were reinforced by returning soldiers who, after living through the horrors of trench warfare, would not willingly stand mutely in awe of their "betters" again. Leonard Thompson, a farm worker from Suffolk, came back after serving in the war to organize a branch of the Agricultural Labourers Union. Others in Britain and on the continent followed similar paths.

One group in particular took on new roles during the war. Women found positions in industries that had traditionally been closed to them, as well as expanded opportunities in areas in which they were already active. It became far more acceptable than ever before for women to have their own apartments, to go out unescorted, and, generally, to make their own decisions about their lives. In Britain and Germany, although not in France, it seemed impossible after the war to deny women the vote. Many people, of course, returned to an older concept of the place of women once the unusual situation created by the war had ended. Many women, however, found it impossible to give up the independence and responsibility to which they had become accustomed. The era of the flapper in the twenties would not have been possible without the changes in attitudes, in both males and females, caused by the Great War.

Peasants and Agriculture

The peasantry was perhaps the class least affected by the Great War, and the one class that did not share in the general prosperity of the later 1920s. Food prices, on which the income of farmers depended, were low throughout the 1920s and competition from abroad was stiff. Many peasants in western Europe had borrowed either during or right after the war to purchase land or equipment. These debts were difficult to repay in the later 1920s.

Many peasants had served in the army or had in other ways become more aware of the nature of life beyond their own region. They expected more in the 1920s and in some cases were willing to work in new and different ways to obtain their demands. In Britain many agricultural laborers joined organizations to improve pay and working conditions. The interwar period was one of bitter struggle as organized agricultural laborers tried to persuade their fellow laborers to join and fight to gain recognition from the landlords. In Italy an attempt in the early 1920s to reform landholding patterns was defeated in the postwar violence that led to Fascism. In Germany many peasants left the land for the cities; those who remained on the land began to support movements such as the Nazi Party, which promised to protect the farmer and the small agricultural enterprise. Although some French and German peasants resorted to lobbying groups, cooperative movements, and the promise of technology to improve their condition, little changed in terms of agricultural practices and lifestyles. Peasants continued to lead largely isolated, family-centered existences. The peasants in western Europe had been brought into contact with the modern world before the Great War through the development of the market economy, the spread of public education, expansion of national institutions like the army, and the improvement of transportation and communication facilities, but their contact was still slight and episodic even in the late 1920s.

In eastern Europe, the process of rural adaptation—that had taken place in western Europe and America before the Great War—had barely begun by the end of the 1920s. The power of the landed elites and traditional aristocracies was still formidable. In some countries, Bulgaria for example, the small peasant landholders remained an important group. In most countries, Hungary being perhaps the best example, the large estate owners dominated agriculture. In every case, rural populations continued to grow, placing additional pressure on the agricultural economy. In much of eastern Europe, poverty, superstition, ignorance, and isolation were the rule among the peasantry. Some new ideas circulated as a result of service in the war, the impact of the Russian Revolution, and the work of peasant political movements, but most peasants lived in ways scarcely different from those of their ancestors in the early 1800s. Only in the Soviet Union was a large-scale effort made to introduce the peasant to the modern world, an effort that took on revolutionary proportions in the early 1930s.

The Working Class

In general, the working classes benefitted from the war. Labor supported the war effort in each country by ensuring labor stability and thus war production. In return, the working classes received higher wages, recognition of the right to unionize and bargain collectively, and even participation by labor's leaders in government decisionmaking. When the war ended, labor was determined not to yield any of its newly won status or influence.

Although in the 1920s the organized working class was stronger and more influential than it had been before the war, it was not as strong as it might have been. This was due to two related developments. First, the organized working class split in the immediate postwar period into a communist movement that centered on the Comintern and a socialist movement that continued the policies of the old Second International. The German Social Democratic Party (SPD), faced competition from the left in the Communist Party of Germany (KPD); and there were similar divisions elsewhere in western Europe. The split was also reflected in the trade union movement and many other specialized organizations. Precisely because the communist and the socialist parties referred to the same heritage (Marxism) to interpret political and social events and because both appealed to the same social group (the working class), they were bitter rivals. The communists in particular thought competition of the socialists caused the working class to divide into mutually hostile groups. The split also made it difficult for social democratic parties to moderate their stance toward bourgeois society and government. Even in Germany, where the SPD was often a crucial element in coalition governments, the official line was unremitting hostility to the existing order. Any serious compromise of Marxist doctrine might have driven even more of the working class into the Communist Party.

Although a united working class would have been stronger than a divided one, a divided one was still impressive. Socialists were not only represented in large numbers on the national level, but they also played important roles in municipal and provincial governments in Italy (until the Fascists came to power), Germany, and France. Unfortunately, despite generally responsible attitudes and actions, working-class representatives never gained the trust and full cooperation of their middle-class counterparts. Particularly in Germany, most members of the middle class resented the new political power of the workers on the local and state levels.

Organized labor faced even stronger resistance to its influence in the economic sphere. At the end of the war the labor movement had pushed hard for economic changes, including higher wages, better working conditions, shorter hours, and worker participation in the management of industry. The dislocation of national economies (e.g., Great Britain) made it difficult for organized labor to maintain its wartime gains. This, together with the determination of returning veterans to gain what they believed was fairly theirs, and promises of a better life by politicians and business leaders, fueled strike movements in 1919 and 1920 in France, Britain, Germany and Italy.

Efforts to resolve these economic and social problems in the immediate postwar period met with little success. In part this failure was due to the short depression that Europe experienced at the beginning of the 1920s. The split within the labor movement at the same time also weakened it. Employers rapidly organized groups in the early 1920s to influence the government and to provide mutual aid against strikes; the rate of defeat of strikes went up. Governments became less sympathetic to labor goals and in some cases, notably that of Fascist Italy, obviously hostile. Still, by 1924 and 1925 general prosperity led to better conditions for most groups of workers. Many worked eight-hour days with Saturday half-holidays. Real wages rose between 1924 and 1929. Workers participated with other groups in the new possibilities for entertainment and recreation. The major exception to the general labor peace in the latter part of the 1920s was the British General Strike in 1926, but Britain was plagued by high levels of unemployment in the 1920s and by a particularly troubled but important sector of the economy, the coal mining industry. Perhaps the main result of the resounding defeat of the coal miners, who had stayed out on strike after other groups involved in the General Strike had gone back to work, was the reduction of overt labor unrest in Britain despite the troubled economy.

The Middle Class

Historically, the middle class (or bourgeoisie) was the driving force and backbone of liberalism. Indeed, the nineteenth century was the "golden age" of both liberalism and the middle class. But the stability of the middle class rested upon its ability to accumulate wealth and pass it on to the next generation. The validity of its world view was based on traditional morality. Middle-class people believed that by their industriousness, frugality, and defense of the nuclear family and traditional values, they played a major role in creating a better world. The middle class had retained its faith in progress because of its self-confidence. One of the most important effects of the Great War was that it undermined that self-confidence.

The spiritual crisis confronting Western civilization at the turn of the century (as noted above) undermined the religious foundations of middle-class morality. Since the middle class traditionally viewed everything in moral terms, the emergence of a new world view had serious implications for it. Likewise, the emancipation of women (e.g., greater employment op-portunities, loosening of divorce laws and traditional moral codes) furthered by the war effort, together with the growth of public education and a mass culture, undermined the importance of the family. Individuals increasingly sought their fulfillment outside of the home.

The financial base of middle-class ascendancy was also weakened by the war and its economic repercussions. Some historians have speculated that one of the most important effects of the Great War was the financial impoverishment of the middle class due to taxes, inflation, and the expropriation of wealth through nationalization, land reform, and rent controls. Taxes, virtually nonexistent or very light before 1914, became burdensome after 1919. Inflation was often devastating for the middle class. In France, for example, a capital investment of 500,000 francs in 1914 would allow one to live in style off the annual interest income. That same capital investment in 1924, although producing a higher annual income, was not sufficient to maintain the same standard of living. The cumulative impact was demoralizing for the middle class, who began to question the value of its work and its other contributions to civilization. Also, the middle class began to question the validity of liberalism, both economic and political.

Businessmen, for example, tended to believe that parliamentary democracy was a weak and ineffectual means of government. A strong national state required a more authoritarian kind of leadership and, in any case, one sympathetic to business. Those who lived in small towns and provincial centers identified Europe's problems with the increase of urbanization. It was the city, especially Berlin in Germany and Paris in France, where all that was wrong and dangerous was spawned. For the middle class, the late 1920s were good times, but, having experienced war, revolution, depression, and inflation in recent memory, this segment of the population was wary and somewhat insecure. Waiting in the wings to benefit from that sense of insecurity during the 1930s were the demagogues, those who considered themselves the supermen of Nietzsche's vision.

Suggested Books and Films

Otto Friedrich, *Before the Deluge: A Portrait of Berlin in the 1920's* (1972). A very readable and entertaining history of the cultural life of Weimar Germany.

Robert Graves and Alan Hodge, *The Long Week-End: A Social History of Great Britain, 1918–1939* (1963). The ever-popular account of everyday life in interwar Britain.

Paul Johnson, *Intellectuals* (1988). Short, well-written biographies of important cultural figures including Bertolt Brecht, Bertrand Russell, and Jean-Paul Sarte.

Abraham Pais, *Subtle Is the Lord: The Science and Life of Albert Einstein* (1982). A look at the life and ideas of the man who "reordered" the universe.

H. R. Rookmaaker, *Modern Art & the Death of a Culture* (1970). Discusses art as a vehicle for world view.

Raymond J. Sontag, *A Broken World, 1919–1939* (1971). Still one of the best introductions to Europe during the 1920s.

Roland N. Stromberg, *Makers of Modern Culture: Five Twentieth-Century Thinkers* (1991). A concise examination of five individuals—Sigmund Freud, Albert Einstein, Ludwig Wittgenstein, James Joyce, and Jean-Paul Sarte—who transformed the world.

Metropolis, 1926. Fritz Lang's silent film classic that powerfully portrays the dehumanization of modern science and urbanization. A good example of the German cinema of the 1920s.

Cabaret, 1972. A popular musical based loosely on Christopher Isherwood's autobiographical novels *The Last of Mr. Norris* (1935) and *Goodbye to Berlin* (1939). It captures the mood and atmosphere of Berlin in the early 1930s.

Chronology

1919	German National Assembly drafts the Weimar Constitution
1921	Russian Civil War ends
	Lenin introduces the New Economic Policy (NEP)
1922	Washington Naval Conference
	Rapallo Treaty between Germany and the Soviet Union
1923	"Beer Hall (Munich) Putsch" led by Adolf Hitler
	Ruhr Occupation (June 1923–August 1924) triggers Great Inflation in Germany
1924	Lenin dies; power struggle between Leon Trotsky and Joseph Stalin
1925	Locarno treaties between Germany, France, and Belgium
1926	General Strike in Great Britain
1928	Kellogg-Briand Pact
1929	Joseph Stalin succeeds Lenin as the leader of the Soviet Union
	Lateran Accord between Italy and the Papacy

5
Recovery and Prosperity, 1919–1929

THE GREAT WAR HAD BEEN FOUGHT to "make the world safe for democracy."
It was also the "war to end all wars." To some perceptive individuals in
1919, these were hollow utopian slogans that concealed the approach of
the grim reaper to harvest the bitter seeds of resentment and hatred sown
and watered at the Paris Peace Conference. Looking back after a second
and more destructive world war, it is tempting to view the events of the
1920s and 1930s with the clarity of historical determinism. But if one
views the events of the 1920s without the benefit of hindsight, it is possible to sympathize with those who chose to see the Great War as a brief
and unfortunate interruption in the forward march of civilization. The
Great Depression would abruptly end the "Roaring Twenties" and reveal
how fragile were the foundations of the return to "normalcy." But a look
at international relations and the internal affairs of the major European
states reveals a collection of mixed signals.

The most obvious outcome of the Great War was the passing of the
ancient empires of Germany, Russia, Austria-Hungary, and Turkey. With
the departure of those antique dynasties, and with them a host of lesser
princely houses, a new era appeared to be dawning, when, as President
Woodrow Wilson had foretold in 1917, those who submitted to authority would have "a voice in their own government." Where in 1914 there
had been seventeen monarchies and three republics, in 1919 there were
thirteen monarchies and thirteen republics. Germany, Austria, Hungary,
Czechoslovakia, and Turkey were all proclaimed republics. In Russia, the
autocratic rule of the Tsar was replaced by what Lenin called "democratic
centralism," a Soviet republic that was soon revealed as more autocratic
than tsarist Russia. In nearly every country, a communist party emerged
from the old social democratic and trade union movements to challenge
what communists termed "bourgeois democracy." The various communist
parties were connected with one another in an organization called the Communist, or Third, International (the Cominterm), which seemed, potentially

at least, very dangerous to democracy. Attempts to establish the new soviet style "democracy" in Germany (1919, 1921, and 1923) and Hungary (1919) were defeated by the army, assisted in Germany by paramilitary forces (the Freikorps) and in Hungary by the Romanian army.

A constitutional and parliamentary government, republican more often than monarchical, was the norm by the mid-twenties. Universal male suffrage was generally accepted; some nations had adopted female suffrage as well after the war. On the continent, socialist parties had to face the question of active participation in government. In Germany, the Social Democrats (SPD) formed a major component of the coalition government. In France, the Socialists backed away from full participation. Everywhere the centrist parties formed the backbone of the ministries. It was still nearly a decade before William Butler Yeats's prophetic line "Things fall apart; the centre cannot hold" would come true.

There were several examples of cooperation in international relations during the 1920s. In 1922, the Washington Naval Conference made progress towards limiting the size of navies among the five postwar great powers. Some seventy ships were scrapped; a ten-year moratorium on the construction of any new battleships was declared; and the five signatories agreed to limit the tonnage of capital ships to a ratio of: 5, Great Britain; 5, U.S.A.; 3, Japan; 1.75, France; 1.75, Italy. In April 1922, Germany and Soviet Russia signed the Rappallo Treaty, by which they reestablished diplomatic relations, renounced all financial claims against each other, and pledged cooperation. It initiated five years of close cooperation between the two ostracized powers. Also in 1922, the "Little Entente" of Czechoslovakia, Yugoslavia, and Romania was formed under French auspices to dampen the fears of both France and the east European successor states of a revived Germany.

Perhaps the most promising development was the Locarno treaties concluded in December 1925. In the principal treaty signed by France, Belgium, and Germany, and guaranteed by Great Britain and Italy, Germany accepted as final its western borders with France and Belgium as fixed by the Versailles Treaty. The inviolability of the demilitarized Rhineland was also confirmed. The Locarno treaties were the work of Gustav Stresemann (1878–1929), Aristide Briand, and Austin Chamberlain (1863–1937)—all of whom received the Nobel Peace Prize—three foreign ministers committed to international cooperation based upon the fulfillment of the Paris Peace Settlement. A new spirit of conciliation swept through Europe in the wake of the Locarno agreements. Even the French were beginning to suspect that the Germans were becoming civilized. The fact, however, that Germany specifically refused to accept as permanent its eastern borders should have cast a shadow over the "spirit of Locarno."

Perhaps the best expression of the widespread optimism engendered by the spirit of Locarno was the Kellogg-Briand Pact of 1928, which outlawed war as an instrument of national policy. Proposed to United States Secretary of State Frank B. Kellogg (1856–1937) by Aristide Briand, it was signed by sixty-four nations. The Kellogg-Briand Pact was given more immediate significance due to the fact that Germany and the two leading non–League members, the United States and Soviet Union, signed it. As the following decade was to demonstrate, outlawing war and calling for peaceful resolution of international disputes while not providing any means for enforcement was only a pious gesture, or as one U.S. senator put it, an "international kiss." In 1928, spirits were high amidst economic prosperity and international conciliation. No one could see the Great Depression waiting ominously in the wings to shatter the illusion. A closer look inside the European powers during the 1920s reveals disturbing signs of future distress.

Great Britain

On the eve of the Great War, three major problems had threatened to overwhelm the British government: 1) the question of Irish home rule, 2) the vote for women, and 3) a broad-based dissatisfaction among workers. At the end of the war, the first two issues were resolved, although not to everyone's complete satisfaction. Agreements in 1920 and 1921 resulted in the division of Ireland into Northern Ireland, which remained attached to Great Britain as an autonomous area, and the Irish Free State, which gained Dominion status. It was a far-from-definitive solution, but one which largely removed the Irish problem from British politics for the first time in over a century. The second issue was resolved when women over thirty were given the vote in 1918 (ten years later women received the vote on the same terms as men).

The third issue was more intractable. Great Britain's problems between the wars were rooted in the economic impact of the Great War. As an island nation with an empire upon which the sun never set before 1914, British prosperity, and with it British influence, depended upon foreign trade. But Britain's dominant position in world trade was severely shaken by the war. Many old reliable trading partners either developed their own industries and reduced imports, or established new trade relations with other nations (e.g., the U.S.A. and Japan). Still others were themselves too impoverished by the war to continue as major trading partners. An example of the latter was Germany, Britain's leading continental trading partner before 1914. At the same time, the cost of the war had increased the national debt by about 1,000 percent. In the course of the war, Britain had exchanged its position of creditor for that of debtor.

In some important ways, Britain had become less competitive industrially. It had not participated to the same extent as Germany in the rapid development of electrical and chemical industries. A large part of its industrial base consisted of the older coal, iron, steel, textiles, and shipbuilding industries. Britain had lost the competitive edge in these key labor-intensive industries. When in 1925 the Exchequer put Britain back on the gold standard, the problem was only exacerbated. British goods became too expensive, resulting in decreased exports. For a while the "invisible exports" (e.g., income from shipping and foreign investments) offset the losses. But the drop in exports hit especially hard those traditional industries which employed large numbers of workers. The result was chronic unemployment of at least 1, often 2 or more, million persons during the 1920s.

Chronic unemployment led to frequent strikes that culminated in the General Strike of May 3–12, 1926. The general strike began with a strike by the coal miners. The miners were joined by most of Britain's organized labor as the Trades Union Congress (TUC) called for a general strike. The strike collapsed after nine days, although the miners continued to strike for six months until starvation forced them to return to work on the mine owners' terms.

The dominant theme in British politics during the 1920s was the decline of the Liberal Party and the rise of the Labour Party amidst a generally conservative political mood among voters. Until 1922, the Liberal Party governed with the support of the Conservatives. In the parliamentary elections of 1922, Labour emerged for the first time as "His Majesty's Loyal Opposition." Twice during the 1920s Labour led a minority government headed by Ramsey MacDonald (1866–1937) and supported by the Liberals. Neither during their first tenure in office, from January to October 1924, nor their second, from May 1929 to August 1931, did the Labour government attempt anything radical. Rather by governing very timidly, largely in line with the policies set by the Conservatives, they earned respect among middle-class voters, something they needed in order to become the normal alternative to the Conservatives. The most daring action taken by the Labour governments was to establish diplomatic relations with the Soviet Union. The Conservatives, with their belief in deflation, strict economy in government spending, and a passive foreign policy, best represented the mood of most British voters during the 1920s.

France

During the 1920s, France was preoccupied with Germany. This was due to both economic and security considerations. France had suffered greater proportional losses than any other country in the war. Northeast France had been a battlefield for almost four years. Much of the nation's prewar industry had been devastated. It borrowed heavily in order to rebuild the war-ravaged areas. Plagued with inflation, a rising national debt, and an unbalanced budget, the French looked to war reparations from Germany for financial relief.

The hard line toward Germany also seemed necessary because of France's feelings of insecurity. When both the United States and Great Britain refused to ratify the defensive alliance with France, the French were left to fend for themselves. Thus France adopted an intransigent attitude towards Germany, determined to keep Germany weak and isolated. At the same time it sought to replace the old prewar Franco-Russian alliance with alliances with the new eastern European states (e.g., the Little Entente in 1922). It was a dangerously shortsighted policy that could only hope to succeed so long as both Germany and the Soviet Union remained prostrate.

The political situation in France remained confused and unstable during the 1920s. The Socialist Party split in 1920 into the French Communist Party, affiliated with the Comintern, and the Socialist Party. In May 1924, the Left Cartel, a coalition of Socialists and Radicals, assumed control of the government from the National Bloc, a coalition of centrist and rightist parties. The Socialists and Radicals disagreed on how to deal with the troubled economy. Between April 1925 and June 1926, six cabinets came and went as Socialists and Radicals remained deadlocked.

In July 1926, Raymond Poincaré (1860–1934) returned to power at the head of a National Union ministry that governed France until July 1929. With the support of the Radicals and the centrist and rightist parties, Poincaré pursued a conservative economic policy. Poincaré had headed the government between 1922 and 1924, when France (together with Belgium) occupied the Ruhr industrial district of Germany with disastrous results for the Weimar Republic and France. Between 1926 and 1929, however, Poincaré's conservative policies restored financial stability to France.

In 1928, with the franc worth about one-fifth its prewar value (as opposed to one-tenth at its low point two years before), France went on the international gold standard. The devaluation of the franc was a disguised repudiation of much of the national debt, which had been contracted in terms of the prewar franc. It was a difficult blow for many in the middle classes, the value of whose savings and investments had been undermined. The determination grew never to allow the franc to be touched again. Devaluation brought financial stability, however, and "normalcy" to France. In fact, mainly because of Poincaré's measures France was better prepared than most European countries for the worldwide economic difficulties that began in 1929.

Weimar Germany

In January 1919, while Berlin was in revolution, German voters elected a National Assembly to draft a constitution for what became known as the Weimar Republic. In February, the delegates met in the town of Weimar. The National Assembly chose as president Friedrich Ebert, the leader of the Social Democrats and former saddlemaker, bartender, journalist, and party bureaucrat. A constitution was drafted that was a model of a democratic constitution. Two aspects of the constitution were to prove fatal for the Republic, however. Article 48 allowed the president to rule by decree during times of national emergency. Also, the lower house of the Reichstag was to be elected by universal suffrage, but according to a system of proportional representation that made it virtually impossible for any one party to achieve a majority. Indeed, during the life of the Republic, no party ever achieved a majority.

The survival of the Republic became dependent upon the cooperation of the so-called "Weimar parties"—Social Democrats (SPD), Catholic Center Party (Z), and German Democratic Party (DDP). These parties were ideologically incompatible, but willing to collaborate because the alternative was too frightening to contemplate. Important differences of opinion on both economic and political questions were only papered over. Most Germans did not prefer the Republic and even associated it with defeat and betrayal. The traditional elites of army, judiciary, bureaucracy, church, and landed and industrial wealth remained openly hostile. Symptomatic of German feeling toward the Republic was the election in 1925 of Paul von Hindenburg, war hero and supporter of the monarchy, as president, following the death of Ebert.

The threat from the right took the form of two attempted coups in 1920 and 1923. On March 13, 1920, a right-wing journalist, Wolfgang Kapp (1858–1922), attempted to seize power in Berlin. Kapp was supported by General Ludendorff and recently disbanded units of the Freikorps. The military refused to come to the Republic's aid as it had during the Spartakus and other communist revolts. Only a general strike called by organized labor saved the Republic. On March 17, Kapp left Berlin for exile in Sweden.

Also from the right was the attempt by Adolf Hitler (1889–1945) to seize control of the government in Munich on November 8–9, 1923, preliminary to a "march on Berlin."Again, General Ludendorff was among the supporters of the attempted coup. The coup collapsed when Hitler, Luden-dorff, and their followers were confronted by armed Bavarian police as they marched into Odeonsplatz. Tried for treason, Ludendorff was acquitted and Hitler was sentenced to five years imprisonment, of which he served only nine months. The failure of the Kapp Putsch and Hitler's "Beer Hall Putsch," as well as separatist revolts in the Rhineland and communist revolts in Saxony and Thuringia during October, indicated that there was by 1923 a relative lack of strength among extremist groups. Of a greater threat was the hyperinflation caused by the Franco-Belgian occupation of the heartland of German industry, the Ruhr.

Reparations were the main sticking point in Franco-German relations and the foremost issue in German domestic politics in the early 1920s. France believed that Germany could pay enough in reparations to finance the reconstruction of France and other costs related to the war. The Germans doubted this. In January 1923, the French and the Belgians occupied the Ruhr in order to force Germany to pay. The German government encouraged a program of passive resistance, which it tried to finance by printing more and more money. Currency quickly lost all value other than the value of the paper for pulping.

In July 1914, one U.S. dollar was worth 4.2 marks. In January 1919, one U.S. dollar would purchase 8.9 marks. When the Ruhr occupation began in January 1923, the figure had risen to 17,972 marks, an unbelievable sum, but nothing compared to the 4.2 trillion marks that a single U.S. dollar

A crowd gathers in front of the Berlin Savings Bank in Germany during the Depression. AP/Wide World.

Table 5.1   Inflation in Weimar Germany

1914	$1=	4.20 marks
1919 (July)	$1=	14.00 marks
1921 (Jan.)	$1=	64.90 marks
1922 (Jan.)	$1=	191.80 marks
1922 (July)	$1=	493.20 marks
1923 (Jan.)	$1=	17,972.00 marks
1923 (Sept.)	$1=	100 million marks
1923 (Oct.)	$1=	1 trillion marks
1923 (Nov.)	$1=	4.2 trillion marks

would bring on November 15, 1923. The material impact was significant; the psychological shock was even greater. Hardest hit was the middle class, whose financial base was wiped out. Many began turning to the rightist parties for an explanation and a solution.

Finally, the government reorganized under the leadership of Gustav Stresemann from the German People's Party (DVP). A new mark was issued at the rate of one new mark for one trillion of the old inflated marks. Soon the mark stabilized at its old prewar value of 4.2 marks to the dollar. Stresemann, who served as foreign minister from 1923 until his death in 1929, carried through a policy of "fulfillment."[1]

"Fulfillment" was based on the assumption that the surest route to revision of the Versailles Treaty was to avoid open confrontation and to work with existing possibilities. Positive results were not long in coming. In 1924, the Dawes Plan provided a realistic scale for reparations payment and a foreign loan (largely provided by American banks) of 800 million gold marks. These measures, together with the end of the Ruhr occupation, enabled the German economy to recover rapidly. By 1928, German industrial production was second only to that of the United States, and unemployment was reduced to 650,000.

In contrast to its own early years of strife and turmoil, the Weimar Republic passed the last half of the decade in relative tranquility. Hitler, following his attempted putsch, spent his time in prison writing his political credo, *Mein Kampf* (1925). After his release, he was able to rebuild the Nazi Party so as to make it stronger organizationally and more intensely loyal to him personally. Yet, he was not able to make much headway in the late 1920s. He was the best-known figure of the extreme right, but not a major politician until his cooperation with the German National People's Party

1 The fact that much of the positive diplomacy of the 1920s was the result of the personal relationship between Stresemann and Aristide Briand made Stresemann's untimely death all the more tragic.

(DNVP) in the 1929 referendum on the Young Plan for the reorganization of reparations. This move brought him into national prominence. The DNVP, based on the hostility of the aristocratic large landowners and some industrialists toward the Weimar Republic, seemed a much more substantial threat to the Republic than any group on the extreme right.

Nonetheless, the major danger to the Republic in the late twenties was not without but within. The army had achieved a position of almost complete autonomy and was even more isolated from the mainstream of life in the Weimar Republic than the Imperial army had been before the Great War. The civil service remained largely composed of people technically competent but uncommitted and often actively disloyal to the Republic. Business interests combined and organized to the point where they possessed enormous powers that the government could not begin to control. The 1925 election of Paul von Hindenburg as President—a man unsympathetic to parliamentary control of government—created another problem for the Republic. A republic with such a president and with so many groups antagonistic toward it could hope to survive only if it avoided the necessity of dealing with serious problems.

Italy

Although Italy was on the wining side in the Great War, its military performance had been less than impressive. The peace conference awarded Italy much less than it felt entitled to by the Treaty of London (1915). Injured national pride was exacerbated by economic and social problems. The aftereffects of the war included a massive national debt, rapid inflation, and increasing unemployment. Between 1919 and 1921, angry workers and peasants began occupying factories and land. Italy appeared on the verge of a "Bolshevik" revolution.

The political system offered little hope for the future. The two largest parties, the Socialists and the Catholic *Popolari*, were each deeply divided. In 1921, the Socialist Party split into socialist and communist factions. The Popolari remained united in its support of the Catholic Church, but divided over economic and social issues. Neither the Socialists nor the Popolari were able to govern alone or able to imagine governing with the other. The smaller Liberal and Radical parties were unable to deal with the political and social crisis of 1919–1922, even when they possessed a working majority in the parliament.

Into this confused situation stepped the small Fascist Party, formed in 1919 by Benito Mussolini (1883–1945), a former school teacher and editor of the Socialist Party newspaper, *Avanti*. Mussolini was expelled from the Socialist Party in 1914, when he called for Italy's entry into the war on the

The fatal attraction between Benito Mussolini and Adolf Hitler eventually led both to defeat and infamy. Courtesy Bildarchiv d. ÖNB, Wien.

side of the Allies. After the war, Mussolini organized the *Fasci di Combattimento* in Milan and began denouncing Marxism and liberal democracy, while talking vaguely of social and economic reform.

From the beginning, Italian Fascism lacked any coherent doctrine or concrete program of reform. Rather, the emphasis was on action. It was a mass movement akin to a religious revival that, like both National Socialism (Nazism) and Marxism-Leninism, claimed to abolish class distinctions and fuse the masses into an organic whole. Once asked to describe the kind of order he was attempting to establish in Italy, Mussolini coined the term "totalitarianism." It must be noted, however, that Mussolini never achieved such total control in Italy. Italian Fascism was in fact a blend of ideas drawn from Nietzsche, Sorel, Bergson, and other pre-1914 intellectuals, dynamic and even romantic.

Mussolini organized a Fascist Party militia, the Black Shirts, which was used to terrorize peasants, organized labor, socialists, and communists alike. In fact, while much of the disorder caused by workers and peasants ended by 1921, the Fascists continued their work and became in that year the actual source of the largest part of the continuing unrest. They were perceived by many, though, as saving Italy from Bolshevism.

Matters came to a head in October 1922. Mussolini demanded that a Fascist cabinet be formed. The premier refused and wanted to declare martial law. King Victor Emmanuel III (1869–1947) would not agree to this, evidently fearing the power of the Fascists and believing also that they might govern responsibly if given the opportunity. The premier resigned and Mussolini was asked to form a government. The "March on Rome" that the Fascists had threatened against the government turned out to be only a train ride into the capital for Mussolini and some of his colleagues.

In the course of the next few years, Mussolini and the Fascists moved rather slowly to gain control of the government. The elections of 1924, held on the basis of the 1923 Acerbo election law which gave the party with the largest number of votes two-thirds of the seats, gave the Fascists an overwhelming position in the Chamber of Deputies. It was not, however, until the murder in 1924 of Giacomo Matteotti (1885–1924), a socialist deputy who had strongly criticized the Fascists, that the party broke with parliamentary and constitutional government in a decisive way. Shortly after the murder, most of the non-Fascist minority of the chamber left in the Aventine Secession. They were not allowed to return. The Fascists had control of both houses of parliament.

Mussolini dreamed of creating a corporate state at home and a new Roman Empire in the Mediterranean. According to theory, the corporate state harmonizes capitalism and socialism through a system of corporations (twenty-two in Fascist Italy), each of which had councils of employers and workers. Strikes by workers or lockouts by employers were forbidden. Ideally, labor and management worked together to resolve disputes, set wages, determine working conditions, and set production levels. Although a National Council of Corporations was established to make policy, the corporate state was a fraud. All decisionmaking remained firmly in the hands of the government which favored the interests of the industrialists over those of the workers.

Neither his domestic nor his foreign policies was successful. The only real success Mussolini had in both domestic and foreign policy was the Lateran Accord of February 1929, which resolved the "Roman Question" that had plagued Italy since the Kingdom of Italy seized Rome in 1870. According to the agreement, Italy paid financial damages to the Catholic Church, recognized the Vatican City as a sovereign state ruled by the pope, Roman Catholicism as the state religion, and church marriages, and approved compulsory instruction in the Catholic religion in the nation's schools. In return, the state received the right to veto the appointment of Italian bishops and, perhaps most important, the church agreed to refrain from any involvement in politics. By the Lateran Accord, Mussolini had effectively neutralized what was potentially the most effective opposition to Fascism. Hitler carried out a similar coup with the Reich Concordat in 1933. During the 1930s, Mussolini's belligerent and unsuccessful foreign policy eventually drew Italy into a fatal alliance with Hitler's Germany.

The Soviet Union

The Soviet Union[2] was the nation that faced the most difficult tasks in bringing about recovery from the war. And interest among Europeans in its fate was probably greater than interest in any other country except Germany. In 1919, there had been, in fact, considerable discussion among the Allies of the wisdom of intervention in Russia.

Civil War raged in Russia between 1918 and 1921. The new Communist government was seriously challenged by several counterrevolutionary armies made up of conservatives and moderates, known as the "Whites." The "Reds," or Red Army of the new Soviet government, were led by Leon Trotsky. The Reds enjoyed the support of the masses, whereas the Whites were often viewed by the populace as fighting for the restoration of the old tsarist regime. Despite Allied intervention in the Civil War, which was never a coordinated effort to overthrow the new communist government, the Whites were defeated. It was during the Civil War, however, that the Communist Party under Lenin's leadership consolidated its control through implementation of what was called "War Communism."

Historians disagree about whether War Communism was a series of emergency measures necessitated by the Civil War, or a means by which the political independence of the people was undermined by eliminating their economic independence. It involved the nationalization of all property, beginning with church, monastic, and crown lands and eventually including all personal property. All banking and commerce, both internal and external, became a monopoly of the state. At one point money was temporarily replaced by an official barter system. Workers' control of industry was ended by decree in 1918, and industry was nationalized over the next two years. At first, agricultural products were requisitioned from the peasants. Then, in November 1918, all land was nationalized. Workers were forbidden to strike and, in 1920, compulsory labor was introduced. Whether a series of ad hoc measures or a coherent policy, War Communism held serious implications for the future.

2 The constitution of 1918 referred to the state as the Russian Soviet Federated Socialist Republic (RS-FSR). In 1924, when additional territory was added, a new constitution was drafted which created the Union of Soviet Socialist Republics (USSR). In 1918, the Bolsheviks began to refer to themselves as the Communist Party.

By 1921 several serious rebellions took place in protest against the harsh policies of War Communism. War Communism was abandoned in 1921, when delegates to the tenth party congress accepted the New Economic Policy (NEP), sponsored by Lenin. The NEP allowed peasants to sell their surplus grain on the open market after payment of a tax based on a percentage of the harvest. Retail trade and private enterprise were partially restored while what Lenin called the "commanding heights" of the economy—banking, large industry, transport, and foreign trade—remained under government control.

The NEP did not come quickly enough to prevent a severe famine in 1921–1922, but it did result in fairly rapid economic recovery over the next few years. By the mid-twenties, standards of living had been improved and illiteracy reduced. By this time, however, Lenin was dead. His death in 1924 marked the beginnings of a struggle for power which by 1929 resulted in the emergence of Joseph Stalin (Iosif Vissarionovich Dzhugashvili) as the most powerful figure in the party and government, and in turn to new experiments with the society and economy of the Soviet Union.

In his "testament," dictated by Lenin in December 1922 following his first stroke, and in a postscript added in early January 1923, Lenin first criticized Stalin, then recommended his removal from the post as General Secretary of the Party. For a time Stalin seemed a rather obscure figure, without much power, but he had, in fact, acquired considerable power through a series of bureaucratic posts.

The power struggle within the Soviet leadership soon focused on two opposed views regarding the future of the Soviet Union represented by Stalin and Trotsky. In 1924, Stalin put forth the idea of "Socialism in One Country." According to this concept, the Soviet Union could create the conditions for socialism, an industrial economy, by itself, without the aid of revolutionary states elsewhere in Europe. This was contrary to Trotsky's ideas about "Permanent Revolution," which called for aid from other centers of revolution. By 1925, Stalin had stripped Trotsky of much of his power and moved into an alliance with the "right" group, while using his position to bring to key posts in the government and party a number of people personally loyal to him.

In 1928, having completely crushed the "left" opposition of Trotsky, Grigori Zinoviev (1883–1936), and Lev Kamenev (1883–1936) the year before, Stalin adopted some of the ideas long associated with the left, ideas concerning economic planning and rapid industrialization based on the control of agriculture. Essentially, Stalin believed that state control of agricultural production was necessary for the rapid industrialization of the Soviet Union. Collectivization of agriculture and industrialization had to be accomplished simultaneously.

At this point, Stalin was extremely powerful but far from all-powerful. His ideas were accepted because they appeared to meet the needs of the Soviet Union as the Communist Party perceived them. Stalin's First Five-Year Plan, in its original form, was ambitious but not unrealistic. Only later, through Stalin's arbitrary modifications, did the five-year plan and collectivization become overly ambitious and even utopian. In 1929 and 1930, then, Stalin and his colleagues implemented plans that would change drastically the lives of four-fifths of the population—those living in the rural areas—and make the Soviet Union into a major industrial and military power.

The Smaller States

Outside the three major democracies of Britain, France, and Germany, democracy was also firmly established in the Lowlands (Belgium, Luxembourg, and the Netherlands), the Scandinavian countries (Denmark, Sweden, Norway, and Finland), and Czechoslovakia. Belgium had been severely affected by the Great War but managed a rapid recovery under the popular King Albert I (1875–1934). The most troublesome question concerned the division of the country between the French-speaking Walloons in the south and the Dutch-speaking Flemish in the north. The Dutch largely escaped the problem of postwar adjustment that most nations experienced. Under Queen Wilhelmina (1880–1962), the Netherlands enjoyed considerable prosperity in the 1920s, much of it based on the great empire of the Dutch East Indies.

In the Scandinavian countries, the 1920s and 1930s were times in which parliamentary governments, universal suffrage, and the welfare state became firmly rooted. Each country instituted a range of social services including various plans to provide for old age, illness, accident, and unemployment. Another characteristic of the Scandinavian societies was the mixed economy, in which some government-run enterprises coexisted with many privately owned businesses and a few others in which both government and private capital actively cooperated. Many developments in the Scandinavian countries between the wars foreshadowed general trends after the Second World War. However, neither the Scandinavian nor the Lowland countries were strong enough, individually or collectively, to affect the course of European affairs in the 1920s and 1930s.

In general, the eastern European states began the 1920s with constitutional and parliamentary governments. With the exception of Czechoslovakia, all had turned to authoritarian government by 1930. Each had been plagued by a combination of lack of experience with parliamentary forms of government, severe economic problems stemming from largely agrarian economies no longer in touch with prewar markets and resources, and problems between ethnic minorities.

Poland, perhaps the most important state in the area in terms of potential influence, experienced all the difficulties typical of the eastern European state following the Great War. Caught between the Soviet Union and Germany, it was plagued by comprising many different ethnic minorities. Its parliamentary system was crippled by a plurality of fifty-nine parties, which made achieving a parliamentary majority virtually impossible. In May 1926, a coup led by Józef Piłsudski (1867–1935) abolished the republic and established a dictatorship behind the facade of a constitutional system.

Hungary had a very brief experience with a republican form of government. The republic, declared in 1918, was transformed by Béla Kun in 1919 into a communist dictatorship which, in turn, was destroyed by the Romanian invasion and the appearance of a counterrevolution. In 1920, Admiral Miklós Horthy (1868–1957), commander-in-chief, became regent and head of state. He declared Hungary a monarchy with the throne vacant. Principal governmental efforts in the 1920s were devoted to maintaining the status quo, which meant reinforcing the power of the great landowners over the peasantry and that of the majority Magyars over the ethnic minorities.

In Yugoslavia, Romania, and Bulgaria, authoritarian monarchies were in power by 1930. Czechoslovakia was a major exception to the rather sad tales of eastern Europe in the 1920s. Tolerant of its ethnic minorities, heavily industrialized and possessing a large urban population in comparison to other states in the area, Czechoslovakia was the only nation with a deeply rooted liberal tradition in eastern Europe. The nation was clearly a success by the end of the 1920s and entered the 1930s able to withstand the rigors of the Depression. In large part, its success was due to the constant efforts of the liberal Tomás Masaryk (1850–1937) and to the enormous prestige and respect he had acquired within the nation.

On the whole, the instability of eastern Europe stemmed from the strength of the older centers of power—the landholding aristocracy, the military, and the dominant ethnic groups—when confronted by some newer forces for democratic forms of government and more modern social and economic arrangements. Exacerbating this were economic problems caused by the breakup of the old economic unit formed by the Habsburg empire and diplomatic tensions brought on by its location between two rival powers that bordered the region west and east, Germany and the Soviet Union.

Conclusion

Taken as a whole, the late 1920s were times of economic prosperity and political stability for large parts of Europe. The liberal, parliamentary governments of the period were, however, seldom more than modestly successful. The experiences of Weimar Germany were a good measure of the lack of strength and popularity of parliamentary government. There were also some resounding failures in eastern and southern Europe where authoritarian regimes came into power. Two important tendencies, which became much more influential in the early thirties, were the decline of the liberal center in politics and, quite closely related, the growth of extremist movements on the margins of parliamentary life.

The prosperity of the later 1920s was already showing signs of faltering before the spectacular crash of the American stock market in 1929. Particularly important was the precarious base for the credit structure in Germany and other areas in central Europe, dependent as it was on American loans. There were indications, even in 1928, that Europeans might have to face a period of economic readjustment. That readjustment turned out to be more severe than anyone had predicted, involving political and cultural ramifications of great significance. The resources for meeting such a serious crisis were lacking. Beneath the glitter lay areas of great vulnerability. Europe entered a time of trial that would extend for the better part of two decades.

Suggested Books

Derek H. Aldcroft, *From Versailles to Wall Street: 1918–1929* (1977). Surveys the complex international economy during the 1920s.

R. Crossman, ed., *The God That Failed* (1950). A collection of "confessions" by Western writers who were attracted to the Soviet experiment and subsequently disillusioned by it.

Bentley Brinkerhoff Gilbert, *Britain, 1914–1945: The Aftermath of Power* (1996). An interpretive study of Britain's decline as a world power between the world wars.

Jon Jacobson, *Locarno Diplomacy: Germany and the West, 1925–1929* (1972). A good survey of the Locarno Conference and the effect it had on reducing tensions in Europe.

Margaret MacMillan, *Paris 1919: Six Months That Changed the World* (2003). A detailed but very readable look at the Paris Peace Conference and the end of the Great War.

Bruce F. Pauley, *Hitler, Stalin, and Mussolini: Totalitarianism in the Twentieth Century,* Second Edition (2003). Compares the origins, development, and final failure of Europe's three would-be totalitarian rulers.

Ignazio Silone, *Bread and Wine* (1937). A popular novel of Fascist Italy, written with passion by a famous opponent.

Aleksandr Solzhenitsyn, *The Gulag Archipelago*, 3 vols. (1973–1975). Traces the origins of the Stalinist dictatorship in the Soviet Union back to Lenin.

Chronology

1928   Soviet Union abandons Lenin's NEP
        and implements the First Five-Year
        Plan (1928–1932)

1929   Great Depression begins in the U.S.A.

1930   Beginning of presidential
        dictatorship in Germany

1931   Japan invades Manchuria

1932   Second Five-Year Plan in the Soviet
        Union (1932–1937)

1933   Hitler appointed Chancellor
        in Germany
        German Reichstag passes Enabling
        Act

1935   Hitler repudiates the disarmament
        clauses of the Versailles Treaty

1936   John Maynard Keynes publishes the
        General Theory of Employment,
        Interest, and Money
        Spanish Civil War (1936–1939)

1937   Japan invades China

1938   Third Five-Year Plan begins in the
        Soviet Union
        Munich Conference

1939   Hitler invades Poland
        Nazi-Soviet Nonaggression Pact

1941   Japanese attack on Pearl Harbor

6
From Depression to War, 1929–1939

WHILE SOME PROSPERED during the Great Depression, most suffered to one degree or another. George Gelies was a New Yorker who worked as a janitor for forty years. Over the years Gelies deposited extra coins and an occasional dollar in a savings account until his balance reached $1,000 in 1930. When informed that the bank had failed and his savings were lost, Gelies went home and hanged himself from a steam pipe. There were many stories of wealthy speculators jumping from windows or otherwise ending their lives after losing their fortunes. In Berlin in 1930, there were five cases of businessmen committing suicide in a single week. Still, some prospered as the Depression deepened. One example was the American millionaire, Andrew Mellon (1855–1937), who paid Leningrad's Hermitage Museum 7 million dollars for twenty-one paintings. The Soviet government needed the cash; Mellon coveted the artworks.

On Tuesday October 29, 1929, the bottom fell out of the New York Stock Exchange. In that one day stocks traded lost a total value equal to more than twice the value of all currency in circulation in the United States. Despite a steady rise in the stock market during the last six weeks of the year, the crisis deepened and became international during 1930. The rapid economic decline in most countries brought into question social structures and political systems as well as economic policies. It has been argued that the Great Depression, not only in America and Europe but all over the world, had an even more pervasive impact than the two world wars of this century; and from it, at least in large part, proceeded a whole chain of consequences which, added to other developments, did not stop until well into the 1950s. Both the middle and working classes began to wonder if liberalism, economic and political, was not obsolete. Perhaps the crises of the 1930s required new theories, new ideologies accompanied by action.

The American Connection

The failure of the New York stock market sent shock waves through Europe. Even before the New York crash, the European economy was experiencing difficulties. Agriculture had been a troubled sector since at least the mid-1920s. Wartime demand had resulted in vastly increased production of agricultural products in North America, some areas of South America, and Australia. But after the war, prices dropped steadily as cheap foreign grain poured into Europe. Canadian or Australian grain could be shipped to Europe cheaper than grain could be shipped from the eastern European agricultural states to western Europe. In 1930, the price of wheat was at its lowest level since the Reformation.

There were other danger signs, largely ignored. As noted above, the British economy was greatly disrupted by the war, leading to chronic unemployment in such key industries as coal and steel production. In eastern Europe, the breakup of the Habsburg monarchy resulted in the creation of several competing national economies, where tariff walls hindered economic recovery.

A hidden weakness in the postwar European economy was its dependence upon American finances. The great prosperity of the period 1924–1929 was financed by American loans, while the prosperity of America itself was financed by credit. In 1924, the American financier Charles Dawes (1865–1951) chaired a committee that produced the Dawes Plan for the payment of reparations by Germany. Included in the plan were arrangements for an immediate loan of 800 million gold marks. By 1925, American banks had loaned Germany 3 billion gold marks. More money flowed into Germany between 1924 and 1929 in the form of loans than flowed out as reparations payments. The German economy prospered, and that prosperity bubbled over into the rest of Europe, as money flowed in a circle from the United States to Germany in the form of loans, to France and Great Britain in the form of reparations payments, and back to the United States as payment of war debts. European prosperity in the "roaring twenties," like that of America, was based more on speculation than on production and consumption of goods and services. If anything should disrupt the flow of credit, the whole edifice would collapse. And so it did between 1929 and 1932.

The prosperity of the 1920s was based upon speculation in stocks, often purchased on credit ("margin") with the stocks themselves serving as collateral. Although even some working-class people speculated in stocks, most workers did not share in the prosperity. Wages remained low for workers, which, together with the depressed agricultural sector, meant that the

A group of unemployed men in England entertain a theatre queue in 1932. The hatless man slightly to the right of the center of the photograph appears to be holding a hat or cap into which people might drop money. Photo by General Photographic Agency/Getty Images.

purchasing power of the masses could not keep up with production. The collapse of the stock market set in motion a vicious cycle, as the financial crisis became an industrial crisis. Bank failures led to the closing of factories and unemployment. As unemployment spread, further reductions in production and plant closings followed. Factories cannot produce what the public cannot afford to purchase.

The Depression spread from America to Europe. Already in 1928, Americans were withdrawing funds from Europe to invest in stocks. As the Depression struck, Americans ceased investing in Europe and began to withdraw funds from European banks in great quantities. Hardest hit were banks in Germany and central Europe. The decline in American industrial productivity, the withdrawal of American capital from the world market, and the low prices paid for agricultural products and raw materials combined to reduce production, trade, and the movement of capital everywhere.

The crisis was international, but not much was done at that level to deal with the problem. In 1931, President Herbert Hoover (1874–1964) of the United States proposed a moratorium of one year on all intergovernmental debts, in recognition of the problems of transferring sums of money for payment of reparations or war debts. This was accepted by European leaders and regarded as an acknowledgment of the connection between reparations and war debts, that is, the latter would not be paid unless the former were paid. That this was not the American understanding became all too clear the following year, when Americans refused to include a plan for setting aside reparations in an agreement on war debts. The question was never resolved by agreement. In the next few years, Germany repudiated reparations and most European states owing money to the United States made only token payments. In 1933 a third international effort floundered when the United States, by then set on a path of economic nationalism, declined to cooperate. Most other countries had already begun their own efforts to find a way out of the morass.

Responses

The Great Depression, or "World Slump," was made all the more severe by the near universal commitment to classic (or orthodox) liberal economic theory. According to classic economic theory the problem was a loss of confidence in the monetary system and the need to become more competitive in the world market. The solution, then, was what is called "deflation," balancing government budgets and reducing the cost of production by, for example, lowering wages. Believing that the economy had to "right" itself, the liberal economists, together with the majority of politicians and businessmen, were prepared to tolerate a high level of public misery. They were convinced by accepted theory that any attempt by governments to maintain wages, or maintain unemployment benefits by deficit financing would only insulate inefficient sectors of the economy, leading to a worse economic disaster in the future.

What the classic liberals feared was just what others, who saw underconsumption as the root problem, believed necessary in order to save capitalism by making it work. Unlike the liberals, these advocates of a "middle road" saw the necessity of some public management and planning of the economy. Also, they advocated what economists call "deficit spending," that is, the use of public funds raised by borrowing. Unlike the socialists, they were committed to preserving private property. Like the economic policymakers of the post–World War II era, theirs was a program that would allow as much planning as necessary and as much freedom as possible. The leading advocate of this new consumer-based economic theory was the Englishman John Maynard Keynes (1883–1946), who expressed his ideas in his *General Theory of Employment, Interest, and Money* (1936).

Keynes's belief that governments could, in effect, spend their way out of economic slumps found many advocates. In Britain, Sir Oswald Mosley (1896–1980), one of the most talented members of the Labour Party, authored a memorandum in 1930 that called for ending the Depression through government intervention and deficit spending. When his ideas were rejected, he bolted the party and founded the British Union of Fascists. Perhaps the best application of what has since become known as Keynesian economics was Franklin Roosevelt's New Deal in the United States. In the end, however, it was the massive spending for defense during World War II, rather than the New Deal programs, that brought an end to the Depression in America. Likewise, it was the massive spending for rearmament after Hitler came to power in 1933, that ended the economic slump in Germany.

The Depression in Germany: The Nazis Come to Power

The Great Depression helped make possible the Nazi "seizure of power" in 1933 by discrediting liberalism, both political and economic, especially for the middle class. It also caused serious doubts among the working class as to the ability (or even desire) of the liberal-democratic government to deal with the unemployment, and its accompanying miseries, caused by the Depression. As both deserted the middle, pro-Republic parties for the extremes, the Weimar Republic, which never really commanded the enthusiastic support of the German people, fell victim to Hitler and the Nazi revival.

On October 3, 1929, just three weeks before "Black Tuesday" at the New York Stock Exchange, Gustav Stresemann died. Stresemann was perhaps the only German statesman who could have led a coalition to resist Hitler. During the previous six years, Stresemann led Germany out of the Great Inflation of 1923, through the Dawes Plan and Locarno treaties, and to an acceptance of the Young Plan just two months before his untimely death. As the Depression began to strike Germany, the Republic was left without a pilot at the helm.

Recession and rising unemployment at the beginning of 1930 led to the fall of the Republic's last truly parliamentary government, the Grand Coalition (1928–1930), led by Chancellor Hermann Müller (1876–1931), a Social Democrat. As unemployment rose, available funding for unemployment insurance proved inadequate. Müller's proposal to reduce benefits while raising the unemployment insurance rates met with strong opposition from both industry and organized labor. The result was the fall of the Müller government and its replacement by a new government headed by Heinrich Brüning (1885–1970) of the Catholic Center Party. Unable to govern through the Reichstag, Brüning resorted to rule by presidential decree. Germany became, in effect, a presidential dictatorship.

The economic and political crisis continued to deepen under Brüning. Germans went to the polls in national elections no fewer than four times in 1932. Twice in 1932, the people elected delegates to the Reichstag, in July and again in November. The results of both elections were similar. Of the old Weimar coalition parties, the Democratic and the People's Parties did badly. From a total of nearly 14 percent of the vote in 1928, they declined to under 3 percent in 1932. The Center Party largely maintained its electorate, but the Socialists, while remaining a major party, lost heavily. They dropped from nearly 30 percent of the vote in 1928 to just over 20 percent in 1932. The center of the political spectrum had won about 55 percent in 1928 but only around 35 percent in 1932. Yeats's line, "The centre cannot hold," had come true.

The extremes gained at the expense of the middle. On the left, the Communists had steadily increased their share of the vote from about 10 percent in 1928 to nearly 17 percent in 1932. On the right, the Nazis became a major political force, rising from under 3 percent of the vote in 1928 to 37.8 percent in July 1932, when they became the largest party in the Reichstag. With 230 seats, the Nazis were almost twice as large as the second largest party, the Social Democrats.

The growing strength of the Nazi movement was evident also in the presidential elections of March and April 1932. In March, Hitler came in second behind President Hindenburg in a campaign featuring four candidates from the extreme right to the extreme left. In the runoff election in April, Hitler again came in second. Hindenburg's reelection was credited to his receiving the support of the left-of-center voters, who saw him as the only means of preventing Hitler's election.

On May 30, 1932, Hindenburg replaced Brüning as chancellor with Franz von Papen (1879–1969), a conservative Catholic aristocrat best known for political intrigue. Although Hindenburg hoped that Papen could put together a majority in the Reichstag, he did not. In the Reichstag elections on July 31, the Nazis received 37.8 percent of the vote, the largest percentage ever received by a party during the Weimar Republic. On September 12, the Reichstag, by a vote of 512 to 42, passed a vote of no confidence in the Chancellor. Papen dissolved the Reichstag and called for new elections for November 6. The Nazis lost 2 million votes, dropping from 37.8 to 33.1 percent of the votes cast. The government crisis continued. Rejecting Papen's suggestion of a military dictatorship, Hindenburg dismissed Papen and replaced him on December 2 with General Kurt von Schleicher (1882–1934). Schleicher's chancellorship lasted only until January 28, when the eighty-five-year-old, and possibly senile, President Hindenburg yielded to the advice of Papen and the president's son, Oskar, and offered Adolf Hitler the chancellorship on January 30, 1933.

It is perhaps appropriate to note that the Weimar Republic had been "hollowed out" even before Hitler came to power by those constitutionally responsible for the republic but actually very much opposed to it as a political system. Hindenburg was a committed monarchist, who assumed the presidency out of a sense of duty to the Kaiser. He saw himself as a caretaker head of state until the exiled Kaiser returned to assume his rightful place.

Article 48 of the Weimar Constitution gave the president, the constitutional head of the state, the power to rule by decree during a national emergency. From the chancellorship of Heinrich Brüning to the end of the Republic in 1933, each chancellor (appointed by, and responsible to, the president, not the Reichstag) governed through emergency decrees issued by President Hindenburg. Since neither Brüning, Papen, Schleicher, nor Hitler was able to command a majority in the Reichstag, the Weimar Republic became a presidential dictatorship after March 1930.

With Papen as Vice Chancellor, the old elites thought they could control, even "use," Hitler. They were wrong. On February 27, 1933, the Reich-stag building mysteriously burned. Hitler convinced Hindenburg to suspend civil liberties. On March 5, against a backdrop of fear and violence, Germans again went to the polls. The Nazis received 43.9 percent of the votes cast. Allied with the German National Peoples' Party, the Nazis commanded a majority, but less than the two-thirds needed to legally establish a dictatorship.

The inglorious end of the Weimar Republic came on March 23, when the Reichstag passed the Enabling Act granting Hitler dictatorial powers for four years. The necessary two-thirds majority was achieved by preventing the Communists and twenty-one Social Democrats from attending. Also, the Catholic Center Party voted for the Enabling Act. Only the remainder of the Social Democratic delegates led by Otto Wels (1873–1939) were courageous enough to vote against it. When the final vote was announced, the Nazi delegates rose to their feet and sang the "Horst Wessel Song," the party anthem.

The New Dictatorships

What followed the Nazi seizure of power in Germany, like what followed the Bolshevik Revolution in Russia and to a lesser degree Mussolini's March on Rome, was the emergence of a new type of authoritarian state peculiar to the twentieth century. These new authoritarian dictatorships[1]

---

1 We are deliberately avoiding use of the term "totalitarian." Although the term was originally coined by Mussolini, its usefulness for the 1930s and 1940s was compromised by its employment during the Cold War.

were very different from the traditional conservative dictatorships that arose as attempts to salvage something of the old order from the threat of advancing liberalism. So long as the citizen-subject paid his taxes, served in the military when called upon, in short was obedient or at least gave passive support, he was allowed considerable personal freedom. Such "garden variety dictatorships" arose during the 1920s and early 1930s in Portugal and the east European "successor states," for example, Poland, Hungary, and Yugoslavia. Their goal was basically conservative, to maintain the status quo. They did not seek a wholly new ideological order based upon a following whose total being, mind and body, were subject to the authoritarian leadership.

The new authoritarian dictatorships of Hitler and Stalin were very different.[2] They were the very antithesis of classical liberalism. Conceived during the total war effort of the Great War, and given birth during the Russian Civil War,[3] they reached maturity in the Nazi Third Reich and Stalinist dictatorship. Like a great religious revival, the new dictators harnessed the masses in an idolatrous worship of the state (or party, or leader) and a never-ending violent struggle against enemies, both within and without. The individual as a rational being possessing certain inalienable natural rights ceased to exist, becoming instead a mere faceless object at the disposal of the state. Not only was individualism denied, but also the traditional liberal belief in reason, progress, and the basic harmony of human society. Loathing the middle class, the mainstay of classical liberalism, the new dictators promised a classless state (never achieved). Employing a large state police apparatus and a carefully crafted program of systemic terror, the masses were recruited for a permanent revolution.

What made possible the success of the new dictators in Germany and the Soviet Union was the fateful confluence of several trends already discussed above. This included the weakening of the Enlightenment Tradition in European thought. As mentioned, Nietzsche, Georges Sorel, Vilfredo Pareto (1848–1923), Sigmund Freud, and others chose to view humans as irrational beings who could be manipulated and motivated by myth and violence. The middle class, the mainstay of liberalism, saw its financial security eroded by taxes, inflation, and various forms of expropriations. Finally, the failure of the liberal-democratic governments to deal effectively with the suffering caused by the Great Depression caused the working class,

---

2 Although Mussolini's Fascist regime had many characteristics in common with the Hitler and Stalin regimes, it was more akin to the traditional dictatorship. *Il Duce* never achieved total power. For example, he did not interfere with the judiciary and himself remained subject to the Fascist Grand Council, which could in theory, and did in fact, dismiss Mussolini in July 1943.

3 Some see its origins as far back as Rousseau's social contract with its emphasis on the General Will arising from the masses, and to which the individual must submit.

like the middle class, to abandon its faith in both political and economic liberalism.

Once legally installed in power by presidential appointment and passage of the Enabling Act, Hitler spent the next two years bringing every aspect of life in Germany under control of the Nazi party, a process referred to as the *Gleichschaltung*, or coordination of society. It was meant to alter totally the relationship between the individual and the state, and also between individuals. It worked as well to alter the way people thought. Joseph Goebbels (1897–1945), Hitler's Minister of Propaganda and Public Enlightenment, summed it up best at the end of 1933, when he said: "If liberalism took as its starting point the individual and placed the individual man in the center of all things, we have replaced the individual by the nation and the individual man by the community."[4] The Nazi dictatorship was meant to be a rejection of European history since the Enlightenment. Germany was to become a *Volksgemeinschaft*, a national or racial community in which traditional social classes would be replaced by a mass of "folk (i.e., racial) comrades."

During the course of 1933, all independent organizations were abolished and/or absorbed into Nazi-led organizations. Thus, for example, all labor unions were abolished and workers required to join the German Labor Front. A Reich Chamber of Culture under Goebbels was established to oversee all aspects of media production and dissemination. In January 1934 the *Reichsrat*, the upper house representing the state governments, and all state legislatures themselves were abolished. For the first time in its history, Germany became a centralized national state.

At the end of 1933, only two key institutions remained outside party (i.e., Hitler's) control—the *Reichswehr* (army) and the churches. To secure the support of the army and to remove any opposition within the party to his personal control, Hitler purged the party leadership in the "Night of the Long Knives" (June 29). Ernst Röhm (1887–1934) and several hundred SA (*Sturmabteilung*, or storm troopers) were shot. The Reichswehr had feared the SA as a potential rival. Now nothing stood in the way of the Reichswehr giving its loyalty to Hitler. After Hindenburg's death on August 2, all in the army swore their personal loyalty to Hitler, now *Der Führer.*

The "coordination" of the churches proved more difficult. Attempts to establish a National Reich Church under Ludwig Müller (1883–1945) as Reich Bishop were less than successful. Evangelical Christians, including Karl Barth (1886–1968), Dietrich Bonhoeffer (1906–1945), and Martin Niemoller (1892–1984), formed the Confessing Church in opposition to the Reich Church. Many of the Confessing pastors, including Bonhoeffer, subsequently suffered martyrdom at the hands of the state.

4 Quoted in Richard Pipes, *Modern Europe* (Homewood, IL: Dorsey Press, 1981), 207.

Hitler was somewhat more successful in neutralizing the Catholic Church as a center of organized opposition. In what was one of his most spectacular foreign policy successes, Hitler signed the Reich Concordat with the papacy on July 20, 1933. By the terms of the concordat, the Catholic Center Party was disbanded and Catholic clergy were required to give up all political activity. Henceforth, Catholics who opposed the Nazi state and its policies (e.g., the Holocaust) had to do so as individuals. In general, however, although there were courageous individuals among both Catholics and Protestants, the organized institutional churches capitulated and openly supported the regime and its policies.

The Stalinist Dictatorship

Old Bolsheviks, members of the Communist Party before the October Revolution in 1917, called the events in the early 1930s "the great change." Western historians have labeled them the "Stalinist revolution." Whatever label one might choose, it was revolution more profound than the revolution of 1917. The primary goal of the second revolution was to transform the Soviet Union into a major industrial power, which in turn would be the basis for a modern military machine capable of securing the Soviet Union from the threat of annihilation by hostile capitalist powers.

The Stalinist dictatorship was constructed between 1928 and 1938. During the first period, from 1928 to 1933, the emphasis was on economic development. Stalin's aim was to make the Soviet Union a major industrial power within ten years through rapid industrialization. In 1928, Lenin's strategic retreat from socialism (NEP) was abandoned in favor of economic planning. The first Five-Year Plan, begun in 1928, aimed at developing heavy industry. Backed by a mixture of dedicated enthusiasm and physical and psychological coercion, the results were impressive. Capitalism was eliminated, a socialist economy established, and agriculture collectivized.

The brutal process of collectivization of agriculture was meant to destroy the independence of the peasants while assuring the food supply necessary for industrialization. The peasants were forced into collective farms, where they were given production quotas to meet. When the peasants resisted by burning their crops and farm buildings and slaughtering their livestock, they experienced severe repression. At least 5 or 6 million, perhaps as many as 10 million, peasants died, mostly in the Ukraine and northern Caucasus. Millions more were sent to labor camps in Siberia and the Arctic regions of the Soviet Union. Some concessions were made to the peasants during the second Five-Year Plan (1932–1937).

A third Five-Year Plan was launched in 1938, but had to be suspended due to the German invasion in 1941. The basis for a modern industrial economy was created in the period of the first Five-Year Plan. At the same time, the basis for the Stalinist state was formed. By 1933, Stalin could not be seriously questioned without calling into question the right of the Communist Party to rule. Those who challenged Stalin in any fashion had to be eliminated. This Stalin set out to do, beginning in 1934, in a series of actions that made Hitler's "Night of the Long Knives" seem benign by comparison.

In the winter of 1934–1935, Stalin began a reign of systematic terror aimed at physically eliminating all individuals and groups that might challenge his regime. A series of show trials was staged in 1936, 1937, and 1938 to convict and execute key party officials (usually close associates of Lenin) on preposterous charges to which the accused confessed following extreme physical and mental torture. Millions were arrested by the secret police (NKVD), often at random to fill quotas, and either executed without trial or sent off to the slow death of the GULAG, the growing network of prisons and labor camps. When the purges ended in 1938, millions of innocent citizens languished in the GULAG; the government and party bureaucracies and the military high commands were decimated; and the population of the Soviet Union lived in fear, but Stalin enjoyed a level of power that would have caused the most autocratic Tsar to blush.

The Road to War in Europe

Virtually all reputable historians agree that the Second World War in Europe was the result of Hitler's aggressive foreign policy. There can be no doubt that Hitler included a war in his plans for the creation of a greater German Reich that would last a thousand years. The war he got, however, was not the limited war in eastern Europe that he desired. Remove Hitler from the equation, and the Second World War was not inevitable.

During his first two years in power, the years of the Gleichschaltung, Hitler pursued a cautious foreign policy. It was necessary to secure his position at home and begin secret rearmament without alarming Great Britain and France. From hindsight it may be concluded that if Hitler were to have been removed from power and war avoided, he would have to have been stopped before 1936. After 1936, his position in Germany was secure and rearmament sufficient that only military defeat could oust him from power. But the aversion to war, the understandable commitment to avoid a replay of the Great War, was so strong among the Western democracies (England and France, not to mention the United States) that appeasement seemed the most logical foreign policy. Certainly, it was the policy that best represented the wishes of the populace of Britain and France in the 1930s.

Hitler removed Germany from both the League of Nations and the Geneva Disarmament Conference in October 1933, while giving assurances of his desire for peace and pledging peaceful cooperation with all countries that treated Germany as an equal. In 1934, to isolate France while also appearing to desire peaceful change, Hitler signed a nonaggression pact with Poland.

Hitler's first overtly aggressive move came in March 1935, when he denounced the disarmament clauses of the Versailles Treaty, introduced military conscription, and announced the existence of an air force. Although the League of Nations condemned Hitler's unilateral action, the British and French took no action to enforce the treaty. In fact, Britain signed the Anglo-German Naval Treaty with Germany in June 1935, implicitly legitimatizing Hitler's violation of the Versailles Treaty.

Table 6.1   Timetable of German Aggression

1935 (Mar. 16)	Hitler repudiates disarmament clauses of Versailles Treaty, restores conscription, announces founding of *Luftwaffe* (the air force), and expands army to over half a million
1936 (Mar. 7)	Hitler sends troops into demilitarized Rhineland
(Oct. 19)	Two-year compulsory military service introduced
(Nov.)	Rome-Berlin Axis formed. Germany and Italy recognize Franco's government and begin intervention in Spanish Civil War. Anti–Comintern Pact between Germany and Japan
1938 (Mar. 11)	*Anschluss* (joining) between Germany and Austria
(Sept. 30)	Munich Conference. Germany occupies the Sudetenland
1939 (Mar. 15)	German troops occupy Bohemia and Moravia; Slovakia becomes German puppet state
(Sept. 1)	Germany invades Poland. Great Britain and France declare war on Germany two days later

Until November 1936, when Hitler and Mussolini formed what Mussolini called the "Rome-Berlin Axis," Hitler was without an ally. In fact,

Fascist Italy stood with Britain and France against Hitler. Mussolini was alarmed by an attempted coup by Austrian Nazis against the government of Engelbert Dollfuss (1892–1934) of Austria in July 1934. When Hitler announced that Germany would rearm, Mussolini joined with Britain and France in the so-called Stresa Front to oppose Hitler. It was the last act of unity between the three Allies of the Great War. What shattered the Stresa Front and sent Mussolini rushing into the waiting arms of Hitler was Italy's attack on Ethiopia in October 1935.

The attack on Ethiopia was an attempt to avenge Italy's defeat at the Battle of Adowa in 1896. The League of Nations condemned Italy's aggression and imposed some economic sanctions on Italy but stopped short of placing an embargo on oil to that nation. Only an oil embargo could have saved Ethiopia. By taking only a weak-willed stand, the League merely offended Mussolini, pushing him into an alliance with Hitler, while effectively ending the League's role as an agent for collective security.

Mussolini and Hitler found an opportunity for cooperation when civil war broke out in Spain in July 1936. Nationalist forces led by Francisco Franco (1892–1975) reacted against increasing bloodshed and political chaos following the election of a left-wing Popular Front government in February. The Nationalists were aided by materiel and some military forces from Italy and Germany. The two dictators used the war to refine military techniques, to strengthen national pride, and to test the resolve of the democratic powers. The Republicans were aided by volunteers, including the International Brigades, but the bulk of the assistance came from the Soviet Union. For its part the Soviet Union hoped to divert Hitler and Mussolini from a possible thrust into eastern Europe, and to rally the democratic powers to a strong antifascist position. Britain and France chose to remain neutral. The subsequent victory of Spain's Nationalists was seen as a victory for Mussolini and Hitler, and a defeat for the western democracies.

On November 5, 1937, Hitler met with his generals. He informed them that Germany's need for living space (*Lebensraum*) in the east would necessitate a war not later than 1943–1945. In the meantime, he meant to destroy both Austria and Czechoslovakia in order to protect Germany's flank. Two weeks later, Hitler met with Lord Halifax (1881–1959), British Foreign Secretary and a leading appeaser. After Hitler spoke of Germany's need to deal with various border disputes and minority problems in the east, Lord Halifax informed Hitler that Britain would accept peaceful change in the status quo. Hitler took Halifax's response as a sign that he could proceed.

First on Hitler's agenda was the annexation of Austria, the so-called *Anschluss*. In February 1938, Hitler summoned the Austrian chancellor, Kurt von Schuschnigg (1897–1977), to Berchtesgaden. Hitler demanded concessions, including Austrian Nazi participation in the government. When Schuschnigg called for a plebiscite on Austrian independence, he was forced to resign and replaced by Arthur Seyss-Inquart (1892–1946), an Austrian Nazi. Seyss-Inquart invited the German army to enter Austria. On March 13, Austria's union with Germany was proclaimed to cheering crowds. Again the western democracies protested, but did nothing.

Hitler was ready to move against Czechoslovakia, the only one of the "successor states" created by the peace settlement still a democracy in 1938. In fact, Czechoslovakia was the only model of democratic government, fair treatment of minorities, and industrial progress in eastern Europe. Also, both France and the Soviet Union had treaties with Czechoslovakia committing them to the maintenance of Czechoslovakia's integrity. Britain favored appeasement.

The Czechoslovakian crisis centered on the fate of the German minority living in the Sudetenland, the region along Czechoslovakia's border with Germany. Encouraged by Hitler, the pro-Nazi Sudeten German party under Konrad Henlein (1898–1945) demanded autonomy for the Sudetenland. The crisis intensified during the summer of 1938; then, on September 12, Hitler threatened intervention unless the Sudeten Germans were allowed to decide their own fate. On the following day, Konrad Henlein called for annexation with Germany.

As war appeared increasingly likely, Britain's prime minister, Neville Chamberlain (1869–1940), flew to Berchtesgaden on September 15, and to Bad Godesberg one week later, in order to assess Hitler's demands and find a way to satisfy them without risking a war. When the Czechs refused Hitler's terms, and war seemed inevitable, Mussolini proposed a conference at Munich. Britain, France, and Germany were invited, but not Czechoslovakia or the Soviet Union. The Soviet Union urged the Allies to resist Hitler's demands and offered military assistance to Czechoslovakia in the event of war.

The Munich Conference convened on September 29. Hitler presented the western Allies with a choice between sacrificing Czechoslovakia or an almost certain war. They chose to sacrifice Czechoslovakia. Czechoslovakia, the only democracy in eastern Europe, was sold out. Hitler once again triumphed over the western democrats and his opponents at home, the generals and the resistance, who were urging the appeasers to reject Hitler's demands. Neville Chamberlain returned home to a cheering crowd, waving a piece of paper with Hitler's signature guaranteeing "peace in our time." The former premier of France, Leon Blum (1872–1950), who opposed the Munich Agreement signed by his successor, Edouard Daladier (1884–1970), was more clear-sighted and spoke of a sense of "cowardly relief" that war had been averted.

Several key developments followed the Munich conference. In mid-March 1939, Hitler destroyed what was left of Czechoslovakia. Bohemia and Moravia were annexed, while Slovakia became a separate satellite of

Germany. It was the first time Hitler had taken territory not containing a German population. Even Chamberlain had to acknowledge this act as aggression. When Hitler then began making demands on the free city of Danzig and the Polish Corridor, Chamberlain reacted by writing out in his own hand a guarantee of Polish sovereignty. Britain's pledge of military assistance for Poland if attacked by Germany was endorsed by France. But Hitler's string of successes made him reckless, and he did not take the warning seriously. On April 3, Hitler ordered his generals to prepare for war with Poland.

Another byproduct of the Munich Conference was a shift in Soviet policy towards Germany. Apparently Stalin felt that the West's sellout of Czechoslovakia at Munich was evidence of a capitalist plot to direct Hitler's aggression towards the Soviet Union. Perhaps as a countermeasure, Stalin began to appease Hitler. The result was the Nazi-Soviet Nonaggression Pact signed on August 23, 1939. A secret portion of the Pact divided eastern Europe into German and Soviet spheres of influence. The Soviet Union was to receive two of the Baltic States (Latvia and Estonia), Finland, Bessarabia, and eastern Poland.

The Nazi-Soviet Nonaggression Pact left Hitler free for his desired little war in Poland. He apparently expected not only an easy victory but also for Britain and France to conclude that there was nothing to be done about it.

Unhappy Czechs line the streets of Prague to watch the German army enter the city. The Germans, by occupying Czechoslovakia in March 1939, violated the agreement reached at Munich the year before. Courtesy AP/Wide World Photos.

After taking Poland he could then look for another angle to work. Thus, on September 1, German forces invaded Poland and annexed Danzig. Two days later, on September 3, Britain and France declared war on Germany. On September 17, the Soviet Union invaded Poland from the east. By the end of the month Poland fell and was partitioned between Germany and the Soviet Union, and a British Expeditionary Force of 158,000 men was on its way to France.

The Road to War in the Pacific

What transformed the war with Germany in Europe into a second world war was the emerging conflict with Japan in the Pacific. Since the end of the Great War, indeed even before, there was rivalry between the two new Great powers, Japan and the United States of America. The Sino-Japanese War (1894–1895), the Russo-Japanese War (1904–1905), and the Spanish-American War (1898) revealed both as imperial powers with a growing conflict of economic interests in China and the Pacific. As events unfolded at the Paris Peace Conference and later during the 1920s and 1930s, each country felt its vital interests in the area threatened by the other. For Japan, at least, the conflict increasingly took on the nature of a struggle for expansion and survival of the Japanese empire

Events around the turn of the twentieth century increased tension between the United States and Japan. As a result of the Spanish-American War, the United States acquired Guam and the Philippine Islands. The latter especially increased American involvement in China and in securing its share of the lucrative Chinese trade. The Open Door policy proposed by Secretary of State John Hay (1838–1905) in 1899–1900 was meant to secure American access to China, while preserving the fiction of China's territorial integrity and independence.

Japan's defeat of Russia in 1904–1905 removed Russia as a major player in the Pacific. Great Britain had already reduced its role in the area, when it concluded the Anglo-Japanese Alliance in 1902. The rising threat of the German High Seas Fleet compelled Britain to turn policing of the Pacific Ocean over to Japan in order to concentrate its naval forces in the North Sea and the Atlantic Ocean. Japan became the dominant naval power in the western Pacific. This fact led some in the United States to conclude that Japan had become the major threat to American interests in the Pacific. The result was America's "War Plan Orange" (1911), a plan for a possible war with Japan that remained valid until 1939.

Japan's seizure of the German territory of Kiaochow in November 1914, and its Twenty-One Demands (January 1915) aimed at gaining a virtual protectorate over China, further aroused suspicions of Japanese imperialism among Americans. Japanese suspicions of American motives were heightened by developments at the Paris Peace Conference (1919) and the Washington Naval Conference (1921–1922).

At the Paris Peace Conference in 1919, Japan requested that a declaration on racial equality be included in the League of Nations Charter. Woodrow Wilson, fearing that such a declaration would assure defeat of the Versailles Treaty (which included the League Charter) in the Senate, refused to agree. As a kind of consolation prize, Japan was awarded a lease on the Shantung Peninsula in China, formerly belonging to Germany.

Additional gains during the Great War in the central Pacific of the former German Caroline, Marianna, Marshall, and Palau islands meant that Japan threatened American supply lines through the Pacific Ocean. To meet the threat, the United States prevailed upon Great Britain to end its alliance with Japan, and join with the United States, Japan, and other great powers to limit the size of their navies and define their interests in the Pacific region. Japanese military leaders would later see the agreements reached at the Washington Naval Conference (November 12, 1922–February 6, 1923) as an affront to Japanese national pride and an attempt to artificially limit legitimate Japanese imperial interests. The conference did, however, afford international recognition of Japan as a major power, if not the major power, in eastern Asia.

Relations between Japan and the United States remained cordial during the 1920s. Both enjoyed immense prosperity. Japan was the only nation, other than the United States, whose investments exceeded its foreign debt. The United States was Japan's number one trading partner, with 40 percent of its industrial product going to the United States. Another 25 percent went to China. As with the world's other industrial nations, the Great Depression brought an end to the prosperity, and set the two great powers of the Pacific on a collision course.

The arrival of the Great Depression brought an end to prosperity in Japan, as it did elsewhere. The effects of the depression in Japan were made worse by an increase of 25 percent in the American tariff on Japanese goods. Wages fell one-third by 1931; rice prices fell below cost, and silk prices collapsed. Soon one-half of Japan's rural population was living in abject poverty. As conditions worsened, real power within Japan's government passed into the hands of a small clique of military leaders, who saw Japan's salvation in an aggressive foreign policy. Under slogans like a "Greater East Asia Co-Prosperity Sphere," Japan set out to establish economic control of China and southeast Asia, and military domination of the whole region. Such an aggressive imperialism meant conflict with both the Soviet Union and the United States

In 1931, Japan invaded Manchuria, an act of unprovoked aggression which was condemned by the League of Nations. Condemnation by the League and its attempt to impose sanctions, provoked the Japanese into withdrawing from the League and renouncing the Washington Naval Conference agreements. The United States also condemned Japan's aggression, but did not join in the sanctions. Manchuria was reconstituted as Manchu-kuo in 1932, under Japanese "protection," and with Henry P'u-i (1906–1967), the last emperor of China, as regent.

Japanese forces invaded China in July 1937. Once again the League of Nations condemned Japan's aggression, but the deteriorating situation in Europe prevented effective action, and even encouraged Japan's militarist leaders. Japanese and Soviet forces clashed along the border between Siberia, Manchukuo, and Korea, despite a nonaggression treaty between the powers, signed in August 1937. Relations with the United States grew more tense when in December 1937, Japanese bombers attacked the American gunboat *Panay* near Nanking, followed by Japan's rejection of the Open Door policy in November 1938.

The United States pursued a cautious policy towards Japan in hopes of avoiding war, until the summer of 1940. With the steady success of German forces in Europe (see Chapter 7), Japan occupied Indochina in 1940–1941. President Roosevelt responded by freezing Japanese assets in America and imposing an embargo on trade with Japan, including oil. When the Dutch East Indies complied with the oil embargo, Japanese imports of the vital resource dropped by 90 percent. Faced with either withdrawing from Indochina and China, as demanded by the United States, or exhausting its oil reserves within two years, Japan saw a solution in gaining control of the Dutch East Indies. That, however, necessitated first defeating, or at least disabling, the American and British fleets in the Pacific. On December 7, 1941, Japanese forces attacked the American Pacific Fleet at Pearl Harbor. On the same day, the Japanese attacked American and British installations at Wake Island, the Philippines, Guam, Hong Kong, and Malaya. On December 8, the United States declared war on Japan. In an act of reckless abandon with few parallels in history, Germany and Italy declared war on the United States on December 11. The war in Europe and the war in the Pacific became World War II, a global conflict that lasted until September 1945, leaving thinking people in the world wondering what had become of civilization.

Suggested Books and Films

William Sheridan Allen, *The Nazi Seizure of Power*, rev. ed. (1984). A classic study of why one small German town succumbed to Nazism (1930–1935).

Karl Dietrich Bracher, *The German Dictatorship* (1970). A scholarly study, and still the best on the origin and structure of the Hitler regime.

Hans Fallada, *Little Man, What Now?* (1932); and W. Greenwood, *Love on the Dole* (1933). Two novels that depict the tragedy of the Great Depression in Germany (former) and England (latter).

Martin Gilbert and Martin Gott, *The Appeasers* (1963). Still a good survey of England's foreign policy during the 1930s.

Ian Kershaw, *Hitler: 1899–1936: Hubris* (2000); and *Hitler: 1936–1945: Nemesis* (2001). Kershaw's two-volume biography is the best available.

Arthur Koestler, *Darkness at Noon* (1956). A classic novel of Stalin's purge trials of Old Bolsheviks.

Charles P. Kindleberger, *The World Depression, 1929–1939* (1973). A standard survey of the Great Depression.

Hugh Thomas, *The Spanish Civil War* (1977). Widely acclaimed history of the Spanish Civil War.

Robert C. Tucker, *Stalin in Power: The Revolution from Above, 1928–1941* (1992). A fascinating picture of Stalin and the creation of the Soviet Union.

The Great Dictator, 1940, directed by Charles Chaplin. A satire of Adolf Hitler by America's favorite "little tramp."

Part 3
Overview: 1939–1967

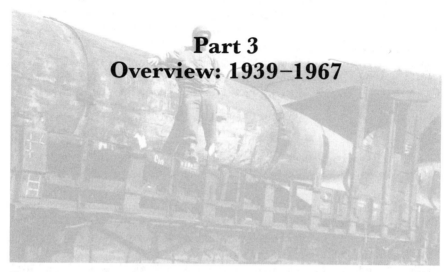

FROM THE START OF WORLD WAR II IN 1939 to the appearance of the European community in 1967, Europe experienced a historical roller-coaster ride. The sickening plunge into global war was followed by a painful climb to recovery. The Europe emerging from wartime destruction and postwar hardships was, however, a different Europe from that which had gone to war.

World War II was a continuation of the Great War, now styled World War I, but it was also a global war, involving the United States, Japan, and China, among others. The outcome completed Europe's descent from its dominant position at the start of the century and pushed two new great powers to center stage, the Soviet Union and the United States.

Barbarism on the one hand and technical brilliance on the other marked the war. The Manhattan Project, the Anglo-American effort to construct an atomic bomb, reflected both facets. Building the bomb required assembling gifted scientists and coordinating their work. The use of the bomb, possibly a factor in the Japanese decision to surrender, horrified large segments of the world population.

The Holocaust caused many to question whether European civilization had not lost its bearings in the twentieth century. There was no military justification for the Final Solution. There was no rational way to understand the Holocaust despite the methodical, business-like manner that sometimes characterized it. That the Holocaust originated in Germany, perhaps the most civilized of European countries, was particularly disturbing. Was this the result of a *Sonderweg*, a special historical path, or something any nation might be capable of doing?

Other aspects of the war offered hope. Advances in such areas as medicine or communications could be transferred to civilian life. Many became convinced during the war of the need for social and economic changes that would provide a better life for the masses. There was also a desire to establish a new international system to prevent future wars.

Three basic developments marked the period from 1945 to 1967. First, Europe found itself in the middle of the so-called Cold War. It also contended with waves of decolonization, as first Asian, then African colonies gained independence. Finally, a divided Europe struggled to recover economically, socially, and spiritually. By 1967, when the European Economic Community, the European Coal and Steel Community, and the European Atomic Energy Commission joined to form the European Community, recovery was complete, especially in western Europe.

The Cold War began to take shape in 1945 and 1946. Already at the Potsdam Conference (July–August 1945), there was an atmosphere of suspicion. The main sources of disagreement were European: the new Poland and occupied Germany. The Soviet Union was anxious to secure a Poland that would defer to Soviet strategic interests. It desperately wanted assurance that Germany would not be able to wage aggressive war again.

Nineteen-forty-seven was a crucial year. First, President Harry Truman of the United States proclaimed the Truman Doctrine, a promise to help governments in danger either from internal subversion or from external aggression. Some saw the Marshall Plan as an economic counterpart to the Truman Doctrine. It was, however, meant to be simply an American initiative to restart European economies, west and east. In the new Cold War atmosphere, however, the Soviet Union saw it as an American plot to gain economic advantage.

Several events, among them a communist coup in Czechoslovakia, the Berlin Blockade (and Airlift), the formation of the North Atlantic Treaty Organization (NATO), the appearance of West Germany and East Germany, and, finally, the victory of the Chinese Communists, convinced Europeans and Americans the Cold War was a reality. The American response to the Korean War in 1950 and the decision to aid the French in Indochina made the Cold War global, even though the essential issues remained Soviet concerns in Europe.

Colonial empires in Asia were, generally, quickly dismantled in the decade following the war. The British left the Indian subcontinent. America granted independence to the Philippines. The Dutch failed in their efforts to retain the Dutch East Indies. The French withdrew from Indochina after a bitter war.

In Africa, decolonization began in the 1950s. With some exceptions, it took place in a orderly manner. One main exception was Algeria, where a million European residents opposed independence. The French army, defeated in 1940 and in 1954, also resisted independence. The British experienced a difficult situation in Kenya with the Mau Mau Movement. Rhodesia and South Africa, white settler colonies, resisted efforts by the black majority in each country to come to power. The Belgians granted the Congo independence without making an effort to insure its success. The Portuguese, however, clung to their colonial holdings until the mid-1970s.

In eastern Europe, the interests of the Soviet Union were paramount. It undertook yet another Five-Year Plan emphasizing defense and heavy industry. After Stalin's death in 1953 there were more efforts to meet the needs of the people. Still, each satellite country experienced a variation on the Soviet model of industrialization in the 1950s, central planning, concentration on heavy industry, and collectivization. By the end of the 1950s, some were finding a national path to economic development. Yugoslavia, since the late 1940s, balanced precariously between East and West, experimented with forms of economic organization neither communist nor capitalist.

In the west, the Marshall Plan played an important role in restarting economies. Each country pursued its own brand of capitalism. The French emphasized planning and government-directed investing. The German *Wirtschaftswunder* (economic miracle) was largely the product of industry and the banks. The major development in the European economy in this period entailed cooperation and integration, first with the European Coal and Steel Community (ECSC) and then with the European Economic Community (EEC).

By the 1960s a divided Europe no longer seemed a novelty. Europeans had also discovered the possibility of life without colonial empires. Europeans, especially in the West, enjoyed a material abundance that only a few had known earlier. The war was a distant memory, the Cold War a threat with which one had learned to live. The situation was not ideal, but the

Chronology

7
Armageddon:
Europe in World War II, 1939–1945

IN THE SPRING AND SUMMER OF 1939 the Soviet Union and Nazi Germany carried out a diplomatic dance that led eventually to the Nazi-Soviet Non-Aggression Pact of August 23.[1] Stalin had given up on the idea of collective security. Instead, he cynically used negotiations with England and France as a means by which to pressure Hitler into agreeing to a nonaggression pact. Hitler, for his part, wanted to begin the invasion of Poland at the start of September, before the fall rains.

Midway through August the tempo of the dance increased rapidly. After much delay, Stalin invited Joachim Ribbentrop (1893–1946), the German foreign minister, to come to Moscow on August 23. Negotiations took very little time. The participants signed the nonaggression treaty. They attached to the treaty a secret protocol that indicated the spheres of interest in eastern and central Europe of the two countries.

In the early morning hours of August 24, Stalin hosted a late supper for Ribbentrop at which he toasted Hitler. Ribbentrop joked that "Stalin will yet join the Anti-Comintern Pact [an agreement between Germany and Japan in 1936, with Italy joining in 1937, that was directed against the Soviet Union]." According to Nikita Khrushchev (1894–1971), a member of the Politburo, Stalin said a couple of days later that he had tricked Hitler. The treaty would keep them out of the war and allow them to save their strength.[1]

The years of war and diplomacy that began with the invasion of Poland in September 1939 completely changed Europe's position in the world. From apparent dominance, Europe fell in 1945 to a position of near impotence before the two great world powers, the Soviet Union and the United States. Furthermore, 1945 marked the beginnings of a process by which the European colonial empires were gradually and painfully dismantled. Of course, part of the explanation for this startling reversal of fortune lies

1 The Non-Aggression Pact may be found on the web at http://www.yale.edu/lawweb/avalon/nazsov/nonagres. The secret protocol is the following document. The record of the conversation of Stalin and Ribbentrop will be found in the document preceding the Non-Aggression Pact.

in the realities that prevailed in 1939: World War I and the Depression in the 1930s had hollowed out European civilization. World War II in many ways only confirmed what some had already noticed. The world was rapidly changing and Europe's easy dominance of it had effectively ended.

Blitzkrieg

The German invasion of Poland, which began on September 1, 1939, made brilliant use of the strategy of *Blitzkrieg* (lightning war). This involved combining mechanized spearheads of troops, tanks massed in groups, and close tactical support by fighters and dive bombers. It was a strategy that both demanded and usually resulted in a rapid, decisive victory. Easy victories in 1939 and again in 1940 led Germany to believe it did not need to prepare for protracted war. This failure to grasp the fundamental reality of modern warfare proved fatal over the next few years.

Blitzkrieg tactics resulted in the rapid defeat of Poland. By September 8 the German forces were outside Warsaw. Soviet forces invaded Poland from the east on September 17. Caught between two massive armies, Poland surrendered on September 28, less than a month after the beginning of the German offensive.

A strange interlude known as the "Phony War" occurred during the eight months following the fall of Poland. Technically a state of war existed between Germany and the two western democracies of Britain and France, yet no military engagements took place. Hitler expected Britain and France to accept his offer of peace. While Britain and France ignored the offer, they had few ideas about how to respond to Germany's conquests.

On November 3, the Soviet Union demanded several small areas from Finland to enhance the defenses of Leningrad. When the Finns refused, Soviet forces invaded Finland, beginning what came to be called the "Winter War," November 1939–March 1940. The Finns did surprisingly well against their much larger opponent, but the massive resources of the Soviet Union eventually prevailed. After beating the Finns, the Soviet Union moved to incorporate the Baltic States and Bessarabia and Northern Bukovina from Romania.

Germany returned to the offensive in April 1940. Once again, Blitzkrieg tactics brought swift results as Denmark and Norway fell victim this time. In May a massive German effort was launched against the Netherlands, Belgium, and France. The Netherlands and Belgium were quickly beaten. On May 14 Rotterdam's center was flattened by German bombers and 40,000 civilians died, an early indication the new war would be even more senselessly brutal than the previous one.

France crumbled with unexpected quickness after German forces drove to the English Channel, cutting off the British Expeditionary Force and thousands of French troops. In a daring rescue operation between May 26 and June 4, the Allies turned defeat into a kind of victory by evacuating some 200,000 British troops and over 100,000 French at Dunkirk with the help of an armada of small boats. By mid-June the French cabinet voted to ask Germany for armistice terms. The armistice was signed on June 22 in the same railroad car in which the Germans had signed the armistice ending World War I. France was divided into an occupied zone in the north and an unoccupied zone in the south. The French were allowed to govern the unoccupied zone. This was Vichy France, after its capital in the resort town of Vichy.

The Fall of France was due primarily to military mistakes. French generals had prepared for the last war. The Maginot Line, the symbol of France's emphasis on defense, is often seen as the cause of the French defeat, but this oversimplifies the situation. The Maginot Line did what it was supposed to do. The Germans, however, did something no one anticipated. They largely ignored the Maginot Line and went through the wooded and hilly area of the Ardennes to the north. French and British forces in the meantime waited for the Germans to follow the invasion route of World War I along the coast of Belgium. The German invasion caught the Allies by surprise, a surprise compounded by an Allied inability to grasp the techniques of Blitzkrieg. One French commander, the then-Colonel Charles de Gaulle (1890–1970), had long advocated techniques of tank warfare which, had they been employed in 1940, would have made a significant difference. His colleagues had largely ignored him, but German officers had paid close attention.

The Fall of France reflected the dislike many French felt for the Third Republic, the lack of a clearcut national purpose, and the paucity of leaders of imagination and daring. Nevertheless, while the defeat was "strange," as Marc Bloch (1886–1944), a historian and later hero of the French Resistance, put it, it did not result from treason, but rather from bad judgment and failure of nerve.

By mid-summer 1940 only Britain remained to carry on the struggle against Nazi Germany and Fascist Italy. Italy had joined the war against France at the last minute but proved to be a burden rather than an asset. Since May 10 veteran politician Winston Churchill had been leading Britain. Over his long career, Churchill had known many ups and downs, but true greatness had escaped him. Now he became the man to match the hour. More than any other single individual, he became associated with the Allied cause in World War II and generally with its more memorable moments.

If that summer was, in Churchill's words, Britain's "finest hour," it was also a very dark hour. Hitler engaged in planning for Operation Sea Lion, an invasion of Britain. Marshal Hermann Goering (1893–1945), commander of the Luftwaffe, believed he could bomb the British into surrender. The British responded by evacuating urban areas, organizing air-raid defense systems, and by sending up squadrons of Spitfires and Hurricanes. By fall Goering had to acknowledge failure, and Hitler had to call off the invasion. The British had won the Battle of Britain.

Several factors help in explaining British success. Perhaps the most important factors were the nature of the Luftwaffe and the way in which it was commanded. It had been designed more for tactical support of the Blitzkrieg than for bombing runs as such. The German bombers were slow and fighter protection often inadequate. Goering, improvising without a clear plan of attack, changed targets from the planes of the Royal Air Force (RAF) to the terror bombing of London. Had the Luftwaffe concentrated on destroying the RAF on the ground, they might have won. British advantages included new, improved versions of Hurricanes and Spitfires that gave them an advantage in one-on-one combat. Radar, which the British had made a great deal of progress with in the 1930s, provided a crucial few minutes warning. At this point, simply surviving to fight another day was a victory in itself.

Operation Barbarossa

Germany, primarily because of its defeat in the Battle of Britain, decided against attempting an invasion of Britain. Possibly Hitler thought the British would eventually accept peace terms. Probably he and his advisers realized the odds against success were very high. In any case, he had already been thinking about invading the Soviet Union. The decision was taken to launch Operation Barbarossa in the late spring of 1941. Looking back on that fateful decision, it seems odd Germany would take on a country with such vast resources. Ideologically the decision accorded with Hitler's pronouncements in *Mein Kampf.* The east was where Hitler intended to find Lebensraum, space for the rapidly growing Germany he envisioned in the near future. Additionally, Slavs were second only to the Jews as objects of Hitler's hatred. As *Untermenschen,* "subhumans," they would serve as slaves in the Third Reich. Practical considerations also weighed heavily. The Soviet Union appeared still disorganized by the purges and the Five-Year Plans. The Russian army had performed poorly in the war against Finland, but it would only become stronger as time went on. Already the Soviet Union had taken actions conflicting with Germany's interests in central and eastern Europe.

In the meantime, Stalin had been warned repeatedly of plans for a German invasion. Richard Sorge (1895–1944), a German Communist working in Japan, actually provided the date of the invasion. Stalin only decided to send an alert message early on June 22, which was too late. The invasion, which began June 22, 1941, was even more successful than German strategists had hoped. The Russian military, kept from making adequate preparations for a possible invasion by Stalin's fearful insistence on adhering fully to the terms of the Nazi-Soviet Non-Agression Pact, was caught off guard. Whole armies collapsed and were cut off. Attempts to retreat and regroup turned into routs. Much of the Russian air force was lost in the first days of the invasion. Stalin fell apart and sank into depression. It was two weeks before he finally spoke on the radio. Within weeks, Leningrad was under siege, German troops were advancing rapidly toward Moscow, and most of the rich croplands and important industrial complexes of the Ukraine had been conquered.

Yet the Soviet Union did not surrender. Stalin created the State Defense Committee (GKO), which he chaired. The general headquarters of the Soviet supreme command reported to the GKO. It was in charge of basic strategy while the army general staff developed operational plans. Perhaps even more important, the Soviet Union turned to the old traditions and, in particular, to the experience of Napoleon's invasion of Russia in 1812, giving ground and slowly bringing to bear its enormous resources. Stalin called on the patriotism of the masses. The Russian Orthodox Church was pressed into service. Able young leaders emerged in the military and also in the party and government.

The resilience of the Russian people found an unexpected ally in the weather. Winter came early in 1941 and caught the German military totally unprepared. As before, they had counted on a quick victory. They had come close to gaining it, but had failed largely because Hitler insisted on mounting three major campaigns simultaneously: against Leningrad in the north, Moscow in the center, and the Ukraine in the south. Strategic errors were compounded by tactical errors. Rather than regroup and establish winter quarters, Hitler demanded the army push on until, in some cases, major units were cut off and lost. By the end of 1941, if the Soviet Union had only a precarious lease on life, at least it could claim to have stopped the German army short of victory.

The fatal flaw in Nazi strategy was now apparent. Like politics, war making had been a matter of improvisation. Neither the German economy nor society had been mobilized for the kind of prolonged warfare World War II came to demand. Germany had learned nothing from its victories. Britain and the Soviet Union, for their part, had been forced by disastrous defeats to accept the fact that only an extended and long-term effort could possibly lead to victory. American aid to the British and Russians, who had immediately allied in the wake of the German invasion of the Soviet Union, was restricted in the beginning mainly to supplies and money.

In the last month of 1941 the Japanese attack on Pearl Harbor, December 7, 1941, catapulted the United States into war. Although the attack had been highly successful, its architect, Admiral Isoroku Yamamoto (1884–1943), worried that the United States would soon recover and overwhelm Japan. As he had noted the year before, "If I am told to fight regardless of the consequences, I shall run wild for the first six months or a year, but I have utterly no confidence for the second or third year. . . ."[2]

In May 1942, Admiral Yamamoto hoped to involve the U.S. Navy in a decisive battle by attacking Midway Island, which was some 1,100 miles west of Hawaii. In the meantime, American code breakers, their efforts called "Magic," had begun to decipher the Japanese naval code. Many of the Japanese naval messages referred to "AF." Guessing that "AF" was Midway Island, the U.S. Navy had the garrison at Midway radio in early May that the distillation plant was malfunctioning, and they were running short of water. The Japanese took the bait, sending coded messages that "AF" was low on water.

Admiral Chester Nimitz (1885–1996), commander-in-chief, Pacific Fleet, reinforced the garrison at Midway and sent every ship possible to protect the island. When the aircraft carrier *Yorktown* came into Pearl Harbor for repairs it was estimated repairs would take several weeks. Nimitz gave them three days. Working around the clock, workers carried out the most essential repairs. The *Yorktown* was ready to go when the rest of the task force left.

The Japanese attacked Midway on June 4, 1942. As the Japanese bombers were being refitted for a second attack on Midway, a Japanese scout plane spotted the American task force. The Japanese commander reversed the refitting process so that the planes could be sent against the American task force. American planes were attacking his fleet, but not one had scored a hit up to that point. Just at the point when the Japanese fighters, the Zeros, were preoccupied with torpedo planes from the *Yorktown*, a squadron of dauntless dive bombers slipped through, and in five minutes mortally wounded three Japanese carriers, their decks covered with aircraft, fuel hoses, and ordnance.

As historian David Kennedy notes:

> Before Midway, the Japanese had six large fleet-class carriers afloat in the Pacific and the Americans three (four with Saratoga, which was returning from repairs on the west coast at the time of the battle

---

2 Yamamoto to Prime Minister Fumimaro Konoye in September 1940, as quoted in David M. Kennedy, *Freedom from Fear: The American People in Depression and War, 1929–1945*, p. 526.

at Midway). With the loss of just one American and four Japanese carriers, including their complements of aircraft and many of their superbly trained fliers, Midway precisely inverted the carrier ratio and put the Imperial Japanese Navy at a disadvantage from which it never recovered.[3]

Although it took three more years and many casualties, Admiral Yamamoto's nightmare came true. America used its immense resources to push the Japanese steadily back toward the home islands, even while it contributed significantly to the war in Europe. The Battle of Midway was the turning point in the Pacific, just as Stalingrad would be the turning point in Europe.

Stalingrad and D-Day

In 1942 two questions of vital importance appeared on the agenda of the Allies. The first concerned whether the Russian military could hold Stalingrad, a city on the Volga River important both for reasons of strategy and prestige. The other vital question concerned the possibility of the United States and Britain establishing a second front that year.

Hitler pressed the German military to capture Stalingrad at any cost. The Russian military determined to resist the German assault with all the resources it could muster. The struggle was intense, block by block, house by house, and, in some cases, room by room. German soldiers referred to the vicious struggle for Stalingrad as a "Rat War."

While one part of the Russian army held the bulk of the German forces in front of it, other portions of the Russian military massed to the north and to the south of Stalingrad. On November 19, 1942, the Russians launched a gigantic pincers movement, cutting off a large German force in the ruined city. The German military could neither break through and reestablish contact with the surrounded troops nor adequately supply them. Hitler forbade the cut-off troops permission to try to fight their way out of the encirclement. He also gave orders not to surrender. Nevertheless, on February 2, 1943, the remaining German forces, perhaps one-third of the original force, surrendered. Hitler felt he had been betrayed. German soldiers, he said, rather than surrender, should have fought to the death or ended their own lives.

The Russian victory at Stalingrad was the turning point of the war in Europe and probably the greatest military campaign of the war. In the remainder of 1943 the Soviet Union began steadily advancing on all fronts. In January 1944 the siege of Leningrad was lifted and Soviet forces were nearing several key cities in eastern Europe.

3 Ibid, p. 543.

Continuously in 1942 and 1943, the Soviet Union pressed their Allies for a second front in Europe as a means of easing the enormous burden they were shouldering. The United States was largely preoccupied in that period with the war in the Pacific. Britain spent most of 1942 dealing with General Erwin Rommel (1891–1944), the "Desert Fox," in Libya and Egypt. The closest thing to a second front in 1942 was the occupation of French North Africa. This was as much a diplomatic as a military maneuver in that the area was nominally controlled by Vichy France. The Allies risked the possibility Germany would sweep the Vichy government aside or force it to join Germany as an active combatant in retaliation for the invasion. On the plus side, the successful takeover of French North Africa helped the now-General Charles de Gaulle emerge as undisputed leader of the Free French, a military organization created after the French government had signed the armistice with Germany.

The Soviet Union was not satisfied with occupation of French North Africa. It was also not satisfied the following year with the Anglo-American invasion of Sicily and the Italian mainland. The invasion took Italy out of the war when the Fascist Grand Council deposed Mussolini, but this merely led to a German rescue of Mussolini from prison and establishment of a puppet regime in northern Italy. King Victor Emmanuel III (1869–1947) appointed Marshal Pietro Badoglio (1871–1956) as premier to replace Mussolini. Badoglio, after disbanding the Fascist Party, opened negotiations with the Allies, which resulted in Italy switching sides September 3, 1944.

A large number of German troops were committed to the defense of Italy. These troops, combined with the mountainous terrain, meant the campaign up the peninsula was difficult and bloody. For the Soviet Union, however, it was still not the major diversion they sought. They did not consider it the long-awaited second front.

Only with D-Day, June 6, 1944, did the Soviet Union get what it had wanted all along. The landings on the beaches of Normandy by American, British, and Canadian forces were as much a feat of logistics as anything else. Simply to amass and coordinate the equipment and men needed was a tremendous achievement. Waiting for the right combination of weather and tides, and preventing German intelligence from discerning the nature of preparations, constituted an even more formidable task. Germany was now caught in a vise formed by the two massive armies of its opponents.

Home Fronts

Germany lost the war in part because it did not make a commitment to an all-out effort until it was too late. Throughout 1941 this kind of commitment had seemed unnecessary. Quick victories made it possible to re-equip the German military without placing much strain on the civilian economy. Occupied countries had the tops of their economies skimmed off for the German war effort. Additionally, Sweden and Switzerland, both neutral during the war, were important factors in the German war effort. When the Soviet Union did not collapse in 1942, however, it became clear something had to be done to coordinate the economy for military purposes. Goering, who had been in charge of the Four-Year Plan (1936) before the war, made efforts in this direction, as did army personnel. Fritz Todt (1891–1942), Minister of Armaments and Munitions, began a more successful effort that, after his death in 1942 in an airplane accident, Albert Speer (1905–1981) carried on. Speer, Hitler's personal architect, demonstrated considerable managerial ability in reorganizing the German economy. Parallel efforts by Heinrich Himmler (1900–1945) and the SS[4], a virtual state within a state that used vital resources for purposes often having little to do with the war effort, hampered Speer. Nevertheless, he tripled the production of munitions and weapons between 1942 and 1944. However, Allied bombing raids combined with a lack of raw materials and manpower to produce a precipitous decline in production in 1945.

Britain, back against the wall, worked to organize its resources and transform a peacetime economy into one fully mobilized for war. Taking cues from the experience of World War I, Winston Churchill reorganized the War Cabinet and turned over direction of the economy to a small ministerial group called the Lord President's Committee. From 1940 on, Britons suffered materially from the war, but this was borne by most with good grace. It was, first of all, a necessity. Additionally, there was the expectation the postwar period would usher in a new social order, equitable if not egalitarian.

The Soviet Union had the advantage of a tightly controlled command economy from the beginning. Under the Five-Year Plans of the 1930s some industries had been shifted to the east. When war began, entire plants were dismantled, relocated, and put back into production in a matter of weeks. Until 1943, however, Germany controlled large amounts of Russian farmland and significant parts of Russian industry. As the German army retreated, it destroyed as much as possible. Still, the Soviet Union, with its population completely mobilized for the war effort and with considerable American aid in the form of Lend-Lease, built up its productive capacity. The standard of living for the individual Russian dipped below even the previous lows reached in the days of the Civil War or the early 1930s, but

---

4 SS or *Schutzstaffeln*. Originally a protective guard for Hitler and other Nazi leaders, it took charge of the concentration camp system in the 1930s. In World War II it controlled a major part of the German economy and created its own military forces. It organized and ran the Holocaust.

the war effort was sustained. Like the British, the Russians faced both an unavoidable necessity and the prospects of a much-improved situation after a victorious end to the war.

Behind the successful war effort stood the enormous resources of the United States, its productive capacity freed from the Depression by the demands of war. America became, as President Franklin Roosevelt put it, "the arsenal of democracy." Within a year of the attack on Pearl Harbor, American production of armaments equaled that of all Axis powers combined. By 1944 the amount of armaments produced in the United States was double that of the Axis. World War II cost the United States a great deal in both men and money but also made it the richest, most powerful country in the world.

Collaboration and Resistance

The Third Reich made little attempt to use the possibilities for constructing a "New Order" in Europe. Those among the occupied nations who wanted to collaborate with Germany were forced to do so under disadvantageous conditions. Some groups, Ukrainian nationalists for example, who were eager to help in the destruction of the Soviet regime, were treated so badly they had no choice but to resist the Nazis.

In occupied Europe it was frequently difficult to draw a clear distinction between resistance and collaboration. For instance, how should a state functionary see his position? What he did was largely for the welfare of the people in his country, but some of what he did might aid the German war effort. This was the essential dilemma of those governing Vichy France. Pierre Laval (1883–1945), premier during much of the existence of Vichy, argued after the fact that his policies were necessary in order to keep the German occupation at a distance. It was better for Vichy authorities to supervise the recruiting of workers for labor in the German war industry than to turn this task over to the Germans themselves. Similarly, Laval argued it was important for the French police to function as fully as possible, even if this meant cooperating with the Gestapo in tracking down Jews or in dealing with the Resistance.

Not many of those involved in the Vichy government could be accurately labeled as fascists. Most were conservatives who practiced collaboration because it seemed unavoidable, and also because it appeared to offer the chance to carry out a "National Revolution." Between June 1940 and April 1942, members of the Vichy government believed they were working to replace the shopworn values and institutions of the Third Republic with something far better. By 1943, however, Henri-Philippe Pétain, Laval, and the rest of the Vichy government found it possible to do only what Germany allowed or required them to do. What may have been a sensible policy in the shock of defeat in 1940 had become, through a series of almost imperceptible changes, no longer justifiable by 1943 and 1944.

Elsewhere in occupied Europe there was even less possibility than in Vichy France of convincing oneself one was working out a national regeneration within the context of the German occupation. The pressure to supply food, workers for the factories, and Jews for the death camps, was too great. Here and there efforts were made to save the young men from labor service and the Jewish population of the country from transportation. Perhaps the best-known effort to hide Jews was that undertaken by the Frank family and their friends in Amsterdam. It failed, but the diary left behind by Anne Frank has inspired millions in the years since its publication. Corrie Ten Boom (1892–1983) and her family were more successful in their efforts to hide Jews in Haarlem, the Netherlands. Oskar Schindler (1908–1974), whose story has been told in Steven Spielberg's (1946–) *Schindler's List* (1993), protected a large number of Polish Jews by employing them in his business. The extraordinary efforts of the Protestant community of Le Chambon in France also saved the lives of many Jews. Some countries did a better job of protecting their populations than others. Denmark was amazingly successful in protecting its Jewish population, eventually sending most of them to safety in neutral Sweden. Ironically, the record of Fascist Italy was also quite good in this respect.

Organized resistance movements in Europe have often been romanticized and their importance exaggerated. There is a poignant scene in Marcel Orphul's documentary on Vichy, *The Sorrow and the Pity* (1970), in which a man talks about being part of the resistance: he kept a gun hidden under a woodpile throughout the war. This was, of course, dangerous in that he might have been shot had the gun been discovered, but it meant, in reality, his role in the Resistance had been played out only in his mind, and probably after the fact at that. Many in France and elsewhere, once the war ended, repressed any instance of collaboration and blew up all out of proportion anything that might be interpreted as resistance. For those who played an active part, there was always the question of whether it did any good. The moral ambiguity involved in ambushes and assassinations is examined, for example, in Harry Mulisch's powerful novel, *The Assault* (1985), which is about one such incident in Haarlem, the Netherlands.

The resistance movements accomplished much of crucial importance, of course. They furnished intelligence, helped downed pilots and escaped prisoners of war, and, in some cases, severely hampered the German war effort. The most successful resistance movement in the war was the Communist resistance movement in Yugoslavia led by Josip Broz (1892–1980) or Tito. Tito's partisans defeated not only the German occupiers of the country but also their rivals, the conservative Chetniks, who had hoped to restore the monarchy. The liberation of Yugoslavia without outside help was vitally important in the postwar period.

In various other ways, the resistance movements left important legacies. Communists played large roles in most movements because of their previous experience with underground work. Even the noncommunists among the resistance workers tended to reject the old order, which they held responsible for the problems of the 1930s and for the war itself. Many members of the resistance movements hoped to find different ways of organizing society, politics, and the economy after the war. For some this took the form of a "European" approach that would counter the dangers of nationalism. For others, the emphasis was on social justice. Various resistance "charters," such as the Charter of the National Council of Resistance in France, provided guidelines for postwar reconstruction programs.

The tendency to overestimate the importance of the Resistance is perhaps most notable in Germany. Much has been made of the circles, composed largely of military officers and aristocrats, which on several occasions attempted to assassinate Hitler. By 1943 these circles realized Hitler's plans were leading Germany to disaster. There was also considerable uneasiness about the activities of the SS and the Gestapo. Efforts to assassinate Hitler and stage a coup were delayed in part by the reluctance of some to break their oath of loyalty sworn to Hitler as supreme commander and by fears for the integrity of Germany after the coup. Most of those involved in the plot did not envision Germany changing much and were reluctant to open the way to victory by the Allied Powers.

Hitler seemed to lead a charmed life, as attempt after attempt on his life miscarried. The effort by Count Klaus Schenk von Stauffenberg (1907–1944) on July 20, 1944, nearly succeeded, leaving Hitler wounded but alive. The plotters, thinking he had been killed, started the coup. Joseph Goebbels, Hitler's Minister of Propaganda, kept the coup contained until it could be confirmed Hitler was alive. The failure of the plot resulted in the destruction of the German resistance movement. For his loyalty and swift action, the Führer rewarded Goebbels with the office of General Plenipotentiary for the Mobilization of Total War.

The Holocaust

While some Germans had been involved in one capacity or another in the Resistance, others had been active in planning an unprecedented program of genocide. Anti-Semitism had long been a major point in the Nazi program. In the 1930s this had been expressed mostly through measures designed to exclude German Jews (less than 1 percent of the population) from public life and force them to emigrate. With *Kristallnacht* ("The Night of Broken Glass"), November 9, 1938, the regime seemed to be headed in a more violent direction. Once the war began, the Nazis gained control over millions of Jews. At first, emigration, perhaps to the French colony of Madagascar, continued to be stressed. Large numbers of Jews were placed in ghettos. In the meantime, the euthanasia campaign in Germany, designed to eliminate mentally and physically disabled people, so-called "worthless life," provided the occasion for some experiments in killing people efficiently.

The turning point in Nazi efforts to deal with what they termed "The Jewish Problem" came with preparations for the campaign against the Soviet Union. First, the SS created task forces, the *Einsatzgruppen,* which followed the German army as it moved across the Soviet Union. The task forces were instructed to round up communist officials and Jews and to kill them. Thousands of people were forced to dig their own graves and then killed by machine guns. The best-known example of this campaign of slaughter

Inmates of Buchenwald in April 1945. The young man seventh from the left in the middle row bunk is Elie Wiesel who would become an author and Nobel Prize laureate. AP/Wide World.

is Babi Yar near Kiev, where in September 1941, over a period of two days, an estimated thirty-five thousand Jews were slaughtered. Although more than a million Jews were killed in this fashion, it was an inefficient process and difficult for many of the perpetrators to stomach. Late in 1941 plans began to be made for a more organized and coordinated process of slaughter. The Wannsee Conference in January 1942, held in a suburb of Berlin, was merely an effort to resolve remaining logistical problems. The decision to eliminate European Jews had already been made. No direct order from Hitler reflects this decision, but it is highly unlikely that he did not know and approve of the plans. Himmler took the lead in carrying out what he described as the Führer's wishes. The actual paper trail to Hitler only goes as high as a memorandum from Goering authorizing Reinhard Heydrich (1904–1942), an official in the SS, to take steps necessary "for the Total Solution of the Jewish Question within the realm of German influence in Europe."

The Nazis established six killing centers in Poland, the largest at Auschwitz (Oswiecim). Trains came from all over Europe to Auschwitz, which contained industrial enterprises as well as the death camp. After leaving the trains, officials separated people into those headed for the gas chambers and those headed for the labor camp. The Nazis ran the operation with a kind of grotesque efficiency, a terrible parody of a rationalized industrial enterprise. They instructed those intended for the gas chambers first to go to the showers, after which they would receive new clothing and further instructions. Though the gas chambers were constructed in such a way as to resemble showers, it did not take long for people to understand what was happening. Although death came quickly, people experienced panic and intense agony in the few minutes the process took. Evidence of this still exists in the grooves clawed into the concrete ceiling and walls of the chamber.

The Germans made efforts to run the killing centers as productive enterprises. They collected anything of value— mounds of human hair, warehouses full of shoes, handbags, and dresses. They removed gold crowns from the corpses before wheeling them into the crematoria. Nonetheless, the economic irrationality of this enterprise was all too apparent. In the middle of a war beginning to go badly for Germany, vital resources were being squandered for the purposes of slaughter. From the perspective of the Nazis who shared Hitler's racial beliefs, however, the extermination of Jews and other so-called undesirables (gypsies, homosexuals, and others) was precisely the point of the war.

The Holocaust produced a number of acute moral dilemmas. For example, if the perpetrators did not share Hitler's racial fantasies, then how did they justify their participation? Some, of course, insisted they were only

American soldier with captured V-2 rocket, one of the Nazi "miracle weapons," April 1945. Courtesy of Richard B. Hornbeck, private collection.

following orders. Many were active participants in the Holocaust because they saw the war in the east as a crusade against communism. It is now recognized that the army played a larger role in the mass deaths outside the camps than was earlier believed to be the case. Some soldiers simply wanted to remain part of their unit, taking the bad with the good. More frequently than one might wish to think, participation in the mass killings hardened people; others found they actually enjoyed it. To the extent that the victim appeared to be weak, different, or alien, it was possible to consider that person less than human and, therefore, easier to kill. Certainly in the camps, where the system operated in such a way as to degrade people and deprive them of any dignity, it was possible for guards and supervisors to see the prisoners as undeserving of life. Some of the perpetrators and many of the observers were appalled by what they witnessed, but generally felt there was little they could do except on an individual basis.

For the inmates of concentration camps and death centers ethical questions also existed. A few survived by losing every shred of humanity and by taking part in crimes against their fellow prisoners. Most survivors, however, depended on solidarity with others. Invariably, there would come a time when even the strongest and most resourceful would find himself or herself lost without the help of a group. Much has been made of the inmates' passivity, of their failure to do anything to protest. To a large extent, this is unfair. First, the system worked in such a way as to disguise

Table 7.1　Jewish Victims of the Holocaust

Country	Pre-Final Solution Population	Est. Deaths*	Est. Deaths**
Poland	3,300,000	3,000,000	up to 3,000,000
USSR	3,103,000	1,480,000	over 700,000
Baltic countries	253,000	228,000	——
White Russia	375,000	245,000	——
Ukraine	1,500,000	900,000	——
Russia (RSFSR)	975,000	107,000	——
Romania	600,000	300,000	270,000
Czechoslovakia	180,000	155,000	260,000
Hungary	650,000	450,000	over 180,000
Lithuania	——	——	up to 130,000
Germany	——	——	over 120,000
Germany/Austria	240,000	210,000	——
Netherlands	140,000	105,000	over 100,000
France	350,000	90,000	75,000
Latvia	——	——	70,000
Yugoslavia	43,000	26,000	60,000
Greece	70,000	54,000	60,000
Austria	——	——	over 50,000
Belgium	65,000	40,000	24,000
Italy	40,000	8,000	9,000
Estonia	——	——	2,000
Norway	1,800	9,000	under 1,000
Luxembourg	5,000	1,000	under 1,000
Danzig	——	——	under 1,000
Bulgaria	64,000	14,000	——
Denmark	8,000	——	——
Finland	2,000	——	——
Total	8,861,800	5,933,900	5,100,000

*The first two columns of figures are taken from "Estimated Number of Jews Killed in the Final Solution," Appendix B ("The Final Solution in Figures") in Lucy S. Dawidowicz, *The War against the Jews, 1933–1945* (1986), pp. 402–403. See also Appendix A ("The Fate of the Jews in Hitler's Europe: By Country"), pp.357–401, for a detailed discussion of the sources of Dawidowicz's figures.

**The third column is derived from Table B-2 ("Deaths by Country") in Raul Hilberg, *The Destruction of the European Jews* (rev. and definitive ed., 1985), volume III, p. 1220. See also the material in the rest of Appendix B ("Statistics of the Jewish Dead"), pp. 1201–1220, for additional information.

what was happening until it was too late. Second, there were uprisings and protests, even though the odds against their success were impossibly high. Perhaps the most serious moral questions came before people reached the death camps, in villages and towns before deportation orders came. Too many refused to heed the warnings or to organize in their defense. By the time people had been placed in a ghetto, it was too late for escape in most cases. The Jewish councils the Nazis created to administer some aspects of ghetto life had to make agonizing decisions about compliance or resistance. Nonetheless, there were Jewish partisan groups and a few spectacular if also ultimately futile examples of resistance in the ghettos. The Warsaw Ghetto Uprising in April–May 1943 was only the largest and most famous of these acts of defiance.

Finally, there is the question of the many who knew about the Holocaust but did nothing to stop it. While some extraordinarily brave people worked to help Jews hide or escape to a neutral country, most tried to avoid any involvement or knowledge of the scheme. By the middle of the war, Allied leaders knew the broad outlines of the Nazi plan to eliminate all European Jews, yet they took no direct action against it, military or otherwise. In part, this reflected a determination to get on with the war as the surest way to deal with a broad range of problems. In other cases, it reflected a global level of anti-Semitic prejudice that was much higher than many cared to admit. In the United States, for example, influential figures in both the State Department and the Congress blocked attempts to bring in large numbers of Jewish refugees before and during the war.

The Holocaust demonstrated the full range of human behavior. Its scale and the cold-bloodedness with which it was carried out set it apart. Between 5 and 6 million Jews were killed, approximately two-thirds of Europe's prewar Jewish population. Most of those killed came from Poland (3 million) and the Soviet Union (1.5 million). Sizable groups also came from Hungary, Romania, and Germany. Several million other people were killed, a disproportionate number of them Poles and Soviet citizens.

The End of the War

The Holocaust now seems like a crucial element in any consideration of the nature and impact of World War II, but in the minds of those working in 1944 and 1945 to establish the bases of the postwar world, it was a relatively unimportant factor, even when there was some conception of the dimensions of the event. Uppermost in the minds of the leaders of the Allied Powers by 1944 was the war in the Pacific. By then it seemed apparent the Nazi Third Reich was doomed. Planners thought the war in the Pacific might easily continue another year or more, resulting in hundreds of thousands of casualties for the Allies. A second crucial consideration involved political arrangements for European countries that had been either belligerents or occupied territories during the war. For various reasons, it did not seem possible simply to return to the boundaries of 1938 and out of the question to allow some regimes to continue in power unaltered.

At the time of the Yalta Conference in February 1945, the American, British, and French forces had recovered from the Battle of the Bulge, a desperate attempt in December 1944 by the Germans to reverse the Allied offensive in the west, but they had yet to cross the Rhine River. The Soviet Union by that time was approximately one hundred miles from Berlin and had occupied most of the major capitals of eastern and central Europe. The military situation at that time had obvious political implications. Americans continued to resist the idea of using military means to achieve political objectives. Nonetheless, a certain context for the discussions had already been established.

Yalta has often been viewed as either a failure of American diplomacy or a triumph of Russian duplicity. It should not be seen as either, but rather as an agreement that made sense in the context of the times, yet also one badly flawed by misunderstandings. In part, the agreements were shaped by the desire to involve the Soviet Union in the war in the Pacific. This represented a considerable concession on the part of the Soviet Union in that it had borne the brunt of Allied efforts in the war in Europe. The major problem, however, concerned eastern Europe and Russian interests there. Beginning with the Nazi-Soviet Non-Aggression Pact, the Soviet Union had worked consistently to make sure the states along its western borders were sympathetic to its interests and nonthreatening to its security.

Poland formed a major focus of concern. The Soviet Union desired a postwar government in Poland that was at least friendly toward the Soviet Union and willing to accede to its wishes, including incorporation by the Soviet Union of territory that had been disputed by the two states between the wars. The government, however, did not have to be a communist one. The Soviet Union believed it had a natural right to act in its interests and had been encouraged in this belief by Anglo-American practices in Italy, where policies based on American and British institutions and values had been put in place. The so-called "percentages deal" in October 1944 between Churchill and Stalin, dividing central and southeastern Europe into areas in which the Soviet Union or Britain would have predominant influence, was of limited importance but certainly accorded with the Soviet perspective on postwar arrangements.

The problems associated with Yalta came later when the Soviet view, pragmatic and hard-nosed, began to clash with the American view, also pragmatic but colored by ideals drawn from such documents as the "Atlantic

Table 7.2   War Dead in World War I and World War II

Country	World War I*	World War II**
France	1,350,000	600,000
United Kingdom	950,000	400,000
Italy	500,000	410,000
United States	100,000	300,000
Russia	2,300,000	ca. 25,000,000
(Soviet Union)		
Germany	1,600,000	over 4,000,000
Austria-Hungary	1,450,000	
Hungary		430,000
Czechoslovakia		415,000
Rumania		460,000
Yugoslavia		1,500,000 to 2,000,000
Poland		6,000,000
Turkey		400,000
Netherlands		210,000
Canada		34,000

*Statistics are from Table 4, "The balance sheet," p. 227, in Marc Ferro, *The Great War, 1914–1918* (1973).
**Statistics for the Soviet Union, Poland, Yugoslavia, the United Kingdom, the United States, and Germany are from "Conclusions," p. 894, in Gerhard L. Weinberg, *A World at Arms: A Global History of World War II* (1994). The number of dead worldwide in World War II is approximately 60 million. Statistics for France, Italy, Hungary, Czechoslovakia, Rumania, and the Netherlands are from "The Impact of Total War," p. 264, in Gordon Wright, *The Ordeal of Total War, 1939–1945* (1968). For Canada (and other nations as well), see Mattew White's very useful "National Death Tolls for the Second World War," http://users.erols.com/mwhite28/ww2stats.htm. Wright points out that almost half the European dead were civilians. This is compared to 5 percent of the dead in World War I. Statistics from Weinberg and Wright include the approximately 6 million Jews murdered in the Holocaust.

Charter," which had been issued by Roosevelt and Churchill in August 1941. Part of the problem lay in definitions. Phrases such as "free elections" or "democratic governments" might be understood in different ways. From the Soviet point of view, an election was not free nor a government democratic if the result was a state hostile to Soviet interests.

The final and most important issue concerned plans for Germany after the war. Proposals to destroy German industrial capacity were not accepted, but it was agreed that reparations could be extracted, both from current production and from facilities. It was further agreed that the country and its major city, Berlin, were to be divided into four sectors, each to be run by one of the occupying powers but all to cooperate economically. The fate of Germany was the dominant issue for the Soviet Union and the failure of the other Allies to understand this fully created much of the basis for the Cold War that followed the end of World War II.

Between Yalta and the next meeting of the Allied leaders at Potsdam in July and August 1945 the war in Europe ended. In March the Americans crossed the Rhine, the last major obstacle to the conquest of Germany. In the latter part of April, American and Russian troops met at Torgau on the Elbe River. Hitler committed suicide in his bunker in Berlin on April 30, the day after marrying his mistress, Eva Braun (1912–1945). It was left up to the German military commanders to surrender early in May to the Allied forces.

The war in the Pacific ended a little more than three months after the German surrender. On August 6, 1945, the United States dropped an atom bomb on the Japanese city of Hiroshima. The second atomic bomb was dropped three days later on Nagasaki. Also that day the Soviet Union entered the war in the Pacific. On the 14th the Emperor stated the war should end and recorded a radio message to the Japanese people. The following day the message was broadcast, the first time most Japanese had heard the Emperor speak, and the war officially ended.

Suggested Books and Films

Stephen Ambrose, *American Heritage New History of World War II* (1997). A revision and updating of the original text by C. L. Sulzberger, this reliable survey of the war contains hundreds of illustrations and twenty-five full color maps.

Omer Bartov, *The Eastern Front, 1941–1945: German Troops and the Barbarization of Warfare* (1985). An important revisionist study of the war between Germany and the Soviet Union.

Earl R. Beck, *The European Home Fronts, 1939–1945* (1993). A reliable brief treatment of this important topic.

Anthony Beevor, *Stalingrad* (1998). A comprehensive history of one of the turning points of World War II.

Christopher Browning, *Ordinary Men: Reserve Police Battalion 101 and the Final Solution in Poland* (1992). An important study of one aspect of the Holocaust with disturbing implications about human behavior.

———, *The Origins of the Final Solution: The Evolution of Nazi Jewish Policy, September 1939–March 1942* (2004). The best study available of this crucial topic.

John W. Dower, *War without Mercy: Race and Power in the Pacific War* (1987). One of the most important books written about World War II in the past two decades.

Anne Frank (ed. by Otto H. Frank and Mirjam Pressler), *The Diary of a Young Girl: The Definitive Edition* (1995); see also *Anne Frank Remembered* (1995), a documentary film directed by Jon Blair.

Julian Jackson, *France: The Dark Years, 1940–1944* (2001). A recent and exhaustive history of occupation, resistance, and liberation in France.

Michael Marrus, *The Holocaust in History* (1987). A short, very useful introduction to the topic.

Alan S. Milward, *War, Economy and Society, 1939–1945* (1977). A scholarly study of the economic side of war.

Harry Mulisch, *The Assault* (1986). A powerful novel about the Resistance in the Netherlands.

Robert O. Paxton, *Vichy France: Old Guard and New Order, 1940–1944* (1972, 1982). A careful examination of this controversial topic.

Richard Rhodes, *The Making of the Atomic Bomb* (1986). A lengthy but fascinating history of the Manhattan Project.

Art Spiegelman, *Maus*, 2 volumes (1986, 1991). An emotionally gripping personal narrative of the Holocaust using the comic book form. It was awarded the Pulitzer Prize.

Gerhard Weinberg, *A World at Arms: A Global History of World War II* (1994). The best one-volume history of World War II available.

Downfall (2005), produced by Bernd Eichinger, is a riveting dramatic portrayal of the last twelve days in the Bunker. Based on interviews with Hitler's personal secretary, Traudl Junge.

Hitler: The Last Ten Days, 1973, British-Italian production. An excellent portrayal of the final days of Hitler's Third Reich.

Schindler's List (1993), directed by Steven Spielberg. The extraordinary story of Oskar Schindler's efforts to protect Polish Jews by employing them in his business enterprise. See also the basis for the film, *Schindler's List* (1982), a novel by Thomas Keneally.

Chronology

1945	Formation of the United Nations
	Yalta Conference (February)
	Potsdam Conference (July–August)
1946	George F. Kennan's "Long Telegram"
1947	Truman Doctrine launches the era of
	containment in the Cold War
	Marshall Plan offers economic aid to Europe
	Communists forced out of coalition
	governments in France and Italy
	Formation of the Communist Information Bureau
	(Cominform)
1948	Communist coup in Czechoslovakia
	Berlin Blockade and Berlin Airlift (June 1948–
	May 1949)
1949	Federal Republic of Germany (West Germany)
	founded
	German Democratic Republic (East Germany) founded
	North Atlantic Treaty Organiation (NATO) created
	Soviet Union becomes an atomic power
	People's Republic of China (PRC) founded
1950	Korean War (1950–1953)
1953	Death of Stalin
	Uprising in Germany
1954	French defeat at Dien Bien Phu marks the end
	of the war in Indochina
	Vietnam divided into two states at Geneva Conference
1955	West Germany becomes a member of NATO
	Creation of the Warsaw Treaty Organization (WTO)
1956	Khrushchev's speech denouncing Stalin at the
	Twentieth Party Congress of the Communist Party of
	the Soviet Union
	Worker unrest in Poland
	Hungarian Revolution and Soviet intervention
	Suez Crisis
1957	Soviet Union opens a space race with the launching of
	Sputnik
1961	Construction of the Berlin Wall

8
Cold War and Decolonization, 1945–1961

ON MONDAY, JULY 16, 1945, there was a break in the conference at Potsdam. President Harry Truman (1884–1972) decided to take a look at Berlin. Sitting in the back seat of an open Lincoln with James Byrnes (1879–1972), his Secretary of State, and Admiral William Leahy (1875–1959), President Truman was driven past miles of burned-out buildings and rubble. The motorcade went down one of Berlin's best-known streets, Unter den Linden, now stripped of its famous Linden trees, past the Reich Chancellery, the Brandenburg Gate, and the Reichstag. That night he wrote in his diary:

> I thought of Carthage, Baalbek, Jerusalem, Rome, Atlantis, Peking . . . [of] Scipio, Rameses II . . . Sherman, Jenghiz Khan. . . . I hope for some sort of peace—but I fear that machines are ahead of morals by some centuries and when morals catch up there'll be no reason for any of it.[1]

Churchill also toured Berlin that afternoon. Whether Stalin did then or at some other time is not known. Of course, neither he nor Churchill really needed to see the ruins of Berlin in order to know the destructiveness of World War II. They had only to look at the great cities of their own countries.

More than 30 million people were killed in the European part of the war. Slightly more than half were soldiers, the rest civilians. Millions survived with disabilities of one kind or another. Millions more fled before advancing armies or were forced to migrate after the war. The largest group of the latter were Germans forced to move west from what had been East Prussia.

---

1 From Harry S Truman's Diary, July 16, 1945, as quoted in David McCullough, *Truman*, p. 415.

Material losses were enormous. The estimate, in 1945 dollars, was between 2 and 3 trillion. This included damage to farmland, destruction of cattle and other livestock, devastation of villages, towns, cities, bridges, railroads, and highways. Not only Germany, every country that had been involved in the war faced the need to rebuild its economy and to repair the social fabric. Some countries suffered more than others, of course. Denmark was, comparatively speaking, unmarked by the war. The Netherlands, by way of contrast, endured many hardships, particularly in the "Hunger Winter" of 1944–1945. The Soviet Union, victorious and powerful, had nevertheless incurred enormous losses. And, of course, it seemed Germany could not possibly recover. There was much pessimism; some believed Europe had been hopelessly weakened.

This assessment gained force not only from the emergence of two enormously powerful countries on either flank of Europe, the United States and the Soviet Union, but also from the grave weakening of the colonial empires. In different manners, in some cases quickly and in others slowly and painfully, the empires collapsed and disappeared (see the discussion of this process later in this chapter).

Finally, the spiritual cost of war and its aftermath was enormous. Europe had fallen back into a barbarism during World War II that contradicted the previous decades of progress and perhaps simply effaced them. The scale of cruelty was so gigantic as to defy understanding. The "Final Solution" was the major example of barbarism in the war. The firebombing of cities such as Hamburg and of Dresden were also seen as barbarous acts, even if not on the same scale and done with the stated intention of ending the war as soon as possible. Additionally, the use of atomic weapons in the case of Hiroshima and Nagasaki was seen by some as cruel and unnecessary while others claimed it had been done in the interest of forcing Japan to surrender as quickly as possible. All the claims of cultural or moral superiority Europeans had ever made now seemed hollowed out by the events of the war. A spiritual malaise accompanied military impotence and economic devastation.

Origins of the Cold War

Some observers take the long view and see the Cold War as first appearing with the Allied intervention in the civil war after the Russian Revolution. Others prefer to begin with the issue of the second front and other controversial matters in World War II. In both cases, the Soviet Union and the West had reasons for suspicion and distrust of each other. Still, at the end of the war in Europe, there was reason to believe the wartime alliance could be continued in some fashion.

When the Allied leaders met between July 16 and August 2, 1945, at Potsdam, a suburb of Berlin, the intention was to continue the alliance. The end of the war in the Pacific was now in sight, but estimates of when this would actually happen ranged between several weeks and several months. The leaders of the Allies had changed. Stalin continued to speak for the Soviet Union, but Roosevelt died on April 12, 1945, shortly after returning from the Yalta Conference in February. In his place was Harry Truman, inexperienced but astute. Both Winston Churchill from the Conservatives and Clement Atlee (1883–1967) from the Labour Party came to represent Britain. The Parliamentary elections brought a stunning defeat to Churchill and Atlee took over for Britain.

By midsummer of 1945, serious differences of opinion had already begun to surface with regard to postwar Europe. The most important concerned the composition of the Polish government and the question of the administration of occupied Germany. It was largely a matter of misunderstandings at this point. The Soviet Union saw no reason to tolerate a Polish government unreceptive to its ideas about the reordering of eastern Europe. If the Soviet Union installed in Poland a government it sponsored and largely excluded one backed by Britain, this was similar to what it believed the United States was doing in Italy and Britain in Greece. In occupied Germany, the Soviet Union had begun a policy of wholesale confiscation of materiel and facilities in its zone and also in the other three zones. The United States feared this would lead to the economic collapse of Germany and require greatly expanded American aid. The American government could see no point in American taxpayers subsidizing German reparations to the Soviet Union.

Truman took a more aggressive stance at Potsdam than Roosevelt had in earlier meetings. Roosevelt had sometimes been as suspicious of British imperialism as of Russian communism. Truman mainly distrusted the Russians. There is the possibility that Truman wanted to use the American monopoly of atomic weapons to force the Russians to make concessions. There is no evidence for this view, however. Truman did practice a blunt, no-nonsense kind of diplomacy, and he may have hoped the announcement of the new and devastatingly powerful weapon would give him some leverage with Stalin. Atomic blackmail would not have worked in any case. Stalin already knew a good deal about the American efforts to build the bomb through reports on the Manhattan Project sent to the Soviet Union by spies. He wanted the Soviet Union to have similar weapons and had already ordered Lavrenty Beria (1899–1953), Stalin's chief of the secret police, to set up a crash program to build an atomic bomb, but he knew the United States was unlikely to use atomic weapons in most circumstances.

Potsdam, together with Yalta, had created a volatile situation but not one fated to lead to confrontation. After all, the details of treaties with Germany and its allies were yet to be worked out. Whatever problems might appear could be resolved in the various fora now available. The main forum for discussion was the newly created United Nations, in particular, the Security Council, on which both the Soviet Union and the United States had permanent seats. The UN was never the kind of obsession for Roosevelt that the League of Nations had been for Wilson, but it was important to him. And he was not alone in placing great hopes in it. In addition there were meetings of the foreign ministers of the Allies and, on a more local level, meetings of the Allied Control Council in occupied Germany.

There was no Cold War yet in 1946, even though Churchill, speaking at little Westminister College in Fulton, Missouri, on March 5, 1946, noted "From Stettin in the Baltic to Trieste in the Adriatic, an iron curtain has descended across the Continent." Developments were taking shape, however, that moved Europe from the euphoria of war's end to the grimness of the Cold War's beginning.

The two main problem areas, occupied Germany and the new Poland, had become even more intractable. In occupied Germany, there were already signs a common occupation policy was not going to be established. In 1946 the United States and Britain no longer allowed the Soviet Union to take reparations from their zones. In September of 1946 Secretary of State Byrnes called for a revival of the German economy in a speech that signaled a decisive shift in American policy vis-à-vis Germany. Soon after that on January 1, 1947, the British and American zones fused into a single economic and administrative unit, "Bizonia." In the new Poland, a communist government, the so-called "Lublin Poles," had been installed in power in 1945 by the (Soviet) Red Army. A few "London Poles" had been added later to form a coalition government. In 1946 Polish communists worked diligently to break apart the Peasant Party, potentially the most powerful political party in Poland, and to gain control of another popular political force, the Polish Socialist Workers Party (RPPS). The elections scheduled for January 1947 did not look promising for the democratic forces.

Elsewhere, American diplomacy led the Soviet Union to withdraw troops from the northern part of Iran by early May of 1946, but Soviet pressure on Turkey continued. The Soviet Union did not try to influence the civil war in Greece between Greek communists and Greek monarchists, but, even so, by the end of 1946 the British were experiencing difficulties sustaining the monarchists. In all parts of western Europe, there was no sign of economic recovery taking place soon. The communist parties in France and Italy took part in the coalition governments in the two countries, but they seemed likely to be the main beneficiaries if the economies could not be restarted. Finally, in February 1946, George F. Kennan (1904–2005), attached to the U.S. Embassy in Moscow, sent an 8,000-word telegram, the "Long Telegram," back to Washington, D.C., detailing his sense of how Russians viewed their history and the present moment. Russia's historic sense of insecurity, exacerbated by communism's idea of the inevitability of war with capitalism, led Stalin always to seek to improve the country's situation. The Soviet Union, however, did respect strength. A firm response would force Stalin and the Soviet Union to back down. From this essay came the idea of "containment" (of communism), of meeting every Soviet move with a countermove and, later, of anticipating possible Soviet moves in order to preempt them.

Crisis Years, 1947–1948

In 1947 the Cold War began to take shape. The immediate origins lay in the situations in Turkey and in Greece. Turkey had been under considerable pressure from the Soviet Union to allow a Soviet military presence near the straits between the Black Sea and the Mediterranean. Greece was still involved in a civil war between Greek communists and Greek monarchists. Early in 1947 Britain informed the United States it could no longer supply aid to the two countries.

The United States faced the task of maintaining Anglo-American interests in the eastern Mediterranean. Truman, however, in his remarks to a joint session of Congress in March 1947, asked for an open-ended commitment by the United States to help any government threatened by invasion from without or subversion from within. This became known as the Truman Doctrine and, although the Soviet Union was not specifically mentioned in his address, his sentiments were widely regarded as an expression of hostility to Russia and to communism more generally. In effect, the address became the opening gun of the Cold War.

In the months after Truman's speech, Secretary of State George C. Marshall (1880–1959) and others in the State Department concerned themselves with the economic and social problems of Europe. George Kennan, by then the head of the new Policy Planning Staff at the State Department, quickly put together a report on the European situation recommending American aid. It would, he thought, be up to the Europeans to draw up the plans. Aid should be offered to all of Europe. Any decision leading to a division of Europe should stem from the Russian response to the American offer rather than the offer itself. In large part, the aid would be directed at German economic recovery, which Kennan saw as "a vital component of the recovery of Europe as a whole."

Although Marshall had planned to attend the Harvard commencement ceremonies in the spring of 1947, where he was to be awarded an honorary degree, and had been invited to give a speech, it was virtually at the last minute that he decided to use the occasion to launch what became known as the Marshall Plan. In his talk, Marshall indicated he was advocating economic measures to meet economic and social problems.

> Our policy is directed not against any country or doctrine but against hunger, poverty, desperation and chaos. . . . Any government that is willing to assist in the task of recovery will find full cooperation, I am sure, on the part of the United States Government. Any government which maneuvers to block the recovery of other countries cannot expect help from us.

Later seen as the economic counterpart to the Truman Doctrine, the Marshall Plan (or the European Recovery Program as it was formally known) was viewed by Marshall as a means of speeding European economic recovery. He saw, of course, the political implications of social and economic stability in Europe, and he was also aware of the importance to American business of an economically viable Europe.

Although the Marshall Plan was not an American maneuver in the rapidly emerging Cold War, the Soviet Union saw it that way. It walked out of the conference the British and French had called to discuss the initiative and pressured the Poles and Czechs to drop their interest in the plan as well. Stalin saw the plan simply as a means whereby the United States could gain control of the European economies. In particular, he had no intention of revealing the extent to which the war had damaged the Soviet economy.

By the end of 1947 many of the major elements of the Cold War had fallen into place. In May the communist parties in France and Italy had been forced out of the coalition governments. In September the Cominform (Communist Information Bureau), the successor to the Comintern, was established with headquarters in Belgrade, Yugoslavia. This was seen in the West as evidence of the existence of a monolithic communist movement, controlled by Moscow and dedicated to the subversion of democratic governments everywhere. Actually, the main task of the Cominform was to tighten Soviet control over eastern Europe and in particular to try to gain a greater measure of control over communist Yugoslavia.

The Two Germanies

During all this time the Allied Powers found themselves growing farther apart in their ideas about the administration of occupied Germany. The status of Germany was the most important single issue in relations between the Soviet Union and the other Allied Powers. The Soviet Union wanted to make sure Germany could not threaten it again in the twentieth century. The United States was more concerned about feeding Germany and about the connection between its economic recovery and the recovery of the rest of Europe. Neither side seemed to understand very fully the position of the other side. Each side had apparently learned different lessons from the peacemaking process after World War I.

As mentioned, the Soviet Union set out first to strip its zone of Germany of raw materials and factories. It also exercised its rights to take reparations in kind from the other zones. This was in line both with its concerns about security issues and its concerns about its own economic recovery. Initially, the French also followed a policy of extracting reparations from their zone. They began to see, however, as the British and Americans already had, that it was not to their advantage to destroy the German economy if this meant later they would have to send food, goods, and money back into Germany to prevent social unrest and instability.

In the American and the British zones an effort was made to carry out a program of de-Nazification, demilitarization, and democratization, but the programs were only partially successful. In particular, the process of de-Nazification moved slowly and was not especially effective. Many high-ranking Nazis escaped trial because of the often cumbersome process, which attempted to comb through the entire population. Other Nazis managed to escape trial because they were regarded as useful by the United States either for scientific projects or for espionage. The Americans and the British also made efforts to find Germans who had administrative experience but had not been tainted by association with the Nazis for positions of leadership. One such a person was Konrad Adenauer (1876–1967), former Lord Mayor of Cologne, then already seventy-seven years old.

Russian practices differed considerably. In 1946 the Soviet Union virtually eliminated political parties in its zone and put intense pressure on the old Social Democratic Party (SPD) to unite with the Communists (KPD) to become the Socialist Unity Party (*Sozialistische Einheits Partei Deutschlands* or SED). The Soviets also carried out an extensive program of land reform and nationalization of industry. This was based in part on the idea that destruction of capitalism would eliminate the basis for fascism since fascism was a product of "monopoly capitalism."

Two distinct zones were being created. One was composed of the American and British zones, which formally merged economies in January 1947, and, as mentioned, became known as "Bizonia." (The French did not, at first, accept the invitation to join.) The other was the Soviet Zone. When, in 1948, the three western powers announced the introduction of currency reforms, a necessary prelude to economic recovery and the functioning of the zones as an economic unit, the Soviet Union closed down rail, road, and water traffic between Berlin and the west. The Berlin blockade, June 23, 1948, to May 12, 1949, and the Berlin airlift countering it, were the most visible signs of increasing Cold War tension.

In 1949 the division between western Germany, which became known as the Federal Republic of Germany (FRG or West Germany) and eastern Germany, organized as the German Democratic Republic (GDR or East Germany) was officially set. West Germany quickly began to move from the status of former enemy to that of potential ally of the western powers. A divided Germany had not been the intention of any of the Allied Powers at the end of World War II, but in the new context of the Cold War it suited each of them well enough.

The Cold War Launched

The postwar world in 1949 presented a new, ominous look. In addition to the quarrel over the status of Germany and its division into two separate states, there was the phenomenon of tightening Soviet control in eastern Europe. This was symbolized most vividly by the Czech coup in February 1948. In the process of replacing a democratic coalition government with a communist one, Jan Masaryk (1886–1948), Czech foreign minister and son of the founder of the Republic, died in a mysterious fall from his office window. Czechoslovakia, when Eduard Benes (1884–1948) had been president and Masaryk foreign minister, seemed the exception to the rule in Soviet-controlled eastern Europe, a sign of hope that a democratic, freely elected government might coexist with the Soviet Union.

West Europeans and Americans, faced with the events of 1947 and 1948, responded by forming the North Atlantic Treaty Organization (NATO) in 1949. NATO grew out of an earlier pact, the Brussels Treaty (1948), signed by Britain, France, Belgium, Luxembourg, and the Netherlands. In effect, these West European countries invited the United States to participate in an alliance that it would naturally dominate. Europeans agreed to, actually encouraged, the formation of an informal American empire in the interests of collective security. By way of contrast, the Soviet Union imposed its empire on eastern Europe in the interests of the national security of the Soviet Union.

Three developments in Asia also contributed to the shaping of the emerging Cold War world. These were the American occupation of Japan, the victory of the Chinese Communists over the Chinese Nationalists in 1949, and, finally, the Korean War.

Rioters in East Berlin throw stones at Red Army tanks in June 1953 to protest the Stalinist regime of the German Democratic Republic. Cracks appeared in every decade after the formation of the Soviet bloc, but the Soviet Union held its empire together until 1989. AP/ Wide World.

The U.S. exercised complete control over the occupation of Japan. General Douglas MacArthur (1880–1964), commander of the occupation administration, used his authority to reshape Japanese political life, firmly reestablishing a tradition of parliamentary democracy while allowing Emperor Hirohito (1901–1989) to remain as a national symbol. MacArthur had less impact on the contours of economic and social affairs, although he did much to improve the status and rights of women. The Japanese themselves decisively rejected militarism. Although they placed themselves under the American security umbrella and became an important economic component of the Cold War, they did not join, as did West Germany, an Asian equivalent of NATO.

The victory of the Chinese Communist Party under Mao Zedong (1893–1976) shaped the Cold War in two important ways. The People's

Republic of China was an enormous addition to what American and other observers now regarded as a monolithic world communist movement. In reality, Chinese national interests often clashed with Russian national interests. This would not surprise anyone familiar with the long history of contacts between the empires dating back to the seventeenth century, but this perspective seemed to have disappeared in face of the concerns about the newly expanded communist movement. Also, Mao's ideas and the revolutionary romanticism associated with his past accomplishments heightened a fear that every national liberation movement would end up as a victory of the supposedly monolithic world communist movement.

Of the three developments, the Korean War (1950–1953) had the greatest impact on the development of the Cold War. At the end of World War II, the Soviet Union occupied the northern half of the penninsula and the United States the southern half. In the next few years, each power created a Korean administration that conformed more or less to the occupying power's political system. In North Korea, Kim Il Sung (1912–1994), a Korean communist and nationalist, believed his country could easily reunite the peninsula. Additionally, he thought an invasion of the south would lead to a popular uprising. Finally, the Americans seemingly had written Korea off as an area of strategic interest. In any case, they would not have time to intervene. This was the scenario Kim Il Sung presented to Stalin. Although Stalin was generally quite cautious about support for ventures of this sort, he appeared to believe the plan involved little risk. Kim Il Sung then persuaded Mao to lend support as well.

The invasion was initially successful, but the U.S. intervened at the head of an international force under UN sponsorship and drove the North Korean army out of South Korea and up to the Yalu River boundary between North Korea and the People's Republic of China. At this point, China attacked and forced the American forces into a disastrous retreat. The war settled eventually into a costly stalemate with the frontlines more or less on the old borders between the two Koreas. While Europe remained the center of concern in the Cold War up to the building of the Berlin Wall in 1961, the United States increasingly saw danger in every part of the world and sought allies wherever it might find them. It embarked on a policy that went beyond containment, i.e., the idea of blocking overt Soviet attempts to extend the U.S.S.R.'s power. In 1950, the National Security Council, an agency created in 1947 to help manage America's response to the Cold War, issued NSC68. This position paper recommended that the United States oppose the Soviet Union in virtually any situation that might work to the benefit of the latter. According to NSC68, the Soviet Union was "animated by a new fanatical faith . . . and seeks to impose its absolute authority over the rest of the world." The document further recommended greatly increased military spending and foreign-aid programs. Over the next several years, American leaders thought increasingly not simply of containment, but more and more of "rollback," a policy that would lead, they hoped, to a weaker Soviet Union and to the liberation of some of the areas now under its control.

The Soviet Union saw itself as weak and vulnerable. In the late 1940s it was desperate to gain security. Although it apparently did not believe the United States would use its atomic weapons monopoly, the Soviet Union spared no effort to create its own atomic weapons. Its vise-like grip on eastern Europe was another effort to enhance security. Most important of all, its policies toward the two states of East Germany and West Germany betrayed an obsessive, almost irrational fear of German potential. It viewed the United States as an immensely wealthy, powerful, and also hypocritical nation, which denied the Soviet Union what was important to its security while reserving for itself the right to act as it saw fit. Paradoxically, it feared revolution. Although it gave lip service to national liberation movements, it offered little help, and in the case of the Chinese Communists probably hindered their efforts to come to power. In the last years of Stalin's life, the Soviet Union sponsored purges in eastern Europe designed to place communists loyal to Moscow solidly in power. It also attempted to destroy the power of Marshall Tito and other Yugoslavian communists who were attempting to follow a national (read independent) line of development.

Dismantling the Colonial Empires

The dismantling of the colonial empires took place in two large waves. Most of Asia gained independence in the initial wave of national liberation movements in the first several years after the war. Nationalist movements, some heavily influenced or even dominated by communists, had existed in the area before World War II. In some cases, India is the best example, these movements had made considerable progress toward the achievement of self-government if not independence. In most areas, however, the war created conditions which made the conquest of power a distinct possibility.

In those areas where the Japanese had smashed colonial regimes in the process of takeover, a power vacuum existed into which nationalists might move at the end of the war. One such was the Dutch East Indies, where Indonesian nationalists under Ahmed Sukarno (1901–1970) declared independence in 1945. Although the Dutch returned after the war and attempted to regain control by use of armed force, they lacked the resources necessary for that task. The United States was not only unsympathetic to the Dutch cause but actually put them under considerable pressure to grant the Indonesians independence. In 1949 the Dutch recognized the independence of Indonesia. Of the Dutch empire, originally one of the great empires of the world, there now remained only a few fragments. The Dutch had regarded the empire as a very important factor in the economy. They were surprised that its loss had little effect on their ability to recover prewar economic levels and then to surpass them.

The Vietnamese, like the Indonesians, took advantage of the destruction of the colonial government during the war. They did not, however, as the Indonesian nationalists did, work with the Japanese during the war. In August of 1945 they declared their independence in words taken from the American Declaration of Independence. Ho Chi Minh (1890–1969), affiliated between the wars with the Comintern, had created the Viet Minh, a broadly based nationalist movement heavily influenced by Vietnamese communists. He and the Viet Minh took control of the north after the Japanese surrender. The British, who restored order in the south, prevented the Viet Minh from establishing control there and, instead, worked with the French to restore the colonial regime. An uneasy truce existed between the north and the south, but it broke down in December 1946 after a French attack. Over the next several years the Viet Minh defeated French efforts to reestablish control over all of Indochina. At first they used guerrilla tactics similar to those employed by Mao Zedong in China. Later they moved to conventional warfare. The French by the early 1950s counted on large-scale American aid. The United States, influenced by the victory of the Chinese Communists in 1949 and the outbreak of the Korean War in 1950, was eager to assist the French, in sharp contrast to policies followed earlier in connection with Dutch efforts to regain control of Indonesia. The United States did, however, draw the line at sending American troops to help. When the French attempted to defeat the Viet Minh decisively at Dien Bien Phu in 1954 and suffered a major defeat, Americans debated various possibilities including the use of atomic weapons but, ultimately, refused to intervene. At the Geneva Conference in 1954, the Russians and the Chinese pressed the Viet Minh to accept a division of Vietnam at the seventeenth parallel. The north would be under the control of the Viet Minh, the south under a noncommunist Vietnamese government. Elections were to be held by 1956 to determine the government under which Vietnam would unite. Unification came only in 1975, when North Vietnam conquered South Vietnam. Leading up to that moment were years of struggle by the Vietnamese Communists against the United States, which had been increasingly drawn into attempts to support South Vietnam.

Other attempts at national liberation were less successful. The British were able to withstand a challenge in Malaya primarily by Chinese inhabitants influenced by communism. Malaya, which became independent in

Europe During the Cold War

1957, merged with other nations in 1963 to form Malaysia. Singapore, inhabited mostly by Chinese, became an independent city-state in 1965. The United States granted the Philippines full independence in 1946. The Philippines under the charismatic leadership of Ramon Magsaysay (1907–1957) instituted land reforms and successfully ended a guerrilla insurrection by 1951.

India was the major exception to the pattern of national liberation movements and the most important of all the Asian nations gaining independence in the first wave. The British had reluctantly agreed to Indian independence after the war. The major problem concerned whether a separate state should be established for the Muslim population of India. Despite the efforts of Mohandas Gandhi (1869–1948) to keep India intact, Pakistan was carved out of India and the two nations granted independence in 1947. The British rather abruptly brought the two states into existence with the passage of the India Independence Bill in July 1947. Although India (predominantly Hindu) and Pakistan (predominantly Muslim) had not had to fight for independence, thousands were killed as Muslims fled Hindu-controlled areas and Hindus did the same from Muslim-controlled territory. Not long after India and Pakistan gained independence, Ceylon (now Sri Lanka) and Burma (now Myanmar) gained independence.

In North Africa and the Near East, where most of the population was Muslim, two crucial situations took shape in the late 1940s and early 1950s. First, in the British mandate of Palestine, Jewish settlers successfully established Israel as a Jewish state. Palestine had been partitioned in 1947 by the United Nations into a Jewish state and a Palestinian state. When the British left the area, neighboring Arab states attempted to destroy Israel in the Arab-Israeli war of 1948–1949. Israel not only defeated the Arab coalition but enlarged its territory. Arab defeat led to military revolts in Egypt, Syria, and Jordan and to war and terrorism over the next five decades. British and French influence in the area disappeared; an ill-fated effort to regain influence in the joint attack with Israel on the Suez Canal in 1956 misfired. The United States became a major factor in the politics of the area over the next half century with mixed results. On the one hand, it was a major supporter of Israel. On the other, the U.S. worked with most of the other states in the Middle East, making Iran in particular into a major power in the area by the 1970s. The Soviet Union attempted to play a role in Middle Eastern affairs, but generally without success except in the area of terrorism (see Chapter 10 for comments on terrorism). Israel, heavily influenced by the influx of European Jews and by the historical legacy of the Holocaust, became the strongest and most successful state in the area.

In North Africa, the French faced a major challenge in Algeria when the National Liberation Front (FLN) began a revolution in 1954. Although the French had considerable success militarily against the FLN, they steadily lost ground in the court of world opinion. The revolution grew increasingly brutal in the methods used by the two sides. For the French, it was particularly troubling since they could not help but note they were using many of the same methods the Gestapo had used in World War II against the French Resistance. Both Tunisia and Morocco gained independence in 1956, but a similar move for Algeria was out of the question first of all because 1 million Europeans, or *colons*, living in Algeria controlled its economy and government and considered it a part of France. For the French army, holding on to Algeria had become a question of honor, of redeeming itself after humiliating defeats in 1940 by the Germans and in 1954 by the Vietnamese. It was only after the coup in Algiers, the capital of Algeria, and a close brush with civil war, which brought Charles de Gaulle to power in 1958, that a way was found to extricate France from Algeria in 1962 (see Chapter 9 for discussion of de Gaulle's efforts to resolve the Algerian crisis).

By the mid-1950s, in what might be seen as the second wave of independence movements, the British and the French both began moving to grant their African colonies independence. In 1960 the French granted full independence to their African colonies, which had earlier been given autonomy within the French community of nations. The French dream of assimilation, of transforming the inhabitants of colonial areas into people whose culture and heritage were French, did not prepare the former colonies well for independence. Only a tiny elite had been able to follow the path opened up by French education. Most of the population of the new nations were unprepared for living in the modern world.

The British did somewhat better in terms of training a large group of Africans to take over the task of governing themselves. Several areas, however, contained large numbers of white settlers. In these areas there was resistance to independence and considerable violence. In Kenya, the Mau Mau movement (1952–1956) struggled for independence. Most of its terrorist tactics were directed against Africans reluctant to support independence against the British, but white settlers were also killed.

Rhodesia, controlled by white settlers, declared its independence in 1965, but after more than a decade of struggle Rhodesia became Zimbabwe in 1980 and power was handed over to the black majority. The Union of South Africa left the Commonwealth in 1961 and became the Republic of South Africa, a state characterized by an elaborate state system of *apartheid* or segregation. Only after adopting a new constitution in 1993 and holding free elections in 1994 did South Africa leave behind the destructive system that had shaped its society and economy in the twentieth century.

The Belgians, who had not done very much better in managing The Congo after taking it away from the Belgian king in 1908, badly mismanaged the granting of independence. In 1960, with very little advance preparation, the Belgians simply withdrew from The Congo and granted it independence. This led to a five-year period of civil war in which the United States, the Soviet Union, and the People's Republic of China intervened at one time or another. Between 1971 and 1997 the nation was known as Zaire and ruled by Mobutu Sese Seko's (1930–1997) brutally corrupt and inept regime.

By the mid-1960s the second wave of independence movements was over. Only a few white settler regimes and the Portuguese colonies remained in Africa. Elsewhere a handful of colonies in the Western Hemisphere and in the Pacific were still in existence. To all intents and purposes, imperialism in the sense of colonial empires had disappeared from the face of the earth.

Many of the new nations retained ties to the former colonial powers. They did not always, however, follow the political traditions of the ex-colonial powers. The United States, especially, and also the Soviet Union, have maneuvered for influence in the new nations, but with only limited success. A major movement of the 1950s and 1960s was nonalignment, an effort by new nations to avoid commitment to either major bloc.

Many Europeans had spent most or all of their lives in the colonies and found it difficult to return to their home country. They felt considerable bitterness in many cases. Probably the Dutch did the best job of making room for people returning from the old empire. The French, particularly in the difficult case of the colons from Algeria, did the worst job. The British as usual were somewhere in the middle. Europeans as a whole, however, once they had recovered from the trauma of decolonization, found the loss of colonies offset by the freedom from responsibilities the colonies had brought with them. In many cases, they discovered new possibilities. Some countries, the Netherlands may be the best example, built up a far more prosperous and stable economy than they had ever achieved with colonies.

The emergence of dozens of new nations in the 1950s and 1960s began to change the nature of international relations. European nations, like other industrialized and modern states, had to contend with the claims of the so-called "Third World." Political independence was only the first step. The next was to provide, in the form of foreign aid, a fair share of the wealth Europeans gained from the operations of the modern world economy. Europeans wrestled with this issue and by and large did far better by the emerging nations than either the United States or the Soviet Union.

Suggested Books

F. Ansprenger, *The Dissolution of Colonial Empires* (1989). A comprehensive examination of the end of empire.

Carolyn Eisenberg, *Drawing the Line: The American Decision to Divide Germany, 1944–1949* (1996). A fresh look at efforts by the United States to deal with the German question in the 1940s.

Melvin P. Leffler, *The Specter of Communism: The United States and the Origins of the Cold War, 1917–1953* (1994). A brief but very insightful discussion of the many factors contributing to the emergence of the Cold War in the first decade after World War II.

Ralph B. Levering, *The Cold War: A Post–Cold War History,* Second Edition (2005). A good introduction.

John Lewis Gaddis, *We Now Know: Rethinking Cold War History* (1997). An up-to-date review of significant aspects of the Cold War.

Ellen J. Hammer, *The Struggle for Indochina 1940–1955* (1966). An excellent discussion of French efforts to maintain Indochina as a colony after World War II.

Michael J. Hogan, *The Marshall Plan: America, Britain and the Reconstruction of Western Europe* (1987). The best single book on the Marshall Plan.

Alistair Horne, *A Savage War of Peace: Algeria 1954–1962* (1979). A fascinating account of a very important national liberation movement.

Thomas Alan Schwartz, *America's Germany* (1991). An important study of the shaping of West Germany in the postwar period.

Avi Shlaim, *The United States and the Berlin Blockade* (1983). A detailed analysis of this pivotal event.

Robert M. Slusser, *The Berlin Crisis of 1961* (1973). A careful examination of the crisis set off by the construction of Berlin Wall.

Vladislav Zubok and Constantine Pleshakov, *Inside the Kremlin's Cold War: From Stalin to Khrushchev* (1996). The most detailed and authoritative discussion of the role of the Soviet Union in the Cold War from 1945 to 1962.

Messengers from Moscow, 1995. Public television's highly acclaimed four-part series on the Cold War from the Soviet perspective, written and produced by Herbert J. Ellison.

Chronology

1945   Nazi Germany defeated
       Labour party wins elections in Britain
1946   Constitution of French Fourth Republic approved
       Italy becomes a republic
       National Health Service established in Britain
       Beginning of the Indochina War between France
         and the Viet Minh
1947   British rule in India ends
       Truman Doctrine
       Marshall Plan
       Communists forced out of coalition governments in France and
         Italy
1948   Communist coup in Czechoslovakia
       Christian Democrats win elections in Italy
1949   Federal Republic of Germany (West Germany) founded
       German Democratic Republic (East Germany) founded
       Dutch rule in East Indies ends
1950   Schuman Plan
1952   European Coal and Steel Community (ECSC) established
1953   Death of Stalin
1954   France defeated at Dien Bien Phu
       Vietnam divided into two states at the Geneva Conference
1956   Khrushchev's speech denouncing Stalin at the Twentieth
        Party Congress of the Communist Party of the Soviet Union
       Worker unrest in Poland
       Hungarian Revolution and Soviet intervention
       Suez Crisis
1957   European Economic Community (EEC) established by Treaty
        of Rome
1958   Charles de Gaulle becomes president of France
       French Fifth Republic established
1959   European Free Trade Association (EFTA) established
1961   Construction of Berlin Wall begins
1962   Cuban Missile Crisis
1963   De Gaulle vetoes British membership in the EEC
       Franco-German Treaty signed
       West German chancellor Konrad Adenauer retires after fourteen
        years in office
1964   Khrushchev forced to retire—replaced by Brezhnev
1966   Grand coalition of the CDU and SPD in Germany ends
        seventeen years of conservative government
       De Gaulle announces French withdrawal from NATO
1967   Military seizes power in Greece
       EEC, ECSC, and Euratom combine to become the European
        Community (EC)

9
Out of the Ashes:
From *Stunde Null*[1] to a New Golden Age, 1945–1967

IN 1950 LAURENCE WYLIE, then a professor of French at Haverford College, took his wife and children to the commune of Roussillon for his sabbatical year. Situated in the southeastern part of France, Roussillon contained only about 800 people. At that time about half the population of France lived in similar rural communes (a rural commune is defined as containing fewer than 2,000 people). And, as Wylie later realized, many French had lived in such communes at one time or another before moving to towns or cities. A large percentage of the French, then, lived at the start of the 1950s as people lived in Roussillon.

In 1950 farmers had planted wheat instead of the fruit trees they had been told were better suited to the soil and climate. As one of them put it: "Plant an apricot orchard so the Russians and Americans can use it as a battlefield? Thanks. Not so dumb."[2] His comments reflected the fear common to many Europeans in the early 1950s that a third World War would break out.

Eleven years later, Roussillon had changed considerably. Upon revisiting Rousillon in 1961, Wylie noted he could see fruit orchards in every direction from his vantage point at the top of a hill overlooking the commune. More than agricultural practices had changed. Roussillon had become a resort town, a fashionable place to live. A construction boom was underway. Television had made its entrance by the late 1950s and with it the idea of buying on the installment plan.

Roussillon by the early 1960s was representative of one aspect of the new Europe, a Europe that was more urban, more affluent, more egalitarian, and more confident than it had been only a decade before. By the early 1960s, with only a few exceptions, it had left colonial empires behind but, of course, not all the legacies of colonialism. There was also a loosening of the two great blocs, the East headed by the Soviet Union and the West

---

1 *Stunde Null* means "zero hour," but more in the sense of a beginning point. At the end of World War II, Germans felt they were starting over, with absolutely nothing from the past to serve as resources for the present and future.
2 As quoted in Wylie, *Village in the Vaucluse*, 3rd ed., p. 33.

headed by the United States, and indications of détente, a relaxation of tensions between the two great powers. The economy continued to grow and there seemed to be no end in sight for what was increasingly being called a golden age.

Reconstruction

Certain factors worked to make reconstruction easier than was initially expected. First, damage caused by war had sometimes been exaggerated. Also, it occasionally had a "positive" effect. Destruction of a factory in the war became an advantage if that factory were replaced by a more efficient plant. In some cases, the economies of the belligerent nations had expanded during the war and were nearly as large or even larger than the prewar economies, even after wartime damages had been taken into account. Largely intact productive capacity that could be modernized where damaged, together with a great shortage of goods of all kinds, created a basis for a rapid recovery. The most important missing factor was the capital to finance economic growth.

The United States provided much of the capital needed for recovery through the Marshall Plan (1947) and other smaller programs. Before the Marshall Plan, America had already made available nearly 15.5 billion dollars in aid, about 7 billion of that in gifts. From 1947 to 1952 it provided Europe with about 13 billion dollars in aid under the European Recovery Program. After that, Europe financed recovery largely through the expansion of exports.

The Marshall Plan was based on national plans which the Office of European Economic Cooperation (OEEC) helped to coordinate. The national plans gave Americans some assurances as to how their money would be spent and also encouraged participants to use all resources in the most constructive manner.

In many ways, the Marshall Plan's main contribution was psychological. It demonstrated American faith that European economies could be reconstructed and gave Europeans reasons to cooperate with one another in the process. Other factors involved in the recovery included an increase in trade worldwide and several demographic factors in Europe. First, there was a rising birthrate. Additionally, the influx of refugees and, later, the arrival of large numbers of foreign "guestworkers," added to the capacity to produce goods relatively cheaply. Heavy consumer demand, especially in areas of housing and automobiles, was vitally important in maintaining a long-term expansion of the economy.

A new kind of capitalism, characterized by extensive state intervention and by devices such as planning and nationalization, also played an important role in recovery. Governments often used control of banks and investments to determine both the rate of growth of an economy and the direction of that growth. They extended their activities beyond areas having to do with welfare—unemployment, retirement, working conditions, public health, and housing—to the workings of the economy itself. In some cases, housing for instance, welfare and economic expansion went hand in hand. Efforts to make the economy function effectively and equitably followed patterns developed in each of the two world wars. All the factors taken together enabled most western European countries not simply to recover but also to develop at a rapid rate through the first two decades after the war.

Reconstruction in the West: British Problems

Three major developments characterized Britain in the first decade after the war. The most basic was the distressingly slow recovery of the economy and Britain's failure to share fully in the rapid economic growth of the 1950s. Britain was initially handicapped by an enormous war debt and by foreign policy crises in areas such as India, Palestine, Greece, and Malaysia. Even after relinquishing responsibilities around the world, however, Britain still faced a severe balance of payments problem. It had become less competitive on the world market because of a variety of factors. The industrial plant was aging, the labor force more concerned with benefits than productivity, and management reluctant to modernize facilities and encourage innovation. The loss of markets and the sell-off of investments to help finance the war increased the difficulty of balancing imports by exports. Despite economic difficulties, Britain resisted the idea of long-term economic planning and restricted governmental interference in the private sector. Nationalization was regarded more as a rescue operation than as a tool for restructuring or directing the economy.

The expansion of the welfare state formed the second development. The Labour Party erected a comprehensive social security system and a socialized medical care program, beginning with passage of the National Insurance Act and the National Health Services Act in 1946. Criticism was heavy at the time and continued long after Labour had lost power, but both measures quickly became accepted as integral parts of British life. Even during Labour's long absence from power between 1951 and 1964 there were no serious attempts to dismantle the systems.

Finally, Britain spent most of the postwar period in a "retreat from empire." The attempt to reassert its old position in world affairs, the conspiracy with France and Israel to take over the Suez Canal in 1956, failed miserably when the United States and the United Nations forced Britain and its allies to back down.

Labour presided over the initial period of recovery and the elaboration of the welfare state. It became badly divided between left and right wings, however, by 1951 and was defeated in elections that year by the Conservatives. Winston Churchill returned to serve until his retirement due to ill health in 1955. Anthony Eden (1897–1977) served as prime minister only for a short time before the Suez Canal debacle forced him to resign. He was followed by Harold Macmillan (1894–1986), "Supermac," the most able of the three prime ministers. In the 1950s Britain enjoyed a modest economic recovery and the easing of international tensions. By the end of the decade its economy was prosperous if still vulnerable. Heavily dependent on exports, it nevertheless remained relatively uncompetitive because of the various factors already discussed.

Reconstruction in the West: French Success

The general pattern of economic recovery outlined above fits the French experience closely. Wartime destruction and social dislocation demanded strong economic measures. Social and economic programs based on discussions in the Resistance movement during World War II and on the experiences of the Popular Front in the 1930s also had an impact. While some industries were nationalized, the more important factor was the emphasis placed on economic planning. Jean Monnet (1888–1979), the architect of French economic recovery and later of European economic integration, put together a four-year plan that went into effect in 1948. Initial efforts were designed to channel investments into such basic areas of the economy as coal, electricity, steel, and farm machinery. Later plans were directed toward consumer goods, housing, and farm production.

The idea of an economy with a large public sector, planned and guided from above, was a radical departure from past French policy. Owners of small businesses and farmers resisted it, but, nonetheless, during the 1950s and 1960s a "silent revolution" took place, making France industrially and technologically competitive with other nations. At the same time, large numbers of people moved into urban areas and agriculture was thoroughly modernized. In little more than a decade, the French economy changed drastically, despite tenacious rearguard actions.

The French version of the welfare state was not as comprehensive as the British system, but it was a greater break with the past. Aside from some efforts by the Popular Front in the 1930s, French governments had done virtually nothing in the way of welfare reform before the 1940s and 1950s. The new French system provided not only health, maternity, and old-age benefits, but also family allowances paid to families with two or more children. It was meant to provide the population with benefits in such important areas as health services, education, and family life, which would, first, improve the quality of people's lives and, second, protect them from the effects of catastrophes such as long-term illness, accidents on the job, or unemployment.

Success in the social and economic spheres made it possible for the French to ignore for a time the conspicuous political failure of the Fourth Republic. Its initial efforts, after its establishment in 1944 by General Charles de Gaulle, were directed to the writing of a constitution. While the Communists and Socialists favored a strong national assembly, the Popular Republican Movement (MRP) and de Gaulle favored a strong executive. The constitution passed in November 1946 called for neither a strong national assembly nor a strong executive. Instead, it resembled to a large degree the system of the Third Republic.

By the middle of 1947 mounting Cold War tensions forced France to take sides. Shortly after the announcement of the Truman Doctrine, the French Communist Party stopped supporting government efforts to regain Indochina. In April the Communist Party felt compelled to support a strike in the government-owned Renault automobile plant. The premier won a vote of confidence and then demanded the Communists resign from the coalition.

The end of coalition government based on three major parties created nearly impossible political conditions. Coalitions had to be constructed from several different parties and could survive only by doing as little as possible. Any controversial effort might destroy the government. This created the "immobilism" in politics that was the hallmark of the Fourth Republic.

Colonial questions caused the major dilemmas in the 1950s, leading to frequent cabinet changes. Premier Pierre Mèndes-France (1907–1982) was successful in 1954 in ending French involvement in Indochina. Unfortunately for France, the simmering Algerian crisis exploded that same year.

By 1958 France was on the verge of civil war over Algeria. In Algiers, the French army and the colons (European settlers in Algeria) seized power. Next the army and colons seized Corsica and made plans to attack metropolitan France, intending to bring to power a government that would keep Algeria French. Charles de Gaulle, then in self-imposed political exile, appeared the only national figure acceptable to all groups. The French army officers and colons willingly accepted de Gaulle as the one person who could keep the country united and Algeria French. At the time de Gaulle hoped to keep Algeria attached to France, although not necessarily in the same manner as the army and colons wished.

De Gaulle was successful in the next several years both in constructing the type of government he had wanted earlier and in resolving the Algerian crisis. In large part, success in creating a Fifth Republic dominated by a powerful executive allowed him to deal successfully with the colonial impasse. Working quickly in 1958 and 1959, de Gaulle supervised the writing of a new constitution and the referendum approving it. His prestige and force of personality allowed him over the next several years to pursue a number of goals. Absolutely vital was bringing the Algerian crisis to a close. Initially, de Gaulle tried to keep Algeria attached to France in some way, but, when he saw this would not work, he pushed through Algerian independence. For some in the French military, this was completely unacceptable. Although some officers resorted to revolt and assassination attempts, de Gaulle prevailed. France by the early 1960s enjoyed both a strong, rapidly developing economy and a stable, confident government.

Reconstruction in the West: German *Wirtschaftswunder*

The Federal Republic of Germany was a creation of the Cold War, a version of Germany acceptable to the United States, Britain, and France once it became clear no agreement could be reached on uniting all of Germany. Although an artificial construct, West Germany proved to be remarkably successful, both politically and economically, going mostly from strength to strength over the forty-one years of its existence. Even today the united Germany is in the main an enlarged version of West Germany.

As a product of the Cold War, West Germany almost by definition excluded the left from politics. The Communists were formally banned in 1956. On the right, the neo-Nazi Reich Party was also banned. The Social Democrats found acceptance only after adopting a new party program (Godesberg Program) in 1959, with which the SPD abandoned Marxist rhetoric and became a party of reform. The mostly conservative Resistance in Germany had not left a legacy of interest in radical social and economic change. Instead, the major emphasis was on reconstruction of the economy and on establishment of a political system that would not make west Europeans or Americans nervous.

The founding father, or perhaps grandfather, of West Germany was Konrad Adenauer, leader of the Christian Democratic Union (CDU). Adenauer, who had been Lord Mayor of Cologne before the Nazis came to power in Germany, was one of the few German politicians with experience and without the taint of association with the Nazis. He also had good connections with the British and the Americans. Elections in 1949 gave the CDU and the Free Democratic Party a majority. Adenauer became chancellor and remained in that office until 1963, governing in a paternalistic fashion and excluding the *Bundestag* (parliament) whenever possible from discussion of political questions. His style of government, featuring a strong executive and a restricted democracy, has been called "chancellor democracy." It was acceptable in the 1950s, despite its authoritarian overtones, primarily because of Germany's economic success and also because of its delicate situation in international affairs. Adenauer seemed indispensable in the latter area.

Adenauer's lieutenant, Ludwig Erhard (1897–1977) , emphasized economic recovery and expansion. Much was left up to the private sector. A combination of good business management, including efforts by industry to channel investments and to control prices, government intervention when necessary, and a long period of labor peace, enabled German business to become highly competitive in the world market. An expanding economy eventually led in the 1960s to high wages and to a comprehensive welfare system. Some commentators believe Erhard's "socialmarket" approach placed an undue burden on the workers. Others believe labor cooperation formed an essential factor in the robust economy of the 1950s and 1960s.

Although basically a laissez-faire economy, there was always some government intervention, a good deal of cooperation within industry, and sizable efforts by the larger banks to direct the workings of the economy. While no four-year plans on the French model existed, there was a good deal of planning in the private sector. To a large extent, however, German business simply needed to do what it had done so well before. The factors that had worked to make it successful earlier—concentration of capital and other resources, economies of scale, reduction of competition—worked in the postwar period to make it successful again. Economic success, in turn, helped make political questions less significant. One question, however, unification, would not go away. Millions of Germans, displaced from their homes after the war, kept it on the political agenda in the 1950s and the 1960s. Unification, then and later, however, was out of the question. No European state, especially not the Soviet Union, wanted a reunited Germany. Adenauer understood this and worked to place West Germany in European and Atlantic political and economic structures (NATO for example). At the same time, he paid lip service to the desire for unification. As German war refugees were integrated into the new West German society, contributing vital skills and labor, some of the tension of this issue and the even more explosive issue of recovery of lands lost to Poland began to diminish. West Germany by 1961 was divided from East Germany in a very physical way, especially after the construction of the Berlin Wall in August of that year. By then, however, the economy was booming, and many were beginning to live very well indeed. For many West Germans, politics did not matter all that much.

Reconstruction in the West:
Other Countries, Other Stories

Immediately after the war, Italy was governed by a coalition of the Christian Democratic Party (DC), the Communists (PCI), and the Socialists. The 1946 referendum on the monarchy resulted in the creation of the Republic of Italy. The coalition broke up the following year because of increasing Cold War tensions and disagreements over plans for social change.

The United States played a large role in Italian politics in the late 1940s. In the 1948 elections, American officials let it be known that the wrong kind of government from the American point of view would lead to a cutoff in Marshall Plan aid. The DC won a working majority and governed over the next decade in coalitions, usually with the Social Democratic Party, a splinter from the old Socialists. The Social Democrats were distinguished primarily by their refusal to cooperate with the Communists.

Coalition government, in which the most influential politician was Alcide de Gasperi (1881–1954) from the DC, worked reasonably well at first and restored Italy to economic and social stability by the late 1940s, largely with the help of the Marshall Plan. In the 1950s the coalitions grew weaker and less able to take initiatives. A curious political trend developed in which the left gained increasing numbers of votes with each election while at the same time becoming more moderate in its approaches. In particular, the PCI under the leadership of Palmiro Togliatti (1893–1964), moved toward the center under the influence of moderate trade unionists and in reaction to the Soviet suppression of the Hungarian Revolution in 1956. The Socialists (not to be confused with the Social Democrats) moved away from the Communists and openly sought a coalition with the DC.

By the 1950s Italy enjoyed a high rate of growth, becoming a major supplier in Europe of automobiles, refrigerators, office machinery, and other goods. It had an unusual mixed economy. The government-controlled holding company, the Institute for Industrial Reconstruction, and the government energy concern were both administered by private enterprise. Together with FIAT, the giant automobile manufacturer, they contributed concentration of capital, reduction of competition, and economies of scale to economic success. Another major element was formed by sources of cheap labor, particularly in the underdeveloped south. Actually, the south gained little from Italy's reconstruction after the war except through employment in the factories and other enterprises in northern Italy.

The smaller countries in western Europe each had unique political and economic situations, which, with the exception of Spain, Portugal, and Greece, they had considerable success in overcoming. Finland and Austria resolved the problem of relations with the Soviet Union in differing ways: Finland by keeping its foreign policy in line with Soviet wishes; Austria in the form of a treaty in 1955 that ended occupation but obligated Austria to remain permanently neutral. Sweden and Switzerland, both neutral during World War II, achieved standards of living fully comparable with that of the United States by the early 1960s. Both Belgium and the Netherlands faced divisive religious-political problems after the war. In the Netherlands, where an elaborate system guaranteed equity for Protestants and Catholics, rapid economic growth helped to smooth out many of the differences. A rapidly growing and changing economy also helped the Dutch weather the loss of empire.

Reconstruction in the East: The Stalinist Legacy

The Soviet Union had suffered enormously in what it termed "The Great Fatherland War." About 25 million Russians died. Great stretches of European Russia had been devastated by Nazi *and* Soviet scorched-earth policies. Nonetheless, Russians were hopeful a new era was at hand, one in which wartime sacrifices would be rewarded.

Instead, Soviet citizens were bitterly disappointed by a return to the Stalinist practices of the 1930s. The fourth Five-Year plan, introduced in 1946, stressed heavy industry and armaments. Andrei Zhdanov (1896–1948), a major spokesman for the regime, emphasized ideological conformity. Lavrenti Beria, Stalin's fellow Georgian, led the NKVD, the political police. Beria was enormously powerful and greatly feared.

By 1950 the Soviet Union had reached prewar levels in industry and agriculture through the utilization of its own resources, reparations from some nations, and one-sided economic arrangements with its east European satellites. A major industrial power in terms of basic categories like coal and steel production, and closing the gap between itself and the United States in some areas, it nevertheless lacked the technological range of a truly modern industrial society. Much of its production in the 1950s was inferior in quality or outmoded in design. There were serious shortages from the consumer point of view. Agriculture, despite the vigorous efforts of Nikita S. Khrushchev, a rising political star, was inefficient and had not recovered from the effects of collectivization in the 1930s.

By 1952 and early 1953, there were ominous signs that Stalin, aging and in poor health, intended to reinstitute the Purges of the 1930s. One major piece of evidence was the "Doctors' Plot," supposedly a plot by several prominent physicians to murder important party and government officials. Any plans that may have existed to restart the Purges were cut short by Stalin's death in March 1953.

Many Soviet citizens were despondent, believing they had lost that strong ruler who, if sometimes harsh, had kept them from a worse fate and had made the Soviet Union a powerful and respected state. Collective leadership was emphasized since no one dared claim the ability to fill Stalin's role. Georgi Malenkov (1902–1988) became premier. The secretariat of the Central Committee, Stalin's old source of power, was reorganized by abolishing the office of General Secretary. Khrushchev simply became first among equals on the list of secretaries. Beria either made a play for power or his colleagues feared he would. Arrested in June 1953, he was unceremoniously shot. The NKVD was reorganized to curtail its independence and renamed the KGB.

Infighting continued, but methods changed. Malenkov, whose "New Course" had emphasized production of consumer goods, resigned his post in 1955. The other leaders saw his ideas as endangering security. The old survivor Vyacheslav Molotov (1890–1986), long Stalin's closest associate, remained a very important figure, but the dominant political force increasingly was Khrushchev.

In 1956, at the Twentieth Party Congress, Khrushchev made a so-called secret speech in which he severely criticized Stalin for his cult of personality, his leadership in World War II, and many of his actions in the 1930s. It was the beginning of a process of de-Stalinization, which had several goals. By blaming Stalin for many past wrongs, Khrushchev and his colleagues deflected a good deal of the criticism of the existing situation. Criticizing Stalin was also a way to improve relations with those communist movements that had resented Stalin's autocratic behavior toward them. Finally, distancing the present government from Stalin made the relaxation of Cold War tensions more likely. In a sense, Khrushchev was only trying to find a way to get around Stalin's legacy.

In 1956 Khruschev also faced difficult situations with Poland and Hungary. Ironically, the Soviet Union was trying not only to reestablish a good working relationship with Tito and Yugoslavia but also to treat countries in the East Bloc as sovereign states. Thus, the Warsaw Treaty Organization (WTO, commonly called the Warsaw Pact) came into being in 1955, partly in response to West Germany joining NATO but additionally as a way of establishing proper relationships between the Soviet military and the armed forces of the east European states. In the case of Poland, the Polish leader Wladyslaw Gomulka convinced the Soviets of the loyalty of the Polish Communists and of the stability of the political situation in Poland. Hungary, for its part, appeared about to leave the WTO, and the Russians resorted to force to end the Hungarian Revolution. (These events are covered in greater detail later in the chapter.)

Although Stalinism had been heavily criticized, the Stalinists were still a powerful force in Soviet politics. In 1957 they nearly succeeded in deposing Khrushchev. Khrushchev, ever the resourceful politician, took his case to the Central Committee, the members of which mostly owed their careers to him. He also had the backing of the military, in particular Gregori Zhukov (1896–1974), the great Soviet military leader of World War II. It now became clear he was the leading figure in the party, even if not all powerful.

From 1957 until Khrushchev was successfully deposed in 1964, he tried many schemes to create conditions for a more productive, efficient, and technologically sophisticated economy in the Soviet Union. In some respects, he was remarkably successful. The Soviet Union took an early lead in space exploration with the launching of *Sputnik I*, the first satellite, in 1957, and with Yuri Gagarin (1934–1968) as the first man in space (1961). On the other hand, the Virgin Lands campaign, an effort to put into cultivation vast new areas which were fertile but lacked sufficient rainfall, was initially successful but disastrous over the long run. Similarly, efforts

Major Yuri A. Gagarin, the first man to orbit the earth, appears at a press conference in Moscow. AP/Wide World.

Table 9.1   Major Events in Humanity's Journey into Space

1957	*Sputnik I* (USSR), first earth-orbiting satellite
1958	First dogs in orbit (USSR)
1959	First monkeys sent into space (USSR)
1961	Yuri A. Gagarin (USSR), first man to orbit earth
1963	Valentina V. Tereshkova (USSR), first woman to orbit earth
1965	Alexei Leonov (USSR), first man to leave spacecraft and float in space
1966	*Luna IX* (USSR), first soft landing on moon
	Gemini VIII (USA), first link-up in space
1968	*Apollo VIII* (USA), first manned mission to orbit moon and return
1969	*Soyuz IV* and *V* (USSR), first experimental space station
	Apollo XI (USA), first manned landing on moon
1971	*Salyut I* space station (USSR)
1973	*Skylab* space station (USA)
1975	*Apollo XVIII* (USA) and Soyuz *XIX* (USSR) dock while in earth orbit
1984	First untethered space walk (USA)
1986	*Mir I* (USSR), first space station meant to be permanently manned but closed in 1999
	Shuttle *Challenger* (USA) explodes just after takeoff
1989–1993	Magellan mission to Venus (USA)
1989–2003	Galileo mission to Jupiter (USA)
1990	Hubble space telescope (USA) launched (repaired 1993, 1997, and 1999)
1995	Cooperation between USA shuttles and Russian *Mir* space station begins
1997–1998	*Mars Pathfinder* mission (USA)
1997	Cassini-Huygens launched—bound for Saturn
2000	First crew in International Space Station
2003	Mars Rover (USA) launched; landed 2004 and still active at present
2005	Huygens probe (USA) landed on Saturn's moon Titan

to reorganize the bureaucracies of the Soviet Union were well meant but not sufficiently thought out. Ultimately, Khrushchev's downfall came from a streak of adventurism in foreign policy. In particular, the Cuban Missile Crisis in 1962, during which the world ventured to the edge of a nuclear holocaust, prompted his colleagues to bring in someone less erratic. (See the next section for a discussion of Khrushchev and the German question). Ironically, they had to delay deposing him because the Chinese Communists had been extremely critical of him and, at the height of the Sino-Soviet split, the Soviets would not admit the Chinese were right about anything.

Reconstruction in the East: The Seemingly Successful German Democratic Republic

The Soviet Union was ambivalent in its relations with the German Democratic Republic (GDR) or East Germany. For many years it exploited the GDR economically in order to build up its own economy. Set against this, however, was the need to offset the propaganda value of West Germany and, in particular, West Berlin. Additionally, the Soviet Union feared any kind of German resurgence, even if it seemed to be contained by a divided Germany.

Many Germans had returned to the GDR because they had an idealistic vision of what communism might achieve. From their perspective, capitalist West Germany was little better than Nazi Germany. In the first years after the GDR's founding, it was forced to follow the Soviet economic and political model closely and to join in the witchhunt for national deviationists or Titoists. Trials in the GDR, however, did not result in executions and, on the whole, there was less brutality than in Czechoslovakia or Romania.

Crucial events for the later evolution of the GDR took place in 1953. It was a classic case of mixed signals. The SED (Socialist Unity, or Government Party), with Walter Ulbricht (1893–1973) as its most influential figure, agreed to follow a Soviet line emphasizing social and economic concessions. Coupled with the concessions, however, were increases in some work norms, which led construction workers in Berlin to begin protesting on June 16, 1953. The following day the protests spread to all the major cities and towns. It was a large-scale protest but probably should not be seen as an uprising. Only toward the end of the day did the Soviets send in tanks to help restore order.

The irony of 1953 is that it reinforced Ulbricht's position. Over the next few years, he triumphed over a variety of voices within the SED, closing off discussion. The SED became a neo-Stalinist party at precisely the time Khrushchev was launching his de-Stalinization campaign. For the Soviet Union, however, particularly after 1956, it seemed more important to have a strong figure in charge in the GDR than to advance the cause of political reform.

By the late 1950s, the GDR was suffering from the effects of a massive depopulation process. Hundreds of thousands of people each year were flowing out across the border. Almost all the border was sealed off by the end of the decade, but there remained the problem of Berlin, where thousands of people each day crossed from East to West or vice-versa to go to work, to shop, or to visit friends. West Berlin was a hole in the dike threatening to drain the GDR. Khrushchev attempted to resolve the Berlin issue in the late 1950s on several occasions. He threatened to conclude a treaty with the GDR, leaving it responsible for all of Berlin, if the United States, Britain, and France were not willing to renegotiate the status of the city. East German leaders finally came up with a crude but workable solution to the problem: the Berlin Wall. Construction of the Wall, under the supervision of Ulbricht's eventual successor, Erich Honecker (1912–1994), began on August 13, 1961. Well into the fall Berlin threatened to become a flash-point with, for example, American tanks driving full speed right up to the border to face their Russian counterparts only a few feet away.

A portion of the Berlin Wall in the early 1970s. Note that the wall is in fact a series of obstacles, fences, open spaces, and walls. From the collection of Paul Waibel.

The crisis passed, however, and East Germans resigned themselves to life behind the wall.

Reconstruction in the East: The New Poland

Next to Germany, Poland was the country in eastern Europe about which the Soviet Union worried most. By 1948, Poland was on its way to becoming a carbon copy of the Soviet Union. People like Wladyslaw Gomulka, who emphasized a national approach to communism, were arrested, imprisoned, and in some cases even executed.

By 1956, Poles began to believe the situation was improving and things could be somewhat different. At the end of June, riots began in Poznan protesting the low standard of living of the working class. The Polish United Workers Party (PUWP), the official name for the communist party, split between the Stalinists and those who wanted to improve the lot of the workers. Neither the police nor the army would attempt to stop the riots. The government promised the end of collectivization and reforms for the workers. Gomulka was released from prison and returned to power.

Gomulka and his supporters worked hard to convince the Soviet Union of two things: Poland would remain in the Soviet bloc and PUWP would continue to exercise power. The Soviets agreed, not relishing the prospects of fighting the Poles. Aside from abolishing collectivization and de-emphasizing heavy industry, relatively little changed in Poland. Gomulka and the Poles were able to avoid the fate of the Hungarians who, in October and November of 1956, became involved in revolution.

Reconstruction in the East: Hungary and Revolution

Hungary became a People's Republic in 1949 and followed the Stalinist path of economic development over the next four years to the point of economic collapse. Four months after Stalin's death, Imre Nagy, seen as a moderate, was appointed premier. His policies mirrored Malenkov's New Course and included diversion of resources to light industry and an end to forced collectivization. Malenkov's fall from power in the Soviet Union in 1955 led to his protegé, Nagy, being ousted from the premiership. The following year, however, the Hungarian government ran into trouble. In October 1956 it made a fundamental error in calling in the Soviet Army to deal with Hungarian demonstrators. Throughout Hungary councils were formed demanding free elections, the withdrawal of Soviet troops, and an end to the security police.

At first it appeared the Hungarians had won the day. Nagy established a new government October 28, and Soviet troops began to leave. On October

A crowd of Hungarians gathers around a large statue of Stalin knocked off its base in Budapest, October 1956. The Soviet Union used force to suppress the Hungarian Revolution and regained control over the People's Republic of Hungary. AP/Wide World/Arpad Hazafi.

31, Nagy went too far by declaring Hungary's neutrality. After that, Soviet leaders believed they had to crush the revolution by force. The Soviet Union smashed the Nagy government and installed János Kádár (1912–1989) as the new leader. This action had several farreaching consequences. For one, it played an important role in the Stalinists' attempt to oust Khrushchev in 1957. It complicated efforts by the Soviet Union to establish relations with countries in the East Bloc that provided for autonomy and national sovereignty. Communist movements elsewhere in Europe reassessed Soviet Communism and in some cases moved to more independent positions. The West reacted very unfavorably, but, involved in the Suez Crisis and in no case wishing to challenge the Soviet Union directly, it could only criticize and find places for the large numbers of former Hungarian freedom fighters now refugees.

Throughout the 1950s, the Soviet Union dominated the affairs of east and central European countries with the exception of Yugoslavia. The Soviet Union not only shaped the political systems but also the social and economic systems. This meant, leaving aside Czechoslovakia and the GDR, an emphasis on industrialization and urbanization in what had been countries with large peasant populations and small industrial bases before the war. In each nation the pattern was roughly the same: centralized planning, rapid economic growth, and the development of heavy industry at the expense of the production of consumer goods.

On the Way to a United Europe

The division of Europe into two great blocs was both unexpected and unfortunate in the postwar period. Within each bloc, however, there existed considerable interest in European unity. In the East Bloc the Soviet Union limited and distorted any expression of interest in unity. It also repressed expressions of nationalism. In the West, movement toward unity built on ideas and concepts coming from the experience of World War II and followed three parallel paths, two of which reached dead-ends by the mid-1950s.

The first path involved political union. In May 1948 a Congress of Europe took place. Among the participants were such leading Europeanists as Churchill, De Gasperi, Robert Schuman (1886–1963) of France, and Paul-Henri Spaak (1899–1972) of Belgium. The congress proposed the political and economic unification of Europe and established the Council of Europe to that end. The power of decision lay in the hands of the foreign ministers of the member states, organized as the Committee of Ministers. But they guarded the sovereignty of their respective nation states jealously. Political integration was not in the cards.

A second effort at integration concentrated on military matters, specifically the rearmament of West Germany. In 1950 the French proposed to create an European army as a means of circumventing the problem of German rearmament and enhancing the defensive capabilities of western Europe while the United States was embroiled in the Korean War. Before the European Defense Community (EDC) could be organized, however, events passed it by. Stalin's death, the end of the Korean War, and the easing of Cold War tensions in the mid-1950s all worked to remove some of the more pressing reasons for the EDC. The French themselves had second thoughts about such a drastic turn toward supranationalism. The British finished the plan off by declining to participate. Instead, a German military force was created and made part of NATO. NATO remained a collection of armies with some provision for an integrated command structure.

The third path toward unity evolved from the cooperation called for under the European Recovery Program (the Marshall Plan). Two Frenchmen, Commissioner of Planning Jean Monnet and Foreign Minister Robert

Schuman, proposed a pooling of coal and steel resources in Europe in what became known as the Schuman Plan. The plan went into operation in 1952 with France, West Germany, Italy and the Benelux countries (**Be**lgium, the **Ne**therlands, and **Lux**embourg) working together in the European Coal and Steel Community (ECSC).

The ECSC was a great success. Its members pressed on to further economic integration in part because of the obvious potential economic advantage. They were also painfully aware of their vulnerability and weakness as individual states. The failure of the French and British to regain control of the Suez Canal in 1956 only served to underline this. In 1957 the Treaty of Rome established the European Economic Community (EEC) or Common Market. The EEC set out to eliminate customs barriers among its member states and to create a common tariff structure for the rest of the world.

Three significant events affected the development of the EEC in the 1960s. First, French President de Gaulle, worried that Britain's entry into the EEC would weaken French dominance of the institution, vetoed Britain's application in 1963. Second, the Luxembourg Agreement in 1966 resolved clashes between those who favored the Commission, the executive body of the EEC, and those who wanted the Council of Ministers, which represented the individual states, to retain control of the EEC. It required the Commission to consult individual states before making major proposals and noted that no nation could be overturned in the Council of Ministers if it were a matter of national interest. Finally, the so-called Merger Treaty of 1967 combined the EEC, the ECSC, and Euratom into a single institution, the European Community (EC). Despite these various developments, however, by the end of the 1960s the EC had not realized the promise that many saw in it at the beginning of the decade.

The British sponsored a seven-nation European Free Trade Association (EFTA), a much looser arrangement than the EEC. In eastern Europe, the Council for Mutual Economic Assistance (variously referred to as Comecon, CEMA, or CMEA), in existence since 1949, took on a new life. Originally constructed as a counter to the Marshall Plan, but actually little more than a cover for Soviet exploitation of the eastern European economies, Comecon became directed more toward mutually advantageous economic relations. In this, it reflected not only the example of the EEC, but also the desire for autonomy and national sovereignty which had been dampened in some ways by 1956 but also paradoxically accelerated by events of that year.

Although the widespread interest in European unity in the postwar period gave way quickly to political realities like the Cold War and concerns for national interests, it did result in some important steps toward unity on social and economic policies. It also produced processes, particularly in the EEC, by which more could be achieved. It was one of the most significant and characteristic developments of the first two decades after the war.

A Consumer Economy in Western Europe

The main characteristic of this period in western Europe was the extent of prosperity. There was, to be sure, considerable difference between the more industrialized and affluent north and the less developed south. Even within countries there was considerable regional difference. The Italian case offers the best example. The north contained most of the industry and employment opportunities, the south millions of urban and rural poor. But overall, Europe was prosperous to an extent never before realized in its history.

One means of measuring the development of a consumer economy is to examine the composition of the work force. A work force in which the agricultural sector shrinks while the industrial sector remains largely stable and the service sector grows was considered to be moving in the direction of a modern economy, in postwar terms. For the 1950s, using France, West Germany, and Italy as examples, the industrial sector and service sector both increased in size while the agricultural sector declined. In the 1960s the agricultural sector continued to decline, with less than 10 percent of the West German work force engaged in agriculture and related activities. In that same period the industrial sector declined slightly in France, grew slightly in West Germany, and somewhat more in Italy, while the service sector grew substantially in each state. Each economy was becoming increasingly modern.

As the nature of the economy changed, the work force gained larger amounts of disposable income, i.e., more money to spend on food, clothing, and other goods after paying fixed expenses such as rent and taxes. Per capita disposable income increased 117 percent in the United States between 1960 and 1973, but this was greatly exceeded by European figures for the same period: France, 258 percent; Germany, 312 percent; Denmark, 323 percent. Disposable income increased more rapidly in nearly every western European country than it did in the United States, although only Denmark, Germany, Switzerland, and Sweden were close to (or actually higher than in the case of Sweden) the total figure for per capita disposable income in the United States. The rates in France and Belgium, despite large increases, remained substantially below the American figure, while those of Britain and Italy were considerably below.

Old patterns of national affluence also shifted in this period. Britain, the wealthiest country in Europe at the start of the century, continued to lag behind most other western European nations. The beginnings of this trend go back to the interwar period. The French, and especially the Italians, moved dramatically in the opposite direction, constructing much stronger and more affluent economies than they had enjoyed before World War II.

The range of consumer goods and the increasing levels of consumption in this period provide not only a graphic illustration of how much more disposable income Europeans enjoyed but also of a major sociocultural shift in this period. Not just refrigerators, washing machines, and televisions, but automobiles and houses came to be items Europeans might aspire to own in the 1960s. The rapid increase in ownership of automobiles is a particularly sensitive indicator of ways in which the economy and people's habits were changing. By 1969 two of every ten people in Britain, Sweden, West Germany, and France owned automobiles. The United States was still considerably ahead with a figure of four in ten, but the gap was closing.

Table 9.1   Automobiles in 1957 and in 1965

	1957	1965
France	3,476,000	7,842,000
West Germany	2,456,288	8,103,600
Italy	1,051,004 (1956)	5,468,981
The Netherlands	375,676	1,272,898
Sweden	796,000	1,793,000

Sources: *The Europa Year Book 1959* (London, 1959) and *The Europa Year Book 1967*, volume 1 (London, 1967).

Television, a shaper as well as a symbol of a consumer society, provides an even better index of change.

Table 9.2   Televisions in 1957 and in 1965

	1957	1967
France	683,000	6,489,000
Germany	798,586	11,379,000
Italy	367,000	6,044,542
The Netherlands	239,000	2,113,000
Sweden	75,817	2,110,584

Sources: *The Europa Year Book 1959* (London, 1959) and *The Europa Year Book 1967*, volume 1 (London, 1967).

Along with the acquisition of goods came considerable changes in lifestyles and attitudes. The American-style supermarket began to spread in the late 1960s, competing with the neighborhood butcher, greengrocer, baker, and retail grocer. The number of people running routes through neighborhoods selling milk, bread, coal, or sundries began to decline. Once- or twice-weekly markets became smaller and less important in some areas and disappeared in others. It would be easy to exaggerate the extent of the changes, yet the trends were clear by the late 1960s. While most Europeans welcomed the new prosperity, some viewed it with horror as a kind of Americanization of European society.

Social Change

Social change was perhaps most conspicuous among the farming populations of western Europe. First of all, the number of farmers shrank in the 1950s and 1960s while production both per capita and overall increased. This was due to what some have termed an "agricultural revolution." Primarily, it involved greater use of machinery and more attention to scientific techniques in areas such as breeding of livestock, selection of seed, use of fertilizers, and utilization of land. In general, it was connected with market-oriented and capital-intensive rather than labor-intensive farming methods. These changes, together with policies favorable to agriculture in the EEC and elsewhere, led to a decline in the number of marginal, self-sufficient farmers and a growing level of prosperity among those who approached farming as if it were an industry. This approach often robbed farm life of some intangible benefits which many prized, such as a feeling of kinship with nature, but it also helped to close the gap between urban and rural lifestyles. Improvements in transportation and communication also brought the farmer closer to life in the mainstream. The European peasant, long a distinctive social type, had, for better or worse, virtually disappeared.

The working classes were also changing, although not as dramatically as farmers. In some countries a process of "embourgeoisement" was far advanced. This meant that Swedish and German workers, for example, differed less and less from members of the middle classes in terms of housing, clothing, leisure activities, and the like. In other countries, Britain for example, class distinctions continued to remain strong. Practically everywhere in western Europe, however, the working class had sufficient income to participate in the consumer economy. Advertising and the mass media created between them a lifestyle that most of the population, workers or middle class, desired. A common, mass culture began to take shape.

With some reservations and criticisms, workers, whether part of a trade union structure or not, accepted industrial capitalism by the 1960s in western Europe. They were increasingly interested in gaining an equitable share of the national income together with better working conditions, expanded fringe benefits, and an extension of the welfare state.

The generally more cooperative attitude was most fully developed in Sweden and Germany. In Britain, expectations were similar, but relations between workers and employers remained somewhat antagonistic. While in France and Italy unions became more reformist in the 1960s, they achieved fewer improvements for workers than unions in Britain, Germany, and Sweden. In part working-class satisfaction with its situation had to do with the role played in the economy by guestworkers, workers brought in from Yugoslavia, Greece, Turkey, Spain, Portugal, and North Africa to take the lowest-paying, least-desirable jobs. These groups, especially important in Germany, Switzerland, and the Netherlands, and present in large numbers in Sweden and France, provided European economies with a certain flexibility. In good times, they were available to work cheaply. In bad times, they could in theory be shipped back home. Neither for the indigenous working class nor for the other elements of the population was the situation of the guestworker a source of much concern in the 1960s.

By the 1960s the middle classes could be divided into two large groups. On the one hand, a large number of white-collar employees worked as clerks, technicians, sales personnel, lower-ranking professionals (teachers and nurses, for example), and supervisory and lower-level managerial personnel. On the other, a relatively small number of higher-ranking professionals (lawyers, doctors, university professors), upper-level bureaucrats and managers, and technocrats made up an upper segment. The upper segment in the 1960s still controlled a disproportionate share of wealth, political power, and status in European society. It constituted a new elite, composed of the remnants of the older elites and some segments of the traditional middle classes. The aristocracy had either disappeared or was regarded as a quaint anachronism. In Britain and France the new elite was essentially still a continuation of the old establishment. Elsewhere, the new elite was more open. Education, especially a specialized or technical education, increasingly was a necessity. Family ties still played a role, if a declining one. The new elite, like the older upper class, could be generally characterized not only by educational attainment and social background but also by an attachment, genuine or not, to high culture and by distinctive patterns in housing and leisure-time activity. The role of the very rich differed from country to country; it was, for example, very important in Germany and Italy, but minimal in Sweden. The difference had to do mostly with taxation and other income distribution policies. Class differences remained strong in Europe in the 1960s despite the efforts to democratize life. In fact, most of the social tension in western Europe in the 1960s concerned the degree to which social and cultural institutions continued to work to the advantage of those already a part of the elites and against able and ambitious people lower down the social hierarchy.

Détente

Détente was the product of two crises. One, the Berlin Crisis, was actually a series of crises culminating in the construction of the Berlin Wall in August 1961. The second, the Cuban Missile Crisis, edged the world very close to a thermonuclear war. A series of confrontations in the late 1950s and early 1960s, including not only the Berlin crisis but also the U-2 spy plane incident in 1960 (in which the Soviet Union shot down the American high-altitude spy plane), the failed summit meeting between Nikita S. Khrushchev and U.S. president John F. Kennedy, and the construction of the Berlin Wall, had left the two great powers edgy. Khrushchev decided in 1962 to take a chance on installing missiles in Cuba as a means of gaining advantage at little cost. There were several reasons why he pursued this risky policy. One reason, of course, was to back up his guarantee to Fidel Castro to protect Cuba from American threats. A second was probably domestic. A cheap but dramatic victory in the Cold War competition would reinforce his position in the Soviet Union. Various disasters in domestic policy and reservations about the de-Stalinization campaign had eroded Khrushchev's power. Other reasons may have played a part, too. Khrushchev may still have hoped to revise the situation in Berlin. He apparently thought it might be possible to trade removal of missiles in Cuba for removal of American missiles in Turkey.

Kennedy, for his part, badly needed a diplomatic success after the Bay of Pigs fiasco in 1961 (the failed attempt by Cuban exiles to invade Communist Cuba) and the inability of the United States to stop construction of the Berlin Wall. His decision to set up a naval quarantine of Cuba was probably the best move once the crisis had become a matter of public knowledge. Both sides saw the seriousness of the situation and acted to defuse it. Khrushchev agreed to remove the missiles in return for a pledge by the United States that it would not invade Cuba. After the crisis the two powers moved rapidly in the direction of détente. A hot line was installed between Washington, D.C., and Moscow. In 1963 the Nuclear Test Ban Treaty was signed. Even when America began to play an active role in the conflict in Vietnam, détente continued. The Soviet Union continued to support North Vietnam, but did what it could to prevent the war from widening. The United States, for its part, pursued policies designed to keep the Soviet Union or the People's Republic of China (PRC) from taking a more active role in the war. It was caught in a particularly delicate situation where measures that might lead to military victory had to be rejected for fear they would inadvertently bring the Soviet Union or the PRC into the war.

Conclusions

By 1967, Europe had recovered from the war and had broken much new ground. Industry had become the major factor in almost every European economy, even in eastern and southern Europe. The nature of industry was changing as well, especially in northwestern Europe where the emphasis was on the production of consumer goods, the development of new products, and the use of new machines and techniques. Standards of living had surpassed prewar levels. Societies were becoming more homogeneous, even in western Europe where ideology did not work toward egalitarianism as such.

In politics, both east and west, the government became more involved in social and economic issues, resulting in the creation or extension of some kind of welfare state. Greater governmental intervention in economic matters meant not only increased regulation but also government-owned sectors of the economy in most states. Of course, in eastern Europe the private sector was almost completely squeezed out.

The changing political spectrum had resulted in the virtual disappearance of the prewar type of liberal or conservative party. Two major developments were the emergence of Christian Democratic parties, which dominated the first two decades of politics in Italy and Germany, and reform-minded, nonrevolutionary Socialist parties in several states. In many ways, the Christian Democratic parties, attracting members with widely differing interests, replaced the old conservative parties. The Socialists were a partial replacement for the liberals, although far more enthusiastic about government intervention. Politics was less polarized than in the period between the wars. Even the large number of votes given to Communist parties in Italy and France and occasional appearances of right-wing protest movements did not alter the essential moderation of west European politics.

Politics had changed drastically in the east, with communist states subservient to Moscow (with the exception of Yugoslavia and, later, both Albania and Romania) taking the place of the mostly authoritarian right-wing governments that had existed in the 1930s. In the west, parliamentary democracies existed in all states but Spain and Portugal, which still had 1930s-style authoritarian governments.

Europe had not yet made itself into a third great power. In fact, it was actually losing rather than gaining ground in world affairs, as its steadily eroding colonial situation demonstrated. But it had found its own way. European civilization had done far more than merely survive. It had undergone something of a renaissance, becoming by the late 1960s both a guide and example, in terms of social policy and relations with third world countries, for the United States and the Soviet Union.

Suggested Books And Films

P. Duignan and L. H. Gann, *The Rebirth of the West: The Americanization of the Democratic World, 1945–1958* (1996). A useful discussion of all aspects of reconstruction in the decade after the war.

Paul Ginsborg, *A History of Contemporary Italy: Society and Politics, 1943–1988* (1990). An excellent overview.

Stanley Hoffman, ed., *In Search of France* (1963). A classic discussion of many aspects of French life after World War II.

Alan Milward, *The European Rescue of the Nation-State* (1992). An interesting study of the Common Market that sees it not so much a supranational institution as an institution designed to preserve the nation-state.

————, *The Reconstruction of Western Europe 1945–1951* (1984). An excellent study of the difficult first several years after the war in western Europe.

Joseph Rothschild and Nancy M. Wingfield, *Return to Diversity: A Political History of East Central Europe since World War II*, 3rd ed. (1999). A scholarly, country-by-country survey of the history of postwar eastern Europe.

Henry Ashby Turner, *The Two Germanies since 1945: Germany from Partition to Reunification*, rev. ed. (1992). A succinct and instructive review of the parallel histories of West Germany and East Germany.

J. Robert Wegs and Robert Ladrech, *Europe since 1945: A Concise History*, 4th ed. (1996). A dependable and well-informed survey.

The Bicycle Thief, 1948. Vittorio De Sica's neorealist film masterpiece on the hardships of life in Italy right after the war.

The Cranes Are Flying, 1957. Directed by Mikhail Kalatozov, a good example of the new Soviet cinema of the 1950s, with its tendency to glorify and romanticize World War II.

The Marriage of Maria Braun, 1979. Rainer Werner Fassbinder's great film on women and men in Germany in the first decade after the war.

Part 4

THE REVOLUTIONARY YEARS of 1968 and 1989 were bookends for a period of consolidation and attempted reform in response to dissatisfaction with the political, economic, social, and cultural arrangements in both eastern and western Europe. The period also featured efforts to deal with a rapidly changing geopolitical, economic, and technological global situation. In the aftermath of the Cold War in the 1990s, Europe worked with considerable success to overcome the divisions that had characterized the first four decades after World War II and to build on previous accomplishments. It also experienced new and unexpected difficulties, discovering once again that human history is full of surprises.

In the year 1968, when everything seemed possible, the radicalism of the 1960s peaked, both in Europe and in the United States. In western Europe, radicalism was at high tide in the events of May 1968 in France. For a brief moment it seemed students and workers would unite to defeat the government of Charles de Gaulle. Not surprisingly, style and youthful enthusiasm were not enough, and de Gaulle and the Fifth Republic prevailed. In Czechoslovakia, Alexander Dubcek attempted to renew communism in a reform movement know as the "Prague Spring." Widespread national support and earnest attempts by the Czechs to mollify other members of the Warsaw Treaty Organization failed to prevent the Soviet Union, strongly backed by East Germany and Poland, from crushing the movement in August.

193

By way of constrast, 1989 was a year in which the impossible simply happened. Large numbers of people in several eastern European countries responded publically and courageously to economic and political systems that were visibly failing. The disproportionate emphasis on heavy industry had locked communist economic systems into an economic strategy that resisted innovation and failed to match the levels of material comfort achieved in western Europe. Hollowed out economically and led in many cases by gerontocracies, the eastern European satellites of the Soviet Union either gave way to popular discontent, as was the case in Poland and Hungary or resisted ineffectively before completely losing control, as in the case of East Germany, Czechoslovakia, and Bulgaria. Government efforts to hold on to power in Romania led to considerable bloodshed, ending in the trial and televised execution of Nicolae Ceaucescu (1918–1989) and his wife. Perhaps the single most important result of the revolutions was the unification of the two Germanies the following year. This event not only signalled a definitive end to World War II but also marked a resolution of the German Question, a question that had haunted Europe since the formation of the German Empire in 1871.

Between the revolutionary years of 1968 and 1989, western Europe experienced a period of economic dislocation and political turmoil. The oil price shocks of the 1970s caused considerable problems in the West, but the economic crisis of this period had more deeply rooted causes. By the late 1960s the postwar boom had played itself out. The continuous growth of the welfare state in the meantime was becoming a burden to the economy. The economy itself shifted from an industrial focus to one of service. It also shifted to reflect the increasingly global nature of economic affairs. The flexibility of western European economies and the advantages provided by institutions like the European Community helped bring about recovery in the 1980s. Government policy, particularly that developed in Britain under Prime Minister Margaret Thatcher, also helped. Her neocon-servative policies of privatization, union-busting, and downsizing of government were mirrored by President Ronald Reagan's approach in the United States and adopted in varying ways on the continent. Along with economic recovery, however, came a more clear division of society into winners and losers, as reflected in particular in the persistence of high unemployment, even after economic recovery.

The Cold War featured first a period of détente in the 1970s that continued and expanded developments from the previous decade, and then a brief revival of its worst features. The Soviet Union bore the major share of responsibility for revival, primarily because of its military intervention in Afghanistan. President Ronald Reagan, an old Cold Warrior , took a hardline approach in the early 1980s. The activities of his administration, highly visible in the Caribbean and Central America, also worked in the Middle East and Central Asia to create the foundations of twenty-first-century foreign policy dilemmas in those regions. Under the circumstances, it was nothing short of miraculous that Mikhail Gorbachev succeeded by the late 1980s in convincing western leaders to work on defusing the Cold War.

The end to the Cold War came as a result of two events: the revolutions of 1989, which transformed the former satellites of the Soviet Union, and the collapse of the Soviet Union itself in 1991. In the Soviet Union, Mikhail Gorbachev tried a variety of new policies, principally *glasnost'* (openness) and *perestroika* (restructuring), to open up a new era. The fundamental contradiction between perestroika and a powerful and conservative bureaucratic establishment, together with the desires of several of the republics in the Soviet Union to gain independence, created a stalemate that probably could not have been resolved. The attempted coup in August 1991 by communist hardliners led to the collapse of the Soviet Union and the emergence of Boris Yeltsin, the hero of the resistance to the coup, as the leading figure in the Soviet Union.

In the 1990s four quite different developments shaped the European experience. The disintegration of Yugoslavia, while not entirely unexpected, had deeply tragic results. It stemmed to a large extent from the political ambitions of one man, Slobodan Milosevic, but played additionally on nationalist passions and ethnic rivalries. The result was a series of wars and civil wars, ethnic cleansings, and interventions by NATO forces leading to an uneasy peace, particularly in Bosnia-Herzegovina and Kosovo.

Less obviously tragic but much more central to the future of Europe is the failure of the Russian Republic, the major successor state to the Soviet Union, to find its way. Under Yeltsin, Russia fell increasingly under the power of the oligarchs, who had taken advantage of the new economic circumstances to amass wealth and influence. At the same time, Russia squandered resources and good will in failed military campaigns that attempted to restore Russian dominance in Chechnya.

On the plus side, in 1993 the European Community transformed itself into the European Union, simultaneously moving toward wider and deeper versions of the old institution. At the end of 2004 the EU had grown to twenty-five members, with several other prospects in the wings. It had also become far more carefully integrated. Nearing its fiftieth anniversary in 2007, the EU may be fairly regarded as Europe's outstanding achievement in the twentieth century.

Finally, the 1990s and the early years of the twenty-first century witnessed the development of a new kind of terrorism, one based on Islamic fundamentalism. To some extent, the new terrorism stems from the continuing quarrel between the Israelis and the Palestinians. Another and more important source derives from American involvement in the Iran-Iraq war of the 1980s, the Soviet intervention in Afghanistan in the same period, and what may now be seen as the First Gulf War ("Desert Storm") in 1991. The highly visible presence of the United States in the Middle East in the 1990s led to a series of attacks on the United States in that decade and the first part of the twenty-first century, culminating in the tragic events of September 11, 2001. The American response to date has included invasions of Afghanistan and Iraq and a continuing effort to destroy the terrorist group *Al-Qaeda* (The Base).

The development of a worldwide terrorist movement based on Islamic fundamentalism underscores the global context within which Europe now operates. Faced with its own internal difficulties, which include the problems of the Russian Republic, the continuing efforts in eastern Europe to transform the political and economic spheres, demographic changes that include both an aging population and large-scale immigration in western Europe, and the economic challenges the EU faces in a global economy, Europe must also contend with the tides of world affairs. These include, among others, the threat of nuclear proliferation in Iran and North Korea, the emergence of new economic powers such as the People's Republic of China and India, the ongoing AIDs pandemic, and the large question mark of environmental trends.

Europe has long since ceased to be dominant in world affairs, yet it clearly still plays an important, even crucial, role. Most European countries have now achieved levels of political stability and economic prosperity that will allow their populations to take on the roles of wise counselors and arbitrators. Even if the European house is not completely in order, its inhabitants have the wherewithal to help the rest of the world contend with its problems.

Europe's altered role in the world at the end of the millennium is mirrored in its intellectual and cultural history since the end of World War II. In many ways the changes that have occurred in both elite and popular culture grew out of changing assumptions about the nature of reality that were under way already before and after World War I. The shifting philosophical sands after World War II from existentialism through structuralism to deconstructionism resulted from the attempt to make sense out of a world in which all of the old values and certainties had either failed or vanished. To the philosophers, a universe that rejected the existence of God or any other absolute truth that might provide meaning was a universe increasingly without meaning either for the universe itself, or the people who inhabited it.

As with the philosophers, postwar culture, whether high or popular, struggled to make sense of recent events that included war, a great depression, the Holocaust, and the threat of nuclear annihilation. The artists, musicians, poets, and writers displayed in their creative output the growing sense of alienation and despair, and the fragmentation that characterized European civilization in transition. Whether in the fine arts or popular culture, influences from the United States tended to dominate. In the fine arts this was due in part to the interwar flight of creative individuals before the tidal wave of Nazi and communist oppression. The economic dominance of the United States and the presence of American military forces in western Europe assured that European popular culture would mimic American trends.

Chronology

10
Metamorphosis:
An Era of Revolutionary Change,
1968–1989

AFTER THE REVOLUTIONS OF 1989, jokes circulated to help explain why the events of that year had such a significant impact on European history in comparison with the radical developments of 1968. As is usually the case, the jokes provided insight into what was otherwise a somewhat mysterious process One joke asked: "What is the difference between 1968 and 1989?" The answer: "Twenty-one years." While not particularly funny, especially to those who had lived through those twenty-one years, the joke helped make plain that the events of 1968, at least in the Soviet Bloc, were premature. The time was not yet ripe for something like the Prague Spring.

Another joke asked: "What was communism?" The answer: "The stage of transition from capitalism to capitalism." While it did not turn out to be so simple to reestablish capitalism, much less democratic governments, in eastern Europe, it was clear that communism had never taken root, not even in East Germany. Given a choice, most people in the Soviet Bloc opted for free enterprise and free elections.

In western Europe there was no equivalent to the revolutions of 1989 in eastern Europe, yet there were significant changes in both politics and the economy. Perhaps the most significant change involved the rise of Thatcherism and its equivalents on the continent. Conservative politicians (and in some cases, socialist politicians as well) worked to end the continuous growth of the welfare state and to decrease the role of government in the economy. At the same time, western Europe survived a period of economic stagnation and inflation ("stagflation") and moved at the end of the 1980s toward an expanded and more fully integrated European Community.

Radicalism in Western Europe in the Late 1960s

At the end of the 1960s, most western European countries seemed virtually besieged by radicals questioning political frameworks, social institutions, economic arrangements, and even cultural assumptions. Radicals accused governments of ruling in an authoritarian style at home and of aiding

199

"imperialism" and counterrevolution abroad. They viewed social and economic institutions as consciously contrived to perpetuate political and economic power in the hands of ruling cliques while keeping the masses both ignorant of the true situation through manipulation of the media and satisfied through the production of inexpensive consumer goods. Some saw themselves as part of a worldwide revolutionary movement answering the call of the Cuban revolutionary Che Guevara (1928–1967) for "One, Two, Three . . . Many Vietnams!" Few identified with the established socialist or communist parties. Some called themselves Maoists or professed to be anarchists. Many had quite limited aims and concentrated in particular on the reform of what they saw as an undemocratic, elitist educational system designed to reinforce and perpetuate the inequities of the larger political and socioeconomic systems. The organized radical movements, much smaller than the number of protesters who might appear at a demonstration, were mostly students and young intellectuals. They varied widely in terms of their impact on existing systems. France was affected far more than any other western European country. Germany and Italy both confronted large-scale movements but escaped major crises. Britain and the Netherlands had important movements which, however, had limited impact.

In Germany, the German Socialist Student Federation (SDS) protested against the established system with great seriousness. The first major protest was directed against the Shah of Iran, Mohammad Reza Pahlavi (1919–1980), during his visit to West Berlin in 1967. The next focus of SDS attacks was the publications empire of Axel Springer (1912–1985), the influential newspaper and magazine publisher widely regarded as a pillar of conservatism or even counterrevolution. Efforts against the Springer empire were intensified after one of the SDS leaders, Rudi Dutschke (1940–1979) , was shot and seriously wounded in April 1968. Events in Germany in the spring of 1968 were highly dramatic but the government escaped serious challenge. The SDS lacked circumstances similar to France in May, where de Gaulle's policies were widely criticized and student demonstrations brutally supressed. Student radicals in Germany found themselves isolated from a general public largely satisfied with existing political and economic arrangements.

France in May 1968

What happened in France in May 1968 can scarcely be understood unless the influence of Charles de Gaulle in French affairs between May 1958 and May 1968 is taken into account. The structure of the Fifth Republic gave de Gaulle a position of considerable power. In addition to his constitutional powers, and somewhat like Adenauer in West Germany, de Gaulle overstepped the boundaries, taking actions that no politician without his force of personality and moral stature would have been allowed to carry out. While de Gaulle was preoccupied with foreign affairs and contacts with communist bloc and Third World leaders, domestic problems began to surface. One was the odd contrast between the sophistication of French technology and science and the backwardness of some aspects of life in France, two prime examples being the telephone system and housing. Second, society, if increasingly democratic, was still stratified. The different strata were determined in large part by educational achievement, but the way to an appropriate education was paved with money, family background, and connections. The very bright were coopted into the system, but the system worked here as in other areas mostly to perpetuate the elites.

The 1965 presidential elections furnished one glaring indication of the level of domestic dissatisfaction. François Mitterrand (1916–1996), leader of the leftist coalition of socialists and communists, forced de Gaulle into a runoff. De Gaulle won and continued to govern virtually unchecked, seemingly deaf to the rising clamor of opposition.

The events of May 1968, although based on widespread dissatisfaction and on student grievances, began as a spontaneous reaction to a specific event of little significance: the arrest of a number of students demonstrating against the involvement of the United States in Vietnam. On March 22, a meeting to protest the arrests took place at the University of Nanterre, one of the new universities in the French system. A radical movement called the March 22 Movement came out of the meeting. On May 2, "Anti-Imperialist Day," members of the March 22 Movement, finding themselves locked out of Nanterre, went to the Sorbonne, the best-known part of the University of Paris. The following day, the police violated traditions of academic freedom by coming into the Sorbonne and arresting hundreds of students. This was the beginning of a series of demonstrations and confrontations between students and police in the Latin Quarter of Paris. A climax of sorts came on May 10, the "Night of the Barricades," when events in the streets were described minute-by-minute on national radio. On May 13 more than a million people demonstrated in Paris against the government. The day after that workers seized the Sud-Aviation plant. More workers followed their example until 10 million were on strike.

Toward the end of May the government, which had been almost completely ineffective up to that point, dissolved the National Assembly and set a date for elections. De Gaulle, who had been out of the country, appealed for "civic action" against a "totalitarian plot." Many French began to worry about the possibility of anarchy or a communist takeover. Even in Paris, where sympathy for the students had been widespread, people were

French students clash with police in Paris during the confrontation between students and the government in May 1968. AP/Wide World.

tired of the confusion and the disruptions caused by the demonstrations and strikes. There was no consensus among the student radicals as to aims and goals. Workers generally wanted only moderate changes, in particular a substantial pay hike. Almost no one in the general public liked the idea of a genuine revolution.

France, closer to revolution in 1968 than any other western European country, was not, in actuality, all that close. Government inactivity coupled with some blunders had resulted in a situation in which the overthrow of the government seemed possible. The government had, however, a strong position. It had capable leadership in de Gaulle and, especially, in the premier, Georges Pompidou (1911–1974). In the military and the police it had an overwhelming monopoly of force. Even the social and economic strains were not as severe as they appeared at first. Despite the drama and color of events, the government could only fail by losing its nerve.

The radicals had little chance. The "system" was the enemy, but there was no agreement as to how to define the system or what program to follow in order to combat or replace it. While people like Daniel Cohn-Bendit (1945–), "Danny the Red" (so named for his hair as much as his politics), actually a German studying in France, caught the imagination of many, most radicals distrusted leaders and ideas about strategy. Operating almost exclusively on the level of tactics, the radicals were lost once the government took the initiative. Additionally, the radicals did not understand the aspirations of those temporarily allied with them, whether the working class or the middle class.

The major results of the radical movement were changes in the education system, principally possibilities for revised curricula, less elitist student bodies, and less authoritarian structures of university administration. In reaction to the events of May, many turned back to moderate or conservative parties. Parties on the left tried to appear moderate in order to distance themselves from the radicals. The Communist Party in France, which had done nothing to aid the radicals, found itself simultaneously distrusted by moderates and under heavy fire from the radicals. The year 1968, particularly as it played out in France, was the high point of postwar radicalism in western Europe. Radicals had gained a hearing, but the sweeping, comprehensive changes they envisioned were not acceptable to most Europeans. Most found life all right as it was, and worried more that the economy would cease growing or something else might happen to prevent them from achieving goals they had come to see as realistic possibilities.

Brezhnev's Russia

In the 1960s and early 1970s, Leonid Brezhnev (1906–1982) ruled the Soviet Union as President and First Secretary of the Communist Party in tandem with the premier, Alexei Kosygin (1904–1980). They had to acknowledge, however, the importance of several groups within the Soviet system, the military, the KGB, the governmental bureaucracy and, of course, the party. Brezhnev and Kosygin wrestled with basically the same kinds of problems that had plagued Khrushchev, an unresponsive and overly centralized economy, unproductive agriculture, and elements in Russian society that enjoyed privileged positions.

Brezhnev, Kosygin, and other members of the Communist Party's Politburo (Executive Committee) steered a course in the 1960s between the arbitrary terror of Stalin and the adventurism of Khrushchev. Although they experimented briefly with ideas calling for a socialist market approach, i.e., some attention paid to questions of demand and supply and also profitability of enterprises, their policies were largely conventional and followed two major paths. One emphasized highly concentrated efforts to succeed at a particular task. Most tasks had a military payoff. A good example would be the Soviet space effort, which was not intended to race the United States to the moon but rather aimed at a different goal: creating a space station.

The second approach emphasized increasing the number or amount of various components of an industry: more capital, a larger number of workers, a greater supply of energy, and so forth. The first approach achieved some amazing successes but at a high cost. The second worked well as long as larger numbers of workers or greater amounts of capital could make a difference in that industry. What doomed the second approach by the 1960s were first the rapid increases in productivity outside the Soviet bloc, and second the rapid change in technology which quickly began to alter the very definition of a modern economy.

By the early 1960s, the position of the Soviet consumer had begun to improve, with refrigerators and television sets now being items people might be able to purchase. The improvements over earlier periods in Soviet history were heartening, but to those able to make comparisons with the consumer economies of western Europe or the United States, the contrast was startling. Soviet consumer goods tended to be scarce, expensive, and of poor quality. Housing in the cities was difficult to find even twenty years after the war; what was available was cramped and poorly constructed. Long lines to purchase almost anything were customary. One estimate is that Soviet women spent as much as two hours a day waiting in lines.

Some had it better. The "new class" of party officials, high-level bureaucrats, military personnel, technocrats, scientists, ballet and movie stars, world-class athletes, and some literary and intellectual luminaries had not merely higher incomes, which actually was not that much of an advantage, but a range of privileges unavailable to the ordinary citizen. These included a *dacha* (a cottage or even a rather large house in the countryside) for weekends or vacations, special stores with a wider selection than ordinary stores, special clinics for medical treatment without crowds and long waits, official cars for private use, and an "old boy" network that opened up educational and career opportunities to the sons and daughters of the prominent.

Growth rates began to fall in the 1950s and 1960s. By the early 1970s the Soviet economy was scarcely growing at all. Agriculture remained a major problem despite a sizable investment by the state in the early 1970s. To some the answer seemed to lie in technology transfers from the West. Certainly part of the motivation for détente was the idea that western Europe, the United States, and Japan would help the Soviet Union bridge technological gaps and overcome obstacles to rapid economic growth.

In addition to economic problems, the Soviet Union faced growing problems with dissidents. Some emerged in response to the neo-Stalinism that characterized the Soviet Union by the end of the 1960s. Although the Stalin cult of personality and the practice of arbitrary terror were not revived, Brezhnev became increasingly the center of Soviet politics, and

Yuri Andropov (1914–1984) as head of the KGB worked out sophisticated methods utilizing the criminal justice system and mental health facilities to deal with anyone considered troublesome by the regime. Two major dissidents were, first, Aleksandr Solzhenitsyn (1918–), whose *One Day in the Life of Ivan Denisovich* was a revelation to many Russians in the early 1960s. Other than *One Day* and a few short stories, Solzhenitsyn was not allowed to publish in the 1960s. He was also not permitted to accept the Nobel Prize for literature in 1970 and finally was deported from the Soviet Union in 1974. Andrei Sakharov (1921–1989), an eminent Russian physicist and father of the Russian H-bomb, was even more important because of his work with the Committee for Human Rights. Dissidents were restricted generally to *samizdat* (literally "self-publishing"; hand- or typewritten manuscripts circulated illegally) or to occasional interviews with western journalists as ways to spread their views. Critics of the Soviet system as such were relatively isolated and unimportant in Soviet politics, despite the attention paid them by the West. More important, and treated even more harshly, were representatives of the nationalists movements in Lithuania, the Ukraine, and elsewhere. Also, some groups were suspect because of their religious beliefs, among these Russian Baptists and Jehovah's Witnesses. Finally, Soviet Jews were often harassed and their efforts to emigrate were generally not well received.

The Prague Spring

Elsewhere within the Soviet bloc there were attempts to make the Soviet model of communism work better than it did in the Soviet Union. In some cases, mild deviations from the model were allowed. Poland had retreated from collectivized agriculture in the 1950s and enjoyed in the 1960s a much more productive agricultural sector. Hungary, in part to help people forget the events of 1956, was allowed to experiment with different economic structures and to seek some trade ties with western Europe. East Germany, despite Soviet restrictions on the economy, had made considerable economic progress in the 1960s, in part because people realized after the construction of the Berlin Wall that there was no alternative to life in East Germany.

A major disappointment was Czechoslovakia, which had been an urbanized, industrialized state even before World War II. By the early 1960s the Czech economy had deteriorated badly and the political system was regarded as repressive and ineffective. Communist leadership, particularly that of Antonin Novotny (1904–1975), first secretary of the party, increasingly came under criticism. Questions about the fairness of the political trials held between 1949 and 1954 kept coming up within the Czech Communist Party. Slovak communists, who believed, as did Slovaks generally, that Slovakia had been neglected, were especially active in pressing for party reform and a change in leaders.

In January 1968, Novotny was replaced as first secretary by Alexander Dubcek (1921–1992), a Slovak and a leader of the moderate reform impulse. Dubcek moved first to liberalize the economy by decentralizing it, increasing the emphasis on consumer goods and on investments in Slovakia, and establishing more trade with the West. He also lifted censorship and encouraged cultural and intellectual life. Actually, the Prague Spring, a political reform effort that initially appeared in the communist party, owed its existence in large part to a kind of renaissance in the cinema, theatre, and literature starting in 1966. By 1968 this renaissance and the impetus for reform within the party had come together in an impressive, seemingly irresistible, movement for change.

By late spring the reform movement began to get out of hand. The growth of clubs and discussion groups threatened the communist monopoly of political power. Meanwhile, the Russians, East Germans, and Poles grew apprehensive about the movement. The Czechs held two meetings in the summer of 1968, the first with the Soviet Union, and the second with representatives of most of the member nations of the Warsaw Pact. Finally, the Soviets invaded Czechoslovakia on August 20. Czechs tried to block the invasion by such acts as removal of road signs. Demonstrations followed and a few people even set themselves on fire in protest. Brezhnev tried to justify the action by stating that socialist countries had an obligation to come to the aid of a brother socialist country when it was threatened by "counter-revolutionary forces," the so-called Brezhnev Doctrine.

The Soviet Union gradually removed Dubcek and other reformers from power. By the spring of 1969 an orthodox communist regime under Gustav Husák (1913–1991) controlled the country. Ironically, efforts by the Czech communists to construct a "socialism with a human face" failed in part because of the enthusiasm of many participants in the reform movement. They did not sufficiently take into account the rising anxiety of the leaders of the Soviet Union, East Germany, and Poland. Mainly, however, the leaders of these states feared infection from the Czech reform virus. Husák, moderate in comparison to the pro-Soviet hardliners, was successful in establishing pragmatic and moderate policies in Czechoslovakia in the early 1970s. He was not very successful, however, in causing Czechs and Slovaks to forget the promise of 1968. Ironically, the leadership in both East Germany and Poland changed soon after the Soviet invasion ended the Prague Spring. Walter Ulbricht was replaced by Erich Honecker (1912–1994) in 1970 and Wladyslaw Gomulka by Edward Gierek (1913–2001) that same year.

Willy Brandt and Ostpolitik

If the Prague Spring might be seen as a turning point that was not taken, the *Ostpolitik* (Eastern policy) instituted by Willy Brandt in the early 1970s created a small but important bridge between East and West that both could accept with some degree of comfort. Brandt had been the Social Democratic mayor of Berlin at the height of the Berlin Crisis at the end of the 1950s. In the 1960s he led the party into a grand coalition with the Christian Democratic Union (CDU). In 1969, together with the Free Democrats (FDP), the SPD (German Social Democratic Party) became the governing party. The Ostpolitik, part of the larger détente between East and West, created the conditions for the establishment of a dialogue between West Germany and East Germany. In 1970 Brandt negotiated treaties with Poland and the Soviet Union and then in 1972 an agreement that led to East Germany and West Germany according each other diplomatic recognition. In particular, West Germany recognized the Polish-German boundaries. A related agreement in 1971 among the four powers that had occupied Germany after the war protected the rights of the powers in Berlin and also West Germany's particular interest in the city. All of the agreements taken together stabilized the status of both West Germany and East Germany and eliminated the major cause of the Cold War, i.e., the failure to reach a postwar settlement that would prevent the possibility of German militarism reviving.

Brandt, who was awarded the Nobel Peace Prize for the Ostpolitik and what it had led to, enjoyed less success in terms of progress toward social reform in Germany or European unification. Ironically, given Brandt's success with the Ostpolitik, he felt compelled to resign in 1974 after it came to light that a trusted adviser had all along been an East German mole.

The Price of Oil

The oil price shock of 1973 acted as a catalyst to set off a decade of economic problems that explain much of the pessimism and lack of political will marking the 1970s and early 1980s. The Yom Kippur War of 1973 between Israel and several Arab states (Egypt, Syria, Jordan, Iraq) provided the context for the first oil price shock. OPEC (Organization of Petroleum Exporting Countries), founded in 1960, had lacked influence until the Arab members of the organization persuaded the other members to impose an oil embargo on states that supported Israel in the 1973 war. Oil prices increased to four times the previous level, and the evening news began to fill with images of long lines at gas stations and deserted highways.

Even before the oil price shock of 1973, the western part of Europe had experienced some problems with inflation. By 1973 inflation was rampant, and the oil crunch simply made it worse. It was a prime example of one in a series of structural problems European economies faced. The end of the long postwar boom was perhaps the main contributing factor. Reconstruction was largely complete in the west, and people had bought their fill of houses, automobiles, and durable goods like refrigerators. Consumption could not continue to expand indefinitely, especially after the increase in prices of all kinds of articles caused by the increase in the price of energy.

The growth of the welfare state was another important factor. In most countries in western Europe, it had reached a point at which it was straining national economies. As the economy slowed down, unemployment, which had been very low in the 1960s, began to rise. Western Europe was caught in a paradox: inflation meant high prices and interest rates, a recession meant large-scale unemployment. Stagflation was the ungainly term some used to describe the situation. Finally, if the situation were not complicated enough, Europe and other parts of the urbanized, industrialized world experienced a technological revolution in the 1970s and 1980s, which by the end of the period had created an economy radically different from the postwar industrial economy based on heavy industry.

The Welfare State

Leo Tolstoy's opening lines in *Anna Karenina* might be applied to European welfare states in the 1970s: "All happy families are like one another; each unhappy family is unhappy in its own way."[1] Welfare states by the late 1970s were all unhappy families.

The welfare state system has deep roots in the Germany of the 1880s and the Great Britain in the decade before World War I. The prototype of the modern welfare state, however, was Sweden in the 1930s. After World War II, there was consensus in most European countries about the need to ensure the basic necessities of life (food, clothing, shelter, education, and health care) and to guard against catastrophes such as unemployment, injury, and illness. There was particular concern about mothers, infants, and children on the one hand and the retired on the other. While the aims of most nations were similar, the means to accomplish them diverged considerably.

The British system has become synonymous with the welfare state. This is not accurate since not every European country has a National Health Service or a social security system operated entirely by the state. Still, most

1 Quoted from the David Magarshack translation of *Anna Karenina*.

western European countries offered free or virtually free health care and family allowances. Workers' income was covered in case of injury or other disability and in case of unemployment. Some provisions were made for the construction of low cost or public housing. Education, which by the 1970s had become far more widely available even at the university level, was either free or provided for nominal fees.

A major difference among the various systems concerned who paid for services. In Britain and the Scandinavian countries the state, i.e., taxpayers, paid most of the costs. In West Germany employers and employees covered 80 percent of the costs. In France and Italy employers were responsible for about two-thirds of the costs.

By the 1980s the welfare state not only existed to ensure an adequate foundation for people's lives and to guard against the unexpected disaster but also to provide a range of amenities that included parks, libraries, cultural facilities, and subsidies for artists and writers. Additionally, each generation growing up in the system considered what was there as an entitlement and expected the system to be further improved.

A final factor that convinced many the welfare state had to be revised might be subsumed under the term "permissive society." Many critics of the welfare state regarded it as having robbed large groups of people of initiative and self-reliance. Others unfairly blamed the welfare state for new attitudes toward sex and drug use and for problems such as increasing rates of juvenile delinquency. The apparent rise in taxes was more a product of life in a highly industrialized and urbanized society than the existence of the welfare state as such. Whatever the real deficiencies of the welfare state, it became in the 1980s a major target for a new breed of conservative politicians determined to meet head-on the social and economic ills of modern society in western Europe.

Terrorism

Terrorism was a major phenomenon of the 1970s. Added to the mix of social and economic issues confronting Europe at that point, it had the effect of making the situation appear a good deal worse than it was. Not only did the terrorists themselves seem to be an affront to constitutional systems but governments in their response to the challenge on occasion did more damage to civil and human rights than the terrorists.

Terrorism on the left was largely an outgrowth of the failures and frustrations of the 1960s. When revolution had not occurred at the end of that decade, some radicals turned to terrorism: bombing, kidnapping, and murder. The best known of these groups were the *Brigade Rosa* (the Red

Brigades) in Italy and the RAF (the *Rote Armee Fraktion* or Red Army Fraction) in West Germany. They were aided by the existence of what some fearfully saw as a terrorist international on the order of the old Communist International. The reality was less dramatic than this but still lethal. Centers of terrorist activity existed in the Near East where the main players were the Palestinian Liberation Organization (PLO), backed by enormous amounts of petrodollars from sympathetic OPEC members. To this mix could be added the activities of the KGB and other East Bloc intelligence services and the existence of independent nationalist movements like the Irish Republican Army (IRA) in Northern Ireland and the Basque separatists in Spain. The latter appeared about the same time as the Red Brigades and the RAF but for different reasons. On the periphery were terrorists and revolutionaries from Japan and Latin America. While these groups aided one another in securing weapons, in locating sites for training, and with other matters, they seldom worked together on operations. Each group had its own agenda and cooperated with other terrorists only when this served its purposes. The idea of a terrorist conspiracy coordinated by Moscow was simply another variation on Cold War themes.

So far as the Red Brigades and the RAF were concerned, the late 1970s marked the end of any possibility that they would play a major role in national politics. By this time, the RAF had largely moved away from the ideals that had once characterized it to nihilism and criminality. The Red Brigades had also moved in the same direction. In 1978, however, it carried out its most spectacular operation when it kidnapped and later murdered a former premier of Italy, Aldo Moro (1916–1978). The national reaction against this senseless killing was the beginning of the group's downfall; nevertheless, it took the Italian police another five years to destroy the organization.

Sporadic rightwing terrorism, particularly in Italy, continued in the 1980s and disquieting instances of anti-Semitism also appeared. Most of the terrorism of the 1980s, however, was state terrorism sponsored by countries like Libya and Iran. In most cases, this form of terrorism was directed against dissidents from those countries; western Europe merely furnished the location of the action.

Overall, western Europe weathered the outbreak of terrorism in good fashion. While there was much discussion of antiterrorist legislation in West Germany, particularly a 1977 law requiring a political litmus test for civil servants that reminded many of the Nazi *Berufsverbot* (prohibition against entering a profession) used against Jews and others in the 1930s, both West Germany and Italy came through difficult times with their constitutional systems intact.

Recovery

While the economic and social problems of western Europe were genuine and serious, the political problems were more apparent than real. Looked at another way, however, politics seemed to offer a solution to economic and social problems. Certain issues, the welfare state in particular, required rethinking. There was the clear impression among many conservatives that a government willing to divest itself of government-owned operations and to reduce controls and regulations could help create a climate favorable to business. President Ronald Reagan (1911–2004) became the person most closely identified with this political position through his uncanny ability to project an image that matched what large numbers of Americans believed they wanted. It was the British Prime Minister, Margaret Thatcher (1925–), however, who most successfully translated this approach into national policy.

Thatcherism

Margaret Thatcher, probably the most influential woman in Europe in the last half of the century, inside or outside of politics, served as British prime minister between 1979 and 1990, transforming the Conservative Party and Great Britain in the process. As a young woman, she had studied at Oxford and worked as a research chemist. After her marriage in 1951, she studied law and in 1959 entered the House of Commons. Thatcher rose rapidly in the ranks of the Conservative Party and in 1975, at the age of fifty, became its leader. Four years later she led the party to victory in the elections of 1979.

Over the next eleven years, "Maggie" Thatcher became very popular with the public but much disliked by her political opponents. She quickly came to be seen as the "Iron Lady," tough, decisive, strong-willed, and no-nonsense. Her main contribution to British recovery came in the area of economic policy. That policy had three main components: "privatization," reduction of inflation, and weakening of trade union power. The "privatization" of nationalized industries and national utilities received a great deal of press, but it is difficult to say whether it contributed much to overall economic recovery. Probably more important were the largely successful efforts to reduce the power of the trade unions. Trade unions in Britain had contributed to the lack of competitiveness of the economy by a series of regulations regarding work and seniority that made it difficult for companies to reorganize production for greater efficiency. The new political climate favoring business and trade and the greatly weakened trade unions allowed many British firms to take maximum advantage of opportunities to secure profits. The reduction of inflation, which stood at nearly 22 percent in 1979, to 3.7 percent in 1983, created favorable conditions for investment and economic growth. The Thatcher government was also blessed by the discovery of oil deposits in the North Sea.

For many British, the 1980s was a period of new prosperity. In most respects, the economy was stronger than it had been since the early years of the century. One major downside, however, was unemployment. At 6.1 percent in 1980, it rose to 11.6 percent in 1985, then returned in 1989 to about the same level it had been in 1980 (5.3 percent). Some sections of the country, the north in particular, did not share in the general prosperity. The Thatcher years had created a class of big winners, a large group of people who were doing somewhat better or at least okay, and a layer of people who were doing very badly with little prospects of improvement.

Part of Margaret Thatcher's popularity early in her tenure as Prime Minister and vital to her reelection in 1983 was Britain's successful defense of the Falkland Islands from invasion. The Argentine regime that launched the war in the Falklands had few friends. Many observers focused on what was Britain's last imperial hurrah. The spectacle of Britain successfully conducting a long-distance war against Argentina caught the imagination of many Europeans and North Americans. South Americans and Third World countries, not surprisingly, tended to disapprove of British efforts.

Finally, in the realm of international relations, Thatcher could count on friends in high places. In addition to Reagan, her ideological twin, she enjoyed good relations with prominent European leaders such as Helmut Kohl and François Mitterrand. She also became, despite her reflexive anti-Communism, an early champion of Mikhail Gorbachev, whom she recognized as "someone she could do business with." All in all, Margaret Thatcher put her stamp on the last quarter of the century in a way no other European leader other than Gorbachev could match.

France

François Mitterrand served as president from 1981 to 1995. He spent much of the 1960s and 1970s rebuilding and strengthening the Socialist Party. When he and the Socialist Party came to power in 1981, he set in motion an ambitious wave of nationalization involving nine industrial groups including steel, aerospace, armaments, electronics, banking, and insurance. In an era when governments and businesses increasingly were leaner and meaner, Mitterand was something of an anachronism. Within two years, the government quietly abandoned the socialist policies. A more conventional approach, paying more than merely lip service to Thatcher's ideas, came to the fore.

After the 1986 elections, Mitterand remained as president but had to share power with Jacques Chirac (1932–), a Gaullist, as prime minister. Chirac reflected the new rightist majority in the National Assembly. Mitter-and returned in 1988 to win one more term as president.

Over the 1980s the power and appeal of the French Communist Party declined considerably. It gained only 9.7 percent of the vote in 1986, in contrast to the past when it regularly won 20 to 25 percent of the vote. A less powerful Communist Party on his flank allowed Mitterand to moderate his positions to some extent, even if he and Chirac could not reach full agreement on domestic policies.

To some extent, the decline of the Communist Party was reflected in the growth of Jean-Marie Le Pen's (1928–) *Front National* in the 1980s. The Front National is a political movement based to a large extent on hatred and fear. It is racist, chauvinistic, and well to the right in terms of French politics. It is possibly more dangerous than neo-Nazi movements in Germany or Austria, but people do not automatically connect it with Hitler and the Nazis. Le Pen, an astute and charismatic political leader, knows how to play on the fears of ordinary French men and women. Persistent unemployment in the 1980s helped to convince many that Le Pen's perspective was worth taking seriously.

By the end of the 1980s and the celebration of the bicentennial of the French Revolution, the French were doing well despite ongoing political controversy and nagging unemployment. For the majority, the standard of living had greatly improved since the 1960s. France was also characterized by a greater degree of egalitarianism than had been the case before, especially in terms of equality of opportunity as reflected in such areas as education and health care.

West Germany

Helmut Schmidt (1918–) was a worthy successor to Willy Brandt and governed West Germany well in the 1970s and early 1980s. He successfully weathered the challenges of the Red Army Fraction (RAF) and the economic downturns. However, he was not able to maintain the coalition with the Free Democrats after the 1982 elections. At that point, a new coalition between the Christian Democrats and the Free Democrats was formed, and Helmut Kohl became Chancellor.

Helmut Kohl (1930–) liked to say that his generation was fortunate in that it did not have to take part in World War II or the Holocaust and therefore was not burdened with the guilt felt by the generations that had. Critics quickly pointed out that his generation, growing up in the Nazi era as it did, had undoubtedly absorbed much of the Nazi outlook and had therefore as much to overcome as earlier generations. From time to time,

Kohl has made comments that have marked him as something of an opportunist, eager to put the Nazi past behind him for good. He endured, however, as Chancellor from 1982 until 1998.

In the 1980s the Kohl government was successful in leading West Germany to a strong recovery, in part because of policies it introduced and also because of policies Schmidt had set in motion. Additionally, West Germany's powerful central bank, the *Bundesbank* (Federal Bank), and German business leaders made important contributions. The Kohl government largely followed policies West German governments had been following since the 1950s and 1960s. The major exception was an effort to stop the growth of the welfare state. Businesses were also encouraged to slow the growth of wage-and-benefits packages to prevent labor costs from pricing German exports out of the market. By the end of the 1980s inflation had disappeared (6 percent in 1981, but -1 percent in 1986) and exports had shown strong growth. The major disappointment for West Germany was the continuing high unemployment figures, especially in a country that had long enjoyed full employment.

The major political development of the 1980s was the growing appeal of the Greens, an outgrowth of the Extra-Parliamentary Opposition (APO) of the late 1960s. Formed as a party in the 1970s, the Greens were interested primarily in environmentalism, but diverse in outlook. Many in the movement disliked the idea of becoming a political party and participating in institutions like the Bundestag. Green members of the Bundestag introduced new styles of dress and behavior, but learned in the course of the 1980s how work was accomplished in that body and in many cases became quite proficient at advancing the Green agenda. In the 1987 elections, the Greens elected forty-seven members to the Bundestag. The Christian Democrats lost ground, but continued to govern in coalition with the Free Democrats. The Social Democrats remained polarized between a radical left wing and a moderate center. They were also hampered by the lack of an effective standardbearer. Despite the opposition's weaknesses and the relative success of the Kohl government, Kohl's political prospects at the end of the 1980s were not particularly good. As it turned out, however, he stood on the eve of his finest hour.

Some Other States

In the 1970s and the 1980s the Italian Communist Party (PCI) provided a major political story. Under the leadership of Enrico Berlinguer (1922–1984), the secretary-general of the PCI from 1972 to 1984, the party undertook a "historic compromise" in 1979 when it explicitly accepted the rules of the parliamentary system. It fared well in the elections in 1976, gaining 34 percent of the vote and became part of an informal coalition

The Reichstag Building as it appeared in 1985. Although in West Berlin, it was located quite close to the Berlin Wall and had no official function. Since unification it has been completely renovated. From the collection of Michael Richards.

between 1977 and 1979. In addition, the PCI controlled most of the major cities and seven of the sixteen regions, which meant it was often the leading political force on a local or regional basis. In the 1980s, even though the party continued to move rapidly away from Stalinism and even Leninism, its vote totals dipped. Meanwhile the Christian Democrats turned their attention back to the Socialists.

In the 1980s Italians enjoyed a decade of progress. The Christian Democrats continued to dominate national political life but had to concede in the mid-1980s the position of premier to Bettino Craxi (1934–1999), the leader of the Socialist Party. Craxi's government, which lasted from 1983 to 1986, was actually one of the more effective governments in Italian political history. Craxi hoped to emulate the French Socialists, but he was not able to duplicate Mitterand's successes.

For Portugal and Spain the events of the 1970s spelled release from decades of dictatorship and the beginning of efforts to catch up with other western European countries. Portugal began to change after the death in 1970 of Antonio Salazar (1889–1970), dictator since 1932. Marcello Caetano (1906–1980) followed Salazar as prime minister in 1968. Caetano and the remnants of the dictatorship were overthrown by revolution in 1974. Army personnel, radicalized by the long and frustrating struggle to retain the empire, carried out the revolution and established the Supreme Revolutionary Council, which ruled in 1974 and 1975. In 1975 military personnel close to the Portuguese Communist Party attempted a coup, which was unsuccessful. The following year a new constitution was promulgated.

In the late 1970s and in the 1980s the major figure in Portuguese politics was Mario Soares (1924–), a reformist socialist. Soares became president in 1986, the same year Portugal joined the European Community.

The death of Spain's dictator, General Francisco Franco (b. 1892), came in 1975. Franco made arrangements for restoration of the monarchy, with Juan Carlos (1938–), the heir-apparent, succeeding to the throne. Despite serious problems with the ETA (the Basque separatists) and an attempted coup in 1981, which Juan Carlos I played a major role in thwarting, Spain enjoyed in the late 1970s and in the 1980s both a successful transition to democratic politics and impressive economic growth. Spain entered the NATO alliance in 1982 and the European Community in 1986. The major political figure in Spain over the past two decades has been Felipe Gonzales (1942–), who led the Socialist Workers' Party to victory in the 1982 elections. He was forty at the time. Gonzales served as prime minister from 1982 to 1996.

The East Bloc in Decline: The Soviet Union

If western Europe experienced something of a roller coaster ride in the 1970s and 1980s, it was all downhill to the smashup for eastern Europe (1989) and the Soviet Union (1991). The Soviet Union maintained strict control not only domestically but also in eastern Europe in the 1970s with the important exception of the small opening provided by the Helsinki Process. The Soviet Union was itself a terrible kind of paradox, a world power finally, but also failing visibly in terms of the most vital indices of national well-being: infant mortality rates, life expectancy (especially for males), incidence of alcoholism, and accident and suicide rates. By the late 1970s the Soviet Union seemed to have embarked on a kind of Cold War adventurism in Afghanistan, the Horn of Africa, and other trouble spots as a way of denying its economic problems and the disintegration of its social fabric. Leonid Brezhnev, old and ill, had become little more than a parody of a Soviet leader. Trotted out for important state occasions, he had to be helped on and off the podium and often lost his place in speeches.

After Brezhnev's death in 1982, Yuri Andropov, who had played a dark role in Soviet politics as the mastermind of the KGB through the 1970s and early 1980s, appeared ready to make sweeping changes in the Soviet Union. Andropov, as first secretary of the Communist Party, presented to the credulous West as a jazz-loving, Scotch-drinking, spy-novel-reading liberal, never had much of an opportunity to demonstrate what he intended to do. His principal contribution to the 1980s was his sponsorship of Mikhail Gorba-chev. Gorbachev had to wait his turn, however, until after the mercifully brief reign of Konstantin Chernenko (1911–1985) as first secretary. Chernenko was rewarded for his utter loyalty to Brezhnev and will probably be best remembered as an example of the tendency of a decaying system to push to the top those totally incompetent figures who will finally destroy it.

Gorbachev, unlike Andropov, truly was a different sort of Soviet official. A graduate of Moscow University in law, he had come up rapidly through the system, becoming a member of the Politburo in 1980 at the age of forty-nine and in 1985 Secretary-General of the Communist Party. Although Gorbachev was a communist, he saw the need for far-reaching changes in the Soviet system and believed that Leninism provided an adequate basis for those changes. He advanced several important general propositions: glasnost' or openess, perestroika or reformation, and new thinking. Glasnost' was perhaps the easiest of the new approaches to institute. Censorship was gradually abandoned and people encouraged to present the past as accurately as possible in magazines, films, plays, and books. Perestroika was the most difficult to put into practice and ultimately Gorbachev's undoing. Economic reform, particularly the encouragement of modest levels of private enterprise, was stymied by bureaucratic obstructionism, which Gorbachev sought to counter through political reform. This, however, brought into question the primacy of the Communist Party. New thinking was Gorbachev's most successful initiative, perhaps because it was directed mostly at the West and offered a way out of the Cold War impasse. Although President Reagan was initially suspicious, he began to see possibilities in Gorbachev's proposals. In fact, at the summit at Reykjavik, Iceland, in 1986, Reagan had to be restrained by his advisors from responding too enthusiastically to Gorbachev's overtures. The following year the Intermediate Nuclear Forces (INF) Treaty was signed, eliminating all ground-based intermediate-range nuclear missiles. Enormously popular in the West ("Gorby Mania"), Gorbachev experienced increasing difficulty in the Soviet Union in maneuvering between Communist Party hardliners and proponents of radical change

Solidarity in Poland

The contribution of Poland's Solidarity (Solidarnosc) movement to the unraveling of the Cold War can hardly be exaggerated. It grew out of the politics of the 1970s. First, in 1970, strikes protesting increases in food prices led to the replacement of Wladyslaw Gomulka by Edward Gierek. Gierek pushed a policy of economic growth based on foreign loans. By 1976, however, it was apparent that unfortunate choices had been made in pursuit of economic growth (construction of huge steelworks at a time when demand for steel products was declining, for example). Again, attempts to increase food prices led to strikes.

In the next few years, two developments helped to change the terms of confrontation between workers and the government. On the one hand, an organized intellectual opposition, KOR (Committee for the Defense of the Workers), made contact with workers' groups. On the other, the Catholic Church in Poland gained enormously in prestige from the election of a Pole, Karol Cardinal Wojtyla (1920–2005), as Pope John Paul II in 1978. The following year Pope John Paul II made a triumphant tour of Poland and was welcomed by millions of the faithful.

In 1980, for the third time in a decade, the government tried to raise food prices. The strikes this time had a center in the Lenin Shipyards in Gdansk and a leader in Lech Walesa (1943–), an electrician at the shipyards and a participant in the events of 1976. In the negotiations between the workers and the government, the workers pressed for and won the right to organize an independent trade union movement, Solidarity. It began to take on a life of its own in 1981, becoming an enormously large and powerful trade union movement. Although there was no place for Solidarity in the communist system, it began to exercise a kind of de facto power, challenging the authority of the Polish Communist Party (technically the Polish United Workers Party or PUWP). The upshot of this was the appointment of General Wojceich Jaruzelski (1923–) as prime minister and the proclamation of martial law. Walesa and other Solidarity leaders were imprisoned and Solidarity outlawed.

Walesa, who won the Nobel Prize for Peace in 1983, was eventually released from prison. He was able to maintain Solidarity's existence as an organization throughout the 1980s, first as an underground organization, later as an organization unofficially tolerated by the government. As problems mounted for the Polish government and PUWP, the power and influence of Solidarity began to increase. Finally, in 1989, talks between Solidarity and the government began, leading to events that formed one of the most important triggers of the revolutions of 1989.

Eric Honecker's East Germany

East Germany in the 1970s and 1980s seemed to be a success story. There was, first, the connection to West Germany that Brandt's Ostpolitik had developed. For Honecker, it was a double-edged sword. On the positive side stood the prestige involved in formal recognition by West Germany. In addition, entry fees paid by people entering East Germany, West German subsidies of various kinds, and access to the European Community produced income. The negative side was the public's greater contact with the realities of life in West Germany. This, of course, was difficult to avoid, given the widespread availability of West German TV programs. Honecker tried to offset western influences through efforts to encourage East

Germans to distance themselves from West Germany and to take pride in East Germany.

East Germany had about it in the 1970s and 1980s something of the atmosphere of bread and circuses. While it was drab and gray compared to the West, it offered its citizens the highest standard of living in the East Bloc. In effect, this was Honecker's agreement with East Germans. Work hard and you will be rewarded with better housing, good food and clothing, refrigerators, TVs, and the Trabi (the Trabant, the basic East German automobile). As bonuses, the East German regime offered an active cultural life and good health care and educational opportunities. Finally, the government sponsored an amazingly successful sports program, modeled on but surpassing that of the Soviet system.

Behind the bribes was an extensive system of surveillance and repression administered by the Ministry of State Security or the *Stasi*. The Stasi consisted of a sizable bureaucracy which carried out activities both abroad (principally in West Germany) and at home. It was assisted by thousands of people who either volunteered to help or were seduced or coerced into helping. In some cases, husbands spied on wives and friends informed on friends. Even some pastors became agents of the Stasi, informing on members of their congregations. The amount of data gathered was staggering,

A gutted Trabant, or Trabi, sits in a dumpster, symbolic of the initial turning away from anything connected with the old regime. Although East Germans were generally cautious with their money in the first months after unification with West Germany, many could not resist buying a West German or Swedish car. AP/Wide World.

miles of files. An argument could be made that the Stasi by the late 1980s could no longer see the forest for the trees. In any case, it failed to present the East German Politburo with a realistic picture of the country at the very point when one was desperately needed.

A realistic picture would have emphasized an economy that was rapidly becoming uncompetitive, starved for investment capital, and dependent on technologies that were causing enormous ecological damage. The system was failing to provide the kind of life it had promised. While small protest groups existed precariously under the umbrella of the Lutheran Church, thousands of other East Germans had decided it was time to leave. Thousands more were ready to jump at any realistic chance of leaving, should it present itself. It is no small irony that East German leaders directed almost all of their attention to the impending fortieth anniversary of the founding of the state and failed to see how badly those foundations had been eroded.

The Revolutions of 1989

The decisive events of 1989 in eastern and central Europe began in 1985 when Mikhail Gorbachev became the Secretary-General of the Communist Party of the Soviet Union. Gorbachev's policies of glasnost' and perestroika created an attractive model that many in eastern Europe wanted to emulate. Furthermore, Gorbachev began to indicate that the Soviet Union would no longer be willing or even able to intervene in the affairs of eastern European countries, as had been the case in 1953, 1956, 1968, and 1981. By 1989 Gorbachev was telling communist leaders of the satellite nations that they were on their own.

The other essential factor in the events of 1989 was the emergence once again of Solidarity as a major influence in Polish politics. In the summer elections of 1989, Solidarity won all the seats allotted to it in the *Sejm* (the lower house) and all but one of the Senate seats. The first noncommunist premier in more than forty years headed the new coalition government.

About the same time the Polish Communist Party was losing its grip on Poland, its Hungarian counterpart ran into difficulties. In the summer of 1989, Hungarians were able, for the first time since 1956, to discuss the Hungarian Revolution of 1956 openly. In a moving ceremony, Hungarians reburied several of the martyrs of that event.

Hungary also contributed to the developments in the GDR. In the spring of 1989, Hungary removed the barbed wire fence between it and Austria, symbolizing a new relationship with western Europe. East Germans began crossing illegally during the summer. Once in Austria, they were sent to West Germany and a new life. Early in the fall, Hungary stopped all efforts to prevent East Germans from crossing, despite its obligations under a treaty with the GDR. The flood of East German refugees over the border between Hungary and Austria, together with those East Germans who crowded into the West German embassies in Prague and Warsaw, pushed the East German government off balance. Then the uncontested march around Leipzig on October 9 began a process whereby the government responded to events rather than initiated them.

In Czechoslovakia, demonstrators in Prague filled Wenceslaus Square in November. At first, police tried to break up the demonstrations. Within a few days, however, the crowds grew to overwhelming numbers. The Czech government, like its counterpart in the GDR, found itself responding to events, always at least a step behind. The center of political gravity moved to the Magic Lantern Theatre where Vaclav Havel (1936–) and colleagues associated with Charter 77, a group of activists dedicated to monitoring abuses of human rights as defined by the constitution of Czechoslovakia, worked to give direction to the movement against the government. By December, the old government had resigned and a new government headed by Havel had formed. Alexander Dubcek, the heroic figure of the "Prague Spring," emerged from long years of obscurity to lend his presence to the "Velvet Revolution." Tragically, Dubcek died in November 1992 from injuries received in an auto accident.

The revolutionary wave also swept away the communist government in Bulgaria without violence. In Romania, however, Nicolae Ceaucescu, who had ruled in a harsh and increasingly arbitrary manner since the 1960s, attempted to hold on to power. He and his wife were captured by revolutionary forces, who promptly put the couple on trial, declared them guilty, and shot them. Pictures of the dead couple flashed around the world in television reports.

In a few short months, the unthinkable had taken place. The "Iron Curtain" was no more. Instead a series of new governments eagerly began to experiment with the transition to a market economy and to a democratic political system. In the euphoria of early 1990, some thought the transition was a matter of a few hundred days. Instead, years of trial and error lay ahead.

Conclusion

While both eastern and western Europe changed in significant ways in the 1970s and 1980s, the changes in eastern Europe were far more dramatic. Western Europe weathered difficult times in the 1970s and early 1980s. At the end of the 1980s it seemed more economically and politically mature. Though Europe still looked to the United States for leadership, it was increas-

Europe in the 1990s

ingly willing to forge its own path. Particularly in the case of the European Community, western Europe appeared poised to break new ground.

Eastern Europe, euphoric and hopeful after the events of 1989, faced difficult political and economic challenges. Finally free of the Soviet Union, it would not find an easy path to capitalism and democracy. In the 1990s, while both the Soviet Union and Yugoslavia imploded, the latter with particularly grave consequences, the other members of the old Soviet bloc followed various paths, including in some cases membership in NATO and the European Community, to a better, or at least different future.

If Europe still did not resemble the common European house of de Gaulle, it nonetheless was far more united than it had been at any other time in the twentieth century. There were increasing amounts of common ground and seemingly unstoppable processes of integration. However, there were at the same time unforeseen challenges ahead in the last decade of the century.

Suggested Books And Films

Raymond Carr, *Spain: Dictatorship to Democracy* (1986). A thorough discussion of Spain's remarkable recent history by a leading expert.

Mary Fulbrook, *Anatomy of a Dictatorship: Inside the GDR, 1949–1989* (1999).

Timothy Garton Ash, *The Magic Lantern: The Revolution of '89 Witnessed in Warsaw, Budapest, Berlin and Prague* (1993). Classic reportage from one of the keenest observers of the events of 1989.

Paul Ginsborg, *Italy and Its Discontents: Family, Civil Society, State, 1980–2001* (2001). Up-to-date and highly recommended.

Padraic Kenney, *A Carnival of Revolution: Central Europe, 1989* (2003). The best single study of the events of 1989.

Steven Kotkin, *Armaggedon Averted: The Soviet Collapse, 1970–2000* (2001). A thoughtful discussion.

Mark Kurlansky, *1968: The Year that Rocked the World* (2003). A readable overview.

Jean Lacouture, *De Gaulle*, 2 vols. (1991–1992). A detailed biography of the major European political figure in the 1960s.

Charles Maier, *Dissolution* (1999). An excellent anyalsis of the disintegration of East Germany.

Arthur Marwick, *The Sixties: Cultural Revolution in Britain, France, and Italy, and the United States, c. 1958–c. 1974.* An exhaustive discussion of this watershed era.

Kenneth Maxwell, *The Making of Portuguese Democracy* (1995). The best book on the Portuguese Revolution and its aftermath.

H. Gordon Skilling, *Czechoslovakia's Interrupted Revolution* (1976). A fine study of 1968 in Czechoslovakia.

Hedrick Smith, *The Russians* (1976). The first, and in many ways the best, of a string of superb books by reporters on the Soviet Union from the 1970s to the early 1990s.

Henry Ashby Turner, Jr., *Germany from Partition to Reunification*, 2nd edition (1992). A very good survey of German history, East and West, after World War II.

Kieran Williams, *The Prague Spring and Its Aftermath: Czechoslovak Politics, 1968–1970* (1997). Includes new archival matherial.

Hugo Young, *Iron Lady* (1990). A very useful biography of Margaret Thatcher.

Chronology

1940s–1950s	Heyday of existentialist writers, e.g., Albert Camus and Jean-Paul Sartre
c.1945–1950s	New York school of abstract expressionist art promoted by Peggy Guggenheim's Art of This Century Gallery
1949	George Orwell's *1984*
1950s	"Pop Art" emerges in England as a reaction to abstract expressionism
1952	John Cage, leading figure in "music of chance," performs *4'33"*
1950s–1960s	Theater of the Absurd popularizes existential philosophy
1954–1963	"Golden Decade" of rock'n'roll music
1955	Claude Lévi-Strauss's *Tristes Topiques* marks the appearance of structuralism
1964	The Beatles appear on the *Ed Sullivan Show*, launching the "English invasion" of American popular music
1970s	Minimalism displaces Pop Art as the current fad
1973	"Aloha from Hawaii" with Elvis Presley is beamed live around the world on television
1980s	Deconstructionism, or postculturalism, flourishes
1982	Maya Ling Lin's *Vietnam Veterans' War Memorial* opens
1990s	"Postmodernism" becomes a popular description for the contemporary view of the universe as random chaos
2005	Christo and Jeanne-Claude de Guillebon's *The Gates* exhibited in New York City's Central Park

11
New Realities for a New Age

ON THE NIGHT OF FEBRUARY 13–14, 1945, the Tuesday night before Ash Wednesday, more than 800 RAF bombers dropped incendiary and high explosive bombs on the beautiful city of Dresden, Germany. American bombers, 300 on the following day and 200 the day after, stoked the flames of the burning city. A total of 650,000 incendiary bombs, more than one for each of the city's normal population of 630,000, were dropped during the raids. A fire storm of colossal force reaching temperatures of 800 to 1,000 degrees centigrade engulfed the city, converting more than 4,200 acres and 135,000 men, women, and children to ashes.

Dresden was of no strategic importance. It was known as a center of the arts, especially renowned for its beautiful Rococo architecture. Because it had escaped attention from the bombers previously, Dresden had become a center for refugees fleeing the oncoming Russian juggernaut. The decision to fire-bomb Dresden remains one of the most controversial Allied military decisions of World War II, perhaps second only to the subsequent decision to unleash nuclear bombs on Hiroshima and Nagasaki, Japan. Historians agree that the destruction of Dresden and its artistic treasures was one of the war's greatest cultural loses. To obtain some appreciation of the extent of the destruction of Europe's cultural heritage during World War II, one need only view old news reels or old photographs of Europe's, especially Germany's, bombed out cities. Many of central and eastern Europe's great cultural centers were almost totally destroyed.

The damage done to the psyche by the war was far greater than the ruin of the physical landscape. The disintegration of the Enlightenment Tradition begun already before the Great War now appeared complete. Faith in reason, the innate goodness of human beings, and the inherent value of the individual, like the belief in universal truths, values, or principles upon which to construct a humane world, all fell victim to apparent reality. Were

225

reasonable people responsible for such devastation? Were the concentration camps, the fire bombing of cities, and the atomic bombing of Hiro-shima and Nagasaki the acts of reasonable people? The evil of Nazism in Germany and militarism in Japan were finally overcome, but by whom? Stalin, next to Hitler, was the other great villain of the twentieth century. It was the United States, the historical embodiment of the hope created by the Enlightenment *philosophes*, that released from Pandora's box the frightening prospect of a future thermonuclear holocaust. There seemed little hope for the future of civilization viewed from the immediate postwar years.

In their attempt to make sense out of a world in which all the old values and certainties had either failed or vanished, a universe which rejected the existence of God or any other absolute truth that might provide unity and meaning, the intellectuals of the immediate postwar years embraced the philosophy of existentialism. Existentialism appeared to provide a means by which the individual could find (or create) meaning for his or her existence in a universe that seemed increasingly meaningless and frightening. By the 1960s existentialism was giving way to structuralism, which shifted the focus away from the individual as the creator of meaning to universal thought processes that were to provide an underlying structure, or unity, to fragmented reality.

By the 1980s structuralism had mutated into deconstructionism, sometimes referred to as poststructuralism. Deconstruction is a radical rejection of the whole Western tradition, especially as found in the Enlightenment Tradition. It embraces the notion of total fragmentation and denies the possibility of discovering any truth or meaning in the universe. We are back to Nietzsche's assertion in his parable of the madman (*The Gay Science* [1882]) that if God is dead then mankind is adrift in a universe without meaning. By the end of the twentieth century many appeared to have embraced nihilism, at least intellectually and culturally.

The changing views about truth and reality found expression in the works produced by the purveyors of both elite and pop culture. An increasingly fragmented world view during the interwar years was mirrored in the art, music, and literature of the period (see Chapter 5). As the fragmentation of world view continued in the West, even increased, during the second half of the twentieth century, so too did the message and technique of cultural expression. By the end of the century there was no longer any accepted standard by which to judge any work of art, literature, or music. Terms such as "good," "bad," "beautiful," or "ugly" were meaningless, when anything, no matter how outlandish, could qualify as art. This itself was an expression of the new consensus on the nature of man and the universe, and whether that consensus itself had any meaning or relevance.

Existentialism

The roots of existentialism reach back into the nineteenth century with the writings of Soren Kirkegaard (1813–1855), Fydor Dostoevski (1821–1881), and Friedrich Nietzsche (1844–1900). Although most of the existentialists were atheists, or at least ignored the question of God's existence, some were Christians, some were religious—but not Christian—and at least one, Martin Buber (1878–1965), was a believing Jew. Existentialism is not easily defined, for there is no systematic dogma to which all its leading exponents adhered. In general, existentialists asserted that the individual must affirm and give meaning to his or her existence by struggling against the absurdity of a universe that is silent and indifferent to the individual's existence. By choosing to act, the individual gives meaning to his or her existence.

Postwar existentialism was born in the French resistance to German occupation during World War II. Albert Camus (1913–1960), French born and reared in French-ruled Algeria, was the premier example of the existentialist writers who came out of the French Resistance. Camus confronted the predicament of the individual in a world that was without God and therefore silent and indifferent to the individual's existence. Having rejected both suicide and a fatalistic acceptance of nihilism, Camus likened the individual's task to that of the Greek mythic figure of Sisyphus. Like Sisyphus who was condemned to repeatedly roll a great rock uphill, only to have it roll back down again, the individual is condemned to struggle against the absurdity of the universe, knowing all along that his struggle is in vain. Before his death in an automobile accident in 1960, Camus's ideas received wide exposure in three novels—*The Stranger* (1942), *The Plague* (1947), and *The Fall* (1956)—and two philosophical works, *The Myth of Sisyphus* (1942) and *The Rebel* (1951).

Perhaps the best known and most controversial of the postwar French existentialists was Jean-Paul Sartre (1905–1980). Sartre's ideas were popularized primarily through works written during the war. Again, as with Camus, it was through a series of novels, especially *Nausea* (1938), and *The Age of Reason* (1945) and plays, such as *The Flies* (1943), and *No Exit* (1944), rather than serious philosophical studies like *Being and Nothingness* (1943), that Sartre's ideas achieved renown and influence.

For Sartre, an atheist, the starting point is the existence of the individual. There is no reference point in the universe or in time to which the individual relates that validates one's existence. The individual creates his or her own essence, that is, defines his or her own being. The individual is neither the product of environmental forces nor unconscious drives. To be a human

Many individuals at the end of the twentieth century felt as though they were adrift alone in a world where the future was filled with uncertainty and the present haunted by symbols of the past. Photo courtesy of Elizabeth Waibel, private collection.

being is to bear the burden of being one's own creator. One thing that the individual can do, indeed must do, is make authentic choices. By doing so, one takes on the role of what Nietzsche called a superman (Übermensch), the creator of one's essence. In Sartre's own words:

> Not only is man what he conceives himself to be but he is also only what he wills himself to be. . . . *Man is nothing else but what he makes of himself* [emphasis added]. . . . [E]xistentialism's first move is to make every man aware of what he is and to make the full responsibility of his existence rest on him.[1]

Sartre found it impossible to live consistently by the philosophy he espoused. In 1960, Sartre joined with other French intellectuals in signing the Algerian Manifesto, which said that the war in Algeria was morally and ethically wrong. By doing so Sartre seemed to destroy his own philosophical position. There was a standard (an absolute?) by which human behavior could be judged, and the individual could use reason to measure human actions against that standard. Similarly, Sartre's flirtation with Marxism between 1951 and 1955 appeared to place this prophet of radical individualism on the side of a radical mechanical materialism that denied

1 Jean-Paul Sartre, *Existentialism*, trans. by Bernard Frechtman (New York, 1947), 18–19 quoted in Marvin Perry, *An Intellectual History of Modern Europe* (Boston, 1992), 449.

individual freedom. Sartre broke with the Communist Party in 1956 and denounced the Soviet suppression of the Hungarian revolt, once again a moral judgment based upon reason. The contradiction was not overlooked by fellow existentialists. Both Albert Camus and Maurice Merleau-Ponty (1908–1961) broke openly with Sartre. In 1956, before Sartre rejected communism, he was an honored guest in Moscow, where he embarrassed himself by his overindulgence in vodka. Merleau-Ponty voiced the opinion of other existentialists, when he accused Sartre of the sin of "ultra-bolshevism," a betrayal of existentialism's belief in individual freedom.[2]

The following verses by Kendrew Lascelles evoke the sense of isolation that many people felt in the late twentieth century.

When All the Laughter Dies in Sorrow

When all the laughter dies in sorrow
And the tears have risen to a flood
When all the wars have found a cause
In human wisdom and in blood
Do you think they'll cry in sadness
Do you think the eye will blink
Do you think they'll curse the madness
Do you think they'll even think

When all the great galactic systems
Sigh to a frozen halt in space
Do you think there will be some remnant
Of beauty in the human race
Do you think there will be a vestige
Or a sniffle or a cosmic tear
Do you think a greater thinking thing
Will give a damn that man was here[3]

Structuralism

During the 1960s, just as existentialism was filtering down to the masses through the medium of popular culture, even though few of the masses would have been aware of it or able to define the term, the intellectual trendsetters were moving on to structuralism, as if hoping to restore some order to the increasing fragmentation. Once again the birthplace was France, where its appearance is often associated with the publication of

2 Roland N. Stromberg, *European Intellectual History Since 1789*, 6th ed. (Upper Saddle River, NJ, 1994), 260.
3 Kendrew Lascelles © 1970 Mediarts Music, Inc. Used by permission of United Artists.

Tristes Tropiques by Claude Lévi-Strauss (1908–) in 1955. Structuralism entered the United States through Yale University in the late 1960s. By the mid-seventies it was no longer fashionable among French intellectuals, who were turning to deconstruction, a more radical form, or mutation of, structuralism. It remained popular among intellectuals in the United States, England, and Germany through the end of the century.

Structuralism was antihumanist. Whereas the existentialists focused on the individual and the individual's need to find meaning, the structuralists assumed a universal structure, or a kind of hidden harmony, or universal code, that exists independent of human beings. They focused on these universal structures that are independent of humans and determine human behavior. This universal code could be found in the human mind, that is, in universal thought processes that are unconscious but determine consciousness. Since these thought processes are universal, the same for the uneducated native and the sophisticated university professor or corporate executive, there is an alleged unity to humanity that transcends all cultural, racial, and class distinctions. It even transcends history.

Structuralism was a rejection of all Western thought, at least since the Enlightenment. Human beings as the self-conscious creators of a meaningful history were abolished. They were merely the playthings of hidden mechanistic forces, like puppets in the hands of an unseen puppeteer. The autonomous individual, who controlled his or her environment and was master of his or her fate, gave way to the individual as a social creature controlled by his or her environment.[4] History as a linear process that implied progress over time was denied. History was meaningless, and the study of history a waste of time. The study of the past, the gathering of historical data, was a futile activity that could teach nothing of value. Its only result was a collection of factual trivia, empty of any meaning. For Lévi-Strauss, for example, what was important was "the comparative, the universal, the mythic, the immediate rather than the historical and the temporal."[5]

Lévi-Strauss was an anthropologist turned philosopher. His success in spreading the gospel of structuralism was due in part to his beautiful, almost poetic, writing style. His books and other writings are said to resemble musical compositions. In addition to *Tristes Tropiques,* a kind of intellectual

---

4 Structuralism and its successor, deconstruction, were ideally suited for "a world integrated by identification and manipulation of the universal genetic code, computer programs, communications satellites, and multinational corporations, and the absence of major wars. . . . A world fragmented culturally and aesthetically, a world of sub-cultures, small-group choices [made] on aesthetic principles and idiosyncratic, nostalgic recapitulations of the past, but one in which a comprehensive, integrating cultural theory is lacking." (Norman Cantor, *The American Century: Varieties of Culture in Modern Times* [New York, 1997], 434–435).
5 Ibid., 442.

autobiography, *The Savage Mind* (1962), *The Elementary Structures of the Mind* (1969), and a host of other popular writings helped make Lévi-Strauss one of the leading intellectuals in France during the 1960s and 1970s. His ideas were further popularized by Roland Barthes (1915–1989), an existentialist who converted to structuralism. Barthes was editor of *Tel Quel*, an influential Parisian intellectual journal during the 1950s and 1960s.

The ideas of Lévi-Strauss and Roland Barthes became popular during the 1960s and 1970s in the United States, where they were applied to literary criticism. Once again it was the hidden structure behind the words on the page that the structuralist literary critic was seeking. The author's intent was irrelevant to the study of his or her work. As with a newspaper, it was the layout of the newspaper, its structure, rather than the articles themselves, that interested the structuralists. In the end, the structuralists failed to uncover the hidden universal structures that were thought to control the human mind and hence all that human beings produced. By the late 1970s, structuralism was passing out of fashion and yielding the field to decon-struction. Roland Barthes and Michel Foucault (1926–1984) served as a bridge between the two philosophies.

Deconstruction

Structuralism, as one intellectual historian has put it, slid into decon-struction, sometimes called poststructuralism. It did so by assuming that everything had to be decoded in order to discover the hidden meaning of things, which led to the question of whether there was any one meaning, or simply different meanings. It did so, too, by insisting that one's intellect is determined by hidden structures, that is, by linguistics (words). Also, the structuralists were characterized by a sense of alienation that compelled them to play the role of subverters of meaning.[6]

Once again the home of this intellectual movement was France. The leading deconstructionists were the French thinkers Michel Foucault, Jacques Lacan (1901–1981), and Jacques Derrida (1930–). Deconstruction was an open denial of the whole Western intellectual tradition with its emphasis on the individual, the individual's ability to reason, and through reason to arrive at a true understanding of reality, which in turn implied the capacity to make meaningful moral judgments resulting in a reasoned reformation of society.

Deconstructionists held that there was no one hidden meaning to be arrived at as a result of decoding a literary text, for example. There is an infinite number of possible meanings, as many as there are "decoders."

6 Stromberg, 292–293.

The author's intent is no help either, for there is no implicit relationship between the author's mind and the words of the text. The deconstructionist critic may interpret a literary text any way he or she wishes, having deduced that interpretation, not necessarily from what the author wrote down, but from what the author left out, what Lacan calls the "holes in the discourse." Whether what the deconstructionist said of a text had any meaning itself was questionable, for deconstruction itself could be deconstructed. Derrida admitted that by the criteria of deconstruction his own writings were meaningless. Deconstruction had a definite tendency towards nihilism.

The implications of deconstruction for understanding civilization in general and modern European civilization in particular are obvious. When the deconstructionists finish their work, there are no "great books," no treasure trove of wisdom from the past that defines, inspires, or provides a standard for modern civilization. History itself is a text to be deconstructed revealing what Foucault called "non-historical, or discontinuous history." Historical and cultural institutions and forms are revealed to serve the interests of those who rule, who dominate. They are the means whereby the dominant class (e.g., European males) exploits the lower classes. What events of the past are worthy of recording is determined by whatever class is dominant at any given time.

Deconstruction was a logical byproduct of the disintegration of European culture and the growth of cultural pluralism or multiculturalism after World War II. Deconstructionists believe that agreement on a meaningful history was only possible during the nineteenth century when there was a cultural unity among the literate classes of Europe. Historians of different cultural backgrounds would naturally interpret history differently. How, for example, might the history of the nineteenth century appear if written by a middle-class European or an African immigrant? This "discovery" leads to the logical conclusion that one cannot justify requiring today's student to study the history of Western civilization. For the ever-increasing numbers of those whose cultural heritage is largely non-European and non-Western, European history is only the story of deeds done by "dead white males," told by their descendants who seek authority through perpetuating their memory.

Postmodernism

Of the *isms* that have enjoyed a vogue during the latter part of the twentieth century none is more difficult to define than "postmodernism." The term is actually old, having been used historically to characterize various trends in the arts. Since the 1980s, it has become the topic of culture talk shows on educational radio and television and the subject of academic conferences in all of the various disciplines. By the end of the century it took on the characteristics of, as one critic put it, "a trendy buzzword rapidly reaching its sell-by date."[7] At the turn of the twenty-first century, postmodernism and postmodernity were being used commonly to refer to the third and most recent period in a tripartite division of Western intellectual history into premodernity (the Medieval Synthesis), modernity (the Enlightenment Tradition), and postmodernity (the Enlightenment Tradition in disarray).

The term "postmodern" first appeared during the 1870s, when it was used to refer to what was later classified as postimpressionist art. During and following the Great War there was talk of a postmodern man emerging, that is, one who opted for nihilistic or amoral values, having rejected the established values of modern Western civilization. Arnold Toynbee in his monumental *A Study of History* (1947) and some cultural historians of the late 1950s used the term to describe the period after 1875, when the spread of industrialization challenged the established values of "modern" civilization. During the 1960s the term was used most often in reference to Pop Art.

The term really became fashionable during the last quarter of the twentieth century. Applied to the arts and architecture, it describes whatever is at the moment considered avant-garde, an eclectic style that combines elements of earlier, and seemingly incongruous styles which mirror the diversity and pluralism of the contemporary world. Postmodern art and architecture is a kind of collage in which the diverse elements have no unifying theme. It is similar to modernism in that it presents a fragmented view of reality. However, in contrast to modernism which lamented the loss of unity and meaning while holding forth the hope that such could be restored, postmodernism celebrates the fragmentation and loss of meaning. Beginning with the conviction that the world is meaningless, postmodernism sees no value in pretending otherwise. Rather it revels in the chaos and absurdity of everything.

Applied to the areas of thought and history, postmodernism is synonymous with posthumanism. It is a fundamental break with the Enlightenment Tradition (modernity) and the humanism at its core. Whereas the Enlightenment Tradition (some would go back to the Renaissance) emphasized the individual, reason, order, and meaning, postmodernism rejects all of the fundamental assumptions of Enlightenment thought as no longer tenable. Thus postmodernism includes structuralism and decon-struction, or poststructuralism.

As a term commonly used to refer to a contemporary view of reality, postmodernism is best understood when contrasted with premodernity and modernity. During premodernity, roughly the period from the High

---

7 Glenn Ward, *Postmodernism* (Chicago, 1997), 2.

Middle Ages to the Enlightenment (c. 1000–c. 1700), reality was an orderly universe in which there was meaning and purpose for both the individual and history. The individual was understood to be capable of understanding oneself and the universe he or she inhabited, because the individual was a special creation created in the image of his or her creator, that is, God. The experts were the theologians and philosophers who interpreted God's revelation in Scripture and in nature.

According to modernity, roughly the period from the Enlightenment to the mid-twentieth century (c. 1700–c. 1950), reality was an orderly universe of cause-and-effect natural law, but in a closed system, for God, the creator, was now a great architect, or watch maker. God created the universe-machine, but was not involved in its operation. His continued existence as creator, however, kept at bay the troubling questions of why anything exists, and whether or not there was any meaning for the individual or history. The experts were the scientists who could discover, interpret, and exploit natural law. Thus mankind had faith in progress and was optimistic about the future.

In postmodernity, reality is a universe of random chaos, without meaning for either the individual or history. There is no creator, no God, either as the God of biblical revelation or the great architect of Deism. There is only the illusion of order. The ultimate reality is impersonal matter. There are no experts to interpret reality, for reality is only what anyone says it is at any given moment. Any attempt at a metanarrative to explain reality is only the flawed expression of a particular subculture. Another way of looking at the contrast is to understand premodernity as the house that God built, modernity as the house that man built, and postmodernity as the house that never got built.

Culture

War is never kind to the physical manifestations of humanity's cultural achievements. History is impoverished by the loss of cultural monuments due to wars. What wonders of human creativity have disappeared in the flames of warfare? Barbarian hordes put fire and sword to classical civilization in western Europe, and the Vikings did likewise to the early centers of Western Christendom, often leaving behind only written memories. When the dust of World War II had settled and rebuilding began, cultural monuments were not neglected. Reconstruction of the great opera houses and concert halls were sometimes given priority over providing housing for the many homeless refugees. And such reconstruction was made as close to the original as possible. Postwar Europeans seemed to recognize that houses of culture were, like the cathedrals, reservoirs of the national spirit.

As with the philosophers, postwar culture, whether high or popular, struggled to make sense of recent events. The artists, musicians, poets, and writers displayed in their creative output the growing sense of alienation and despair, and the fragmentation that characterized European civilization in transition. It was a continuation of trends already present at the beginning of the century, with perhaps a new reality. Whether in the fine arts or popular culture, influences from the United States tended to dominate. In the fine arts, this was due in part to the prewar flight of creative individuals before the tidal wave of Nazi and communist oppression. The economic dominance of the United States and the presence of American military forces in western Europe assured that European popular culture would mimic American trends.

Art

The dominant artistic style after the war was what became known as abstract expressionism. Its roots were in the surrealism of the interwar era. Like the surrealists, the abstract expressionists looked to the psychoanalytic theories of Sigmund Freud and Carl Jung (1875–1961). Believing that faith in reason and rationalism had guided European culture and politics into the horrors of two world wars, they were seeking a truth beyond reason in the realm of the unconscious. Perhaps what was most characteristic of this artistic style, or concept, was the individualism of the artists associated with it. To really understand and appreciate it one would need to study the output of each individual artist. Such a task is beyond our attempt to identify and describe trends in postwar culture. Hence, we note that abstract expressionism was characterized by a lack of recognizable content and an emphasis upon gesture and/or color. The artist intended to communicate a reality that he or she felt by means of the unconscious, rather than the conscious will.

Abstract expressionism is often referred to as the "New York School," because many of its practitioners were European expatriates and formerly leading figures in surrealism in Europe. Among these were the Spaniard Salvador Dali (1904–1989), the Dutchman Piet Mondrian (1872–1944), and the German artists Josef Albers (1888–1976), Max Ernst (1891–1976), Hans Hofmann (1880–1966), and George Grosz (1893–1959). Max Ernst's third wife (for a period of three years) was the influential art collector and patron, Peggy Guggenheim (1898–1979). Ms. Guggenheim exhibited the works of the European expatriates, as well as new artists whom she "discovered" in her Art of This Century gallery in New York City. Among the latter was Jackson Pollock (1912–1956), arguably the best-known abstract expressionist. Pollock might produce a work of art

"Lobster Telephone (Red and Black)," a sculpture dated 1938 by Salvador Dali at the Philadelphia Museum of Art, 2005. AP/Wide World/Jacqueline Larma.

by merely walking around on a canvas stretched out on the floor, while dripping paint from cans.

It was perhaps inevitable that some artists would react against the abstract expressionists' emphasis on nonrepresentationalism. That reaction came in the mid-1950s with a return to representation. This artistic movement became known as "Pop Art." For these artists, art should depict the real postwar world obsessed with commercialism and mass culture. Influenced by Dadaism, the Pop artists looked to everyday objects and images of mass production for their subject matter—soup cans, comic strips, advertisements of consumer goods, and photographs of movie and rock stars. Although the Pop Art movement originated in England, America was once again the primary home of this movement that was in vogue during the 1960s and early 1970s. Among the leading Pop artists were Jasper Johns (1930–), Robert Rauschenberg (1925–), Roy Lichtenstein (1923–), and Andy Warhol (1930–1987), "The Prince of Pop."

When one thinks of Pop Art, the name of Andy Warhol immediately comes to mind. He burst onto the Pop Art scene in 1962, with an exhibition of paintings that depicted soup cans and Brillo soap boxes. The difference between abstract expressionism with its nonrepresentation and Pop Art's return to representation was noted by Warhol: "Pop artists did images that anybody walking down Broadway could recognize in a split second-comics, picnic tables, men's trousers, celebrities, shower curtains, refrigerators, Coke bottles—all the great modern things that the Abstract Expressionists tried so hard not to notice."[8] Unlike the abstract expressionists who were tuned into the problems of alienation and anxiety inherent in the postwar world as expressed by the existentialists and other philosophers, the Pop artists both celebrated and condemned the middle-class values of the consumer culture of the prosperous 1960s.

By the late 1960s and into the 1970s minimalism displaced Pop Art as the current fad. The minimalists tried to avoid all emotional content or personal meaning. Minimalist painters produced geometric patterns of color, as for example in Ellsworth Kelly's (1923–) *Red, Orange, White, Green, Blue* (1968), a succession of color stripes on canvas. Likewise, minimalist sculptors emphasized simple, symmetrical sculptures. The *Vietnam Veterans' Memorial* (1982) designed by Maya Ying Lin (1960–), and consisting of two polished black granite walls with the names of the 58,000 Americans who died in the Vietnam War, is perhaps the best representation of minimalist sculpture.

In the 1980s and 1990s artistic expression went in various directions, characterized by eclecticism. Some artists probed the limits of abstraction, while others chose a style known as the "new realism," reproducing objects with near photographic exactness. Eclecticism, a kind of "premeditated chaos," is one of the major characteristics of postmodern culture, which borrows at random from the past, but only to revive the past in fragments without any unifying continuity with the past or link to the future.

Europe at the beginning of the twenty-first century is no longer the center of the world, replaced as it is by a faceless, soulless internationalism. In the postmodern "Global Village," there is no accepted historic community or tradition to validate knowledge or artistic experience. In the confusion of a pluralism of cultures, there is no single historic tradition upon which an aesthetic standard can be established by which to distinguish good from bad art, or even what is art, anti-art, or just dabbling on canvas or the wall of a public restroom.

Divorced from any historical continuity, postmodern art is transient, and dependent upon the viewer interacting with it. Lacking any content or meaning, postmodern art has often become more spectacular in order to hold the viewer's attention. The Bulgarian-born Christo Javacheff (1935–) invented *empaquetage*, a technique by which he wrapped anything capable of being wrapped—e.g., the Pont Neuf, The Art Museum in Bern, trees along the Champs Elysees in Paris, or the Reichstag building in Berlin. Christo

---

8 Quoted in Marilyn Stokstad, *Art History* (New York: Harry N. Abrams, Inc., 1999), 130.

and wife Jeanne-Claude de Guillebon (1935–) exhibited *The Gates,* 7,500 saffron-colored fabric panels hanging on sixteen-foot high frames along twenty-three miles of New York's Central Park walkways, in January 2005. As to its message, said Jeanne-Claude, there is none: "It's only a work of art." Roland Baladi proposed transforming the Arc de Triumph in Paris into a giant snow globe. He planned to enclose it in a plastic dome with artificial snow blowing around inside the dome. It was a piece of conceptual art that, fortunately perhaps, remained a concept.

What is called "performance art" of the 1990s was a postmodern version of post–World War I Dadaism. The performance artists meant to be outlandish, to shock, or even offend the viewer. Some of their art was merely amusing, as for example Janine Antoni's (1962–) *Loving Care* (1993), in which she used "her own hair as a paintbrush to 'mop' a gallery floor with Clairol's Loving Care black hair dye,"[9] or Yeves Klein's (1928–1962) use of "living paintbrushes." While an audience listened to a chamber orchestra play a single note for twenty minutes, Klein, dressed in a tuxedo, directed several naked women covered in blue paint (patented as "Klein International Blue") to smear their bodies on a canvas stretched out on the floor of the Galerie Internationale d'Art Contemporaire in Paris.

Not all postmodern art was amusing. Some artists used religious or patriotic symbols or objects in ways many considered offensive or blasphemous. Displays of Robert Mapplethorpe's (1946–1989) photographs of homoerotic and sado-masichistic subject matter were so conroversial that some museums were forced to close their exhibits. Such provocative art brought forth a public outcry from conservatives for an end to the use of public funding to purchase or support the arts.

Literature, Drama, the Cinema, and Music

Postwar writers also tried to find meaning in a world that appeared increasingly without meaning. One of the themes, or issues, that they explored in light of the changing assumptions about truth and reality was the quest for social justice, a continuation of the preoccupation of such interwar writers as Bertolt Brecht and the American, John Steinbeck (1902–1968), both of whom continued to write after World War II, although their best work was done during the interwar period. Another theme, especially during the Cold War era, was an indictment of the new authoritarianism (totalitarianism, in Cold War terminology) of the Soviet Union. Some of the more effective of these writers were among those who had embraced Marxism (socialism, communism) during the early years of the Soviet experiment and now tried to come to grips with their disillusionment. Among these were the Italian

---

9 Perry, *Humanities*, vol. 2, 400.

Ignazio Silone (1900–1978), the Hungarian Arthur Koestler (1905–1983), and perhaps best known, the Englishman George Orwell (1903–1950).

George Orwell's two most memorable works were written right after the war's end and just before his premature death in 1950. *Animal Farm* (1945) and *1984* (1949) are the best known and most widely read indictments of the Soviet Union and totalitarianism. Yet, both end in despair, for although Orwell was deeply committed to the defense of human dignity and freedom, it is "Napoleon" and "Big Brother" who triumph over "Boxer" and Winston Smith. Clearly, Orwell saw those "eternal" values of Western Civilization in grave danger of being extinguished.

During the 1960s and 1970s criticism of the communist regime in the Soviet Union was expressed most effectively in the historical and autobiographical novels of the Russian author, Aleksandr Solzhenitsyn (1918–). In a series of novels beginning with *One Day in the Life of Ivan Denisovich* (1962) that won him the Nobel Prize in 1970 and expulsion from the Soviet Union in 1974, Solzhenitsyn charged that the atrocities committed under Stalin were not his responsibility alone, but must also be attributed to Lenin. After the collapse of the Soviet Union in 1991, Solzhenitsyn returned to Russia in 1994. Since then he has become a harsh critic of the "new " Russia. In an address given at Harvard University in 1978 ("A World Split Apart"), and again in an address given on the occasion of his receiving the Templeton Prize in 1983 ("Men Have Forgotten God"), Solzhenitsyn criticized the West in general for having lost the will to defend the values that made Western Civilization the envy of the world.

In postwar Germany, the two Nobel laureates Heinrich Böll (1917–1985) and Günter Grass (1927–) explored the damage done to the values of European civilization by the war and the failure of the postwar generation to come to grips with its past, or to resist the temptation to allow West Germany's economic prosperity to numb the nation's collective conscience. Böll was a prolific writer of novels, short stories, and nonfiction. The best known of his novels are *Adam Where Art Thou?* (1959), *Billiards at Half-Past Nine* (1959), *The Clown* (1968) and *Group Portrait with Lady* (1971).

Günter Grass, like Böll, wanted postwar Germans living amidst economic prosperity to remember that they once embraced the darkness of National Socialism. In three novels know as the Danzig Trilogy—*The Tin Drum* (1959), *Cat and Mouse* (1961), and *Dog Years* (1963)—Grass tried to understand the attraction that Nazism once held and the power of West Germany's postwar economic miracle to aid in suppressing and forgetting the past. *The Tin Drum* is a particularly disturbing novel that was made into an equally disturbing motion picture.

Art and literature were one means by which philosophical issues and changing world views were communicated to a mass audience. We have noted above how existentialism was communicated more through the novels of Camus and Sartre than through their nonfiction. The theater, the cinema, and music were also powerful means by which serious philosophical statements reached a wider audience. An example from the theater is what was known as the Theater of the Absurd.

The Theater of the Absurd took its name from Albert Camus's description of the human predicament as essentially "absurd." The message of these dramatists who enjoyed a vogue during the 1950s and 1960s was that of existentialism. They portray the individual as inhabiting a meaningless universe in which he or she feels increasingly alone, isolated, bewildered, threatened, even terrified, by an all pervasive sense of angst, yet desperately hoping against all hope to find in oneself some meaning. Among those associated with the Theater of the Absurd were Eugene Ionesco (1912–1994), Fernando Arrabal (1932–), Arthur Adamov (1908–1970), and Samuel Beckett (1906–1989).

Samuel Beckett's *Waiting for Godot* (1952) is the best known example of the Theater of the Absurd. The play portrays two tramps who spend their days waiting for the coming of one Godot, a mysterious individual who may not even exist. Is he like Nietzsche's god, only a belief, but one whose hoped for appearance gives the two otherwise hopeless tramps a reason to go on living? *Waiting for Godot* remains one of the most often performed plays of the postwar theater. Perhaps it is because it, like few others, communicates so well the dilemma of humanity adrift in a postmodern universe.

The European cinema, unlike the American film industry driven by the demands of a mass market, served as a medium through which the search for meaning in an alienated world could be shared with a wider audience. European filmmakers like Ingmar Bergman (1918–), Alain Res-nais (1922–), Michelangelo Antonioni (1912–), Federico Fellini (1920–1993), and Luis Bunuel (1900–1983) powerfully explored the complexities of life in a postwar, postmodern world. Bergman's films are said to be filled with "Nordic angst and gloom."[10] The central characters in Bergman's films are individuals "who wonder whether they are in this world for some reason. They feel themselves alienated from others, meaningless entities walking around on the earth for a few years and then vanishing into endless night."[11] During an interview in which he discussed the making of *The Silence* (1963), Bergman said that he had reached the conclusion that God is dead, and therefore the universe is silent.

Classical music after 1945 developed mainly in two directions. One school, sometimes called the "structuralists," emphasized ever greater

10 James A, Winders, *European Culture Since 1848: From Modern to Postmodern and Beyond* (New York: Palgrave, 2001), 143.
11 Richard Janaro and Thelma Altshuler, *The Art of Being Human* (New York, 2003), 359.

The Seventh Seal, 1957, directed by Ingmar Bergman. Above: Bengt Ekerot as Death. © Svensk Filmindustri/Photofest.

complexity in their compositions. The second school, more in tune with the philosophical assumptions of postmodernism, sought to compose music involving a technique employing random chance. French composer Pierre Boulez (1925–) exemplifies the former, while the American, John Cage, is the best example of the latter.

Boulez's compositions are characterized by their extremely complex structure that gives the composer total control over every element of the music. Building upon the serialism and twelve-tone technique pioneered by Arnold Schoenberg (1874–1951), Boulez aimed at creating a musical structure, the effect of which is "to eliminate any sense of traditional melody, harmony, or counterpoint along with the emotions they evoke."[12] This effort to remove the human element from music led to compositions of "electronic music," beginning in the 1950s.

In electronic music, sounds are arranged, or "ordered," by a computer, and then played on an electronic oscillator, rather than traditional musical instruments. The invention of the synthesizer in 1955 by engineers at RCA greatly simplified the composition (or production) of electronic music. Karl-

12 Cunningham and Reich, *Culture and Values*, 566.

heinz Stockhausen (1928–), a major composer of electronic music, chose to combine electronic music with traditional orchestras in, for example, his composition, *Mixtur* (1965). The structuralists, whether following the example of Boulez's complex serialization or the more "programmed" innovations of electronic music, remained faithful to the most basic premise of Western music, that is, composers create their music according to rules that enable them to communicate with their listeners. This was not true of the second school which turned to creating musical compositions according to random chance.

So-called "music of chance" may be illustrated by the career of John Cage. Cage was inspired by the artist Marcel Duchamp, known for his "ready-mades," and Zen Buddhism, especially the *I Ching*, or *Book of Changes*. Like Duchamp, Cage believed that art and music exist all around us. It does not necessarily originate in the artist's mind. Cage made use of "ready-made sounds" by simply recording the random noises in the surrounding environment. His best known piece is one titled *4′33″* (1952). The pianist approaches the piano, sits down, and, without ever touching the keys, turns the pages of a nonexistent score at random intervals. The actual music of *4′33″* is the random noises produced by the audience. Cage believed that music should reflect the random chaos of the universe that we inhabit.

Popular Culture

Not surprisingly, American tastes and America's spirit of commercialism were major forces shaping popular culture after World War II. The fear, expressed already in the 1920s by novelist Wyndham Lewis (1886–1957), that European culture would become "de-civilized" by its "Americanization" as the world became smaller, appears to have become a reality at the end of the twentieth century. The reasons for American cultural "imperialism" are varied and perhaps not unexpected.

Post–World War II American popular culture offered a very seductive model when compared to the war-scarred landscape of postwar Europe. The mystique of America as a land of prosperity, opportunity, and an exciting, fast-paced lifestyle grew in influence during the 1950s. American consumerism was associated in the minds of the European masses with prosperity, youth, popularity, glamor, and the latest fashions. Increasingly, Europe's youth took their cue from what they saw in America's movies and television programs, or heard in its popular music. The presence of American troops in Europe after 1945, and the broadcasts of the American Armed Forces Radio Network, meant that there was little, if any, real difference between the American hit parade and that of any European nation.

The extent to which postwar European society was shaped in response to the influence of American consumerism would be difficult to overstate. It was particularly true following the collapse of communism in eastern Europe. As the former Soviet Union became a graphic example of the failure of communism, it no longer served as a model for Europeans wanting to build a new future. America, throughout the twentieth century the flag ship of capitalism, and after 1989–1991, the apparent victor in the century-long struggle between capitalism and communism, became the model (for better or worse) for Europe's future. By the end of the twentieth century the symbols of America's commercial dominance could be seen everywhere. The "golden arches" of McDonald's fast food restaurants, and other logos of American franchises like Starbuck's Coffee, dotted the European landscape and threatened to overwhelm national tastes, much as the franchising of America itself largely destroyed regional tastes. More tourists reportedly visit the Disney theme park built outside Paris in 1992, than visit the traditional monuments of France's cultural and historical heritage.

Rock music and the popular cinema were the two main vehicles for the Americanization of European (even world) culture. As with jazz, that other American musical import that swept across Europe between the two world wars, "rock 'n' roll" had roots in the African-American subculture. It was a blend of a variety of popular American music genres, including rhythm and blues, jazz, gospel, country and western, and folk music. However, it was two white performers, Bill Haley (1925–1981)and Elvis Presley (1935–1977), who made rock 'n' roll the music of the new international youth culture during its "Golden Decade" (1954–1963).

Europe's youth were attracted to American rock 'n' roll music as western Europe began to enjoy a measure of economic prosperity. A measure of economic independence allowed European youth to break free of traditional class restraints and indulge their taste for American popular music. What they found in rock 'n' roll was a spirit of revolt and overt sexuality. England's "rockers" donned black leather jackets and rode motorcycles in imitation of their new American idols like Elvis Presley, the "King," and movie star Marlon Brando (1924–2004).

In 1964, leadership in popular music passed temporarily to the English groups, epitomized by The Beatles, who emerged from the working-class bars of Liverpool, England, to chart a new course for popular music. The success of their song "I Want to Hold Your Hand" (1964), the most popular rock hit since Elvis' "All Shook Up" (1957), launched them into superstardom. In February, 1964, they premiered on the *Ed Sullivan Show*, a kind of rite of passage for any popular entertainer, individual or group, who aspired to stardom in America. Fans around the world held a vigil in

December 1964, when drummer Ringo Starr underwent a tonsillectomy. The appearance of their album *Sgt. Pepper's Lonely Hearts Club Band* in 1967, the cover of which was believed to contain hidden messages about the alleged death of band member Paul McCartney, raised the group to enduring cult status. In 1965, Queen Elizabeth II bestowed upon each member of The Beatles the honor of MBE, Member of the British Empire.

The rock groups that followed the Beatles looked and openly lived the rebellious and promiscuous lifestyle they sang about. An example was the Rolling Stones, a rock group that debuted in February 1963 at the Crawdaddy in Richmond, England. Whereas the Beatles' public image was that of clean-cut musicians in mohair jackets with ties and neatly groomed hair, the Rolling Stones were antisocial outlaws in both appearance and behavior. They sang lyrics so explicit that they were sometimes banned. They openly smoked marijuana, abused drugs, hosted wild parties that included nudity, and even were alleged to practice Satanism. The Rolling Stones quickly achieved cult status in the world of rock music, and, despite the questionable quality of their music when compared to the Beatles, were still touring and performing before large crowds in 2003.[13]

Rock music spoke to, or one might say, expressed the soul of post–World War II's youth. The themes found in the lyrics of rock music were the themes of the postwar generation—feelings of isolation, hunger for love, and sexual liberation. By expressing those universal themes rock music had a wide appeal that helped to restore a sense of community for a generation of youth who felt acutely the increasing fragmentation of the postmodern world. Although there were "native" European clones for American and British rock stars, rock culture bore a definite "made in America" stamp.

The evolution of popular music reflected three cultural trends—the changing standards of public morality, the ever increasing role of commercial hype, and a cross-fertilization of cultural influences from around the world that were absorbed into what was becoming by the dawn of the new millennium a popular music that reflected a global culture.

When Elvis Presley made his first television appearance in 1956, his gyrating pelvis was considered so risque that viewers were allowed to see him only from the waist up. During the 1960s the Beatles dared use only suggestive language in reference to the emerging drug culture and relaxed sexual norms. By the mid-1970s British "punk rock" performers like the Sex Pistols were openly and deliberately offensive, even vulgar, in both their performance style and the lyrics of their songs. The 1970s also saw the birth among urban African-American teenagers of rap music. Rap, a kind of chanted poetry that satirizes racism, black culture, and other rappers,

13 Paul McCartney (1942–) of the Beatles, Joan Baez (1941–), Bob Dylan (1941–) and Judy Colllins (1939–) were among the "great ones" of the classic age of folk and rock music, who were still touring and performing before live audiences in 2003.

generally spoke openly and graphically of life in the urban ghetto, of drug use, and of sexual promiscuity as if it were a competitive sport.

The Sex Pistols exemplified the commercialization of popular culture. They were "manufactured" by their promoters as a product to be marketed for profit. This vulgar commercialization was increasingly characteristic of popular music. Styles of music, like differing styles of jeans, were created and marketed with an attentive eye on what might sell. The names of groups or individual artists passed in and out of style like the logos on jean pockets.

Technological advances made possible the cross-fertilization and international marketing of different musical styles. Musical styles from around the world were imported and synthesized. Indian sitar music was popularized by Ravi Shankar (1920–). Reggae, a blending of electric bass and guitars with organ, piano, and drums that originated among the poor of Jamaica, introduced a Caribbean influence into popular music. The appearance of music videos and live transcontinental television broadcasts (e.g., *Aloha From Hawaii* with Elvis in 1973 and the famous Live Aid show in 1985) demonstrated that rock had become the world's choice in popular music and the chief medium of popular culture.

The cinema, like rock music, did much to create a common popular culture. European directors, often enjoying government subsidies, continued to dominate the motion picture genre commonly referred to as the "art film." These were "gourmet" films intended for a very small but discriminating audience. The popular cinema, like popular music, was dominated by American-made action films, comedies, and sentimental romances, heavy on the entertainment, but making very little demand on the viewer's intellect. As the growing popularity of television lured more and more people away from the movie houses, Hollywood turned during the 1950s to blockbuster epics like *The Ten Commandments* (1956), *Around the World in 80 Days* (1956), and *Ben Hur* (1957).

American dominance of the silver screen continued during the last quarter of the twentieth century and into the twenty-first century.[14] American filmmakers like Francis Ford Coppola (1939–), the *Godfather* (1972), and George Lucas (1944–), *Star Wars* (1972) and *Raiders of the Lost Ark* (1981) made lavish blockbuster adventure films that enjoyed international popularity. No filmmaker of the late twentieth or early twenty-first centuries could trump Steven Spielberg (1946–) in box office receipts or artistic achievement. Spielberg produced films such as *E. T. The Extra-Terrestrial* (1982) that warmed the heart and reduced movie goers to tears, as well as serious films such as *The Color Purple* (1985) and *Schindler's List* (1993) that raised the social consciousness of his audience.

14 Hollywood did not have total control of the world market in actions films. Britain's "James Bond, 007" film series based upon the best selling fiction of Ian Fleming (1909–1964) achieved international success comparable to any American produced film series.

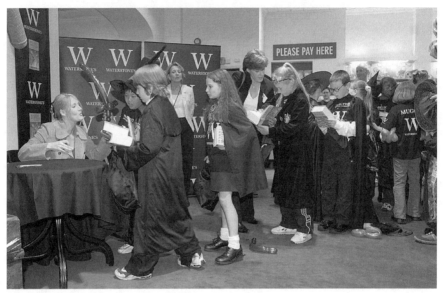

The author of the Harry Potter books, J. K. Rowling (left), signs her books for children dressed as characters from her series, 2003. AP/Wide World/ Ian Torrance.

The rapid spread of television from the 1950s on and the development of new technology such as video tapes (VHS), digital video disks (DVD), and cable and satellite television networks assisted creation of a universal pop culture. Since American commercialism was the major driving force behind the new technology, the culture that it nurtured reflected that of middle-class American youth. American films and television programs were now available to virtually unlimited audiences, and American entertainment stars became international stars. Lucille Ball (1911–1989), Bill Cosby (1937–), Peter Falk (1927–), the bungling lovable detective, and many others were as familiar to Europeans as Mickey Mouse.

We began this chapter with the postwar intellectuals searching for meaning amidst the physical ruins of European civilization at the end of World War II. Those intellectuals who pondered the meaning of history, and of life, concluded that human beings were adrift, alone in a cold and meaningless universe. At the end of the century and the beginning of the new millennium, there were signs that the masses did not agree with that conclusion. There is evidence in the popular culture that people did not accept the conclusion that a human being is only a cosmic cipher in a cold, dark universe. This could be seen in the phenomenal popularity, both in book publishing and the cinema, of two megamyths—the *Lord of the Rings*

15 *Left Behind* (1995), a science fiction series based loosely on the biblical book of Revelation may be cited as another example. Definitely a distinctively American product, and lacking any literary merit, it has been a phenomenal best-selling series internationally.

trilogy by J. R. R. Tolkien (1892–1973) and the seven-volume Harry Potter series by J. K. Rowling (1965–)—both British authors.[15]

Both the *Lord of the Rings* and the Harry Potter series are adventure stories centered around a cosmic duel between good and evil. Upon the outcome of each struggle, both of which affirm the ultimate triumph of good, hangs the future of the universe. Tolkien, an Oxford professor of medieval literature, conceived of his story and worked on it during the interwar years. He was a member of the Inklings, a group of writers associated with C. S. Lewis (1898–1963), a professor of medieval and renaissance literature at Oxford University. J. K. Rowling, who published her first Harry Potter novel in 1997, has acknowledged that she was influenced by her reading of Tolkien and Lewis. Both series have broken all sales records in the publishing industry worldwide. Both have been made into motion pictures that likewise have established new records for attendance. Clearly, though the intellectual dream spinners may be adrift in a fog, the average man or woman living under the influence of European civilization is living in a world of hope, a world in which the future is brighter than the past.

Suggested Books and Films

William Barrett, *Irrational Man* (1958). Still regarded as the best introduction to existentialist philosophy, it discusses the views of Kierkegaard, Nietzsche, Heidegger, and Sartre.

Norman F. Cantor, *The American Century: Varieties of Culture in Modern Times* (1997). A provocative look at the cultural history of the twentieth century, which focuses on Europe and the United States.

Louis Giannetti and Scott Eyman, *Flashback: A Brief History of Film*, 4th ed. (2000). A well written, richly illustrated, popular history of "fiction movies," which views film as "both art and an industry."

Romano Guardini, *The End of the Modern World* (2001). A contemplation of the condition of modern man in the wake of two world wars, the Holocaust, and other horrors of the postwar world.

John Lukacs, *At the End of an Age* (2002). Believing that we are living at the end of an age that began with the Renaissance and is often called "modern," Lukacs examines what it means to live in a new age of post-modernism.

The Rolling Stone Illustrated History of Rock and Roll (1992). A comprehensive history of the musical styles and artists of rock and roll.

Roland N. Stromberg, *After Everything: Western Intellectual History Since 1945* (1975). A somewhat dated but very useful introduction to the main themes of Western thought after WW II.

Aloha from Hawaii with Elvis, 1973, 1991.

Chronology

1990	Czechoslovakia's "Velvet Divorce" results in the formation of the Czech Republic and the Republic of Slovakia
	Unification of Germany; Kohl reelected chancellor in the first free all-German elections since 1932
1991	John Major replaces Margaret Thatcher as leader of the British Conservative Party and as Prime Minister
	First Gulf War
	Dissolution of the Warsaw Treaty Organization
	Attempted coup in the Soviet Union; Gorbachev resigns as president of the Soviet Union, which is dissolved at the end of the year
	Slovenia and Croatia leave the Yugoslav Federation; beginning of the disintegration of Yugoslavia
1992	Bosnia withdraws from the Yugoslav Federation
	Maastricht Treaty sets the process by which the EC will become the EU
1993	European Community becomes the European Union (EU)
1995	Austria, Finland, and Sweden join the EU
	Dayton (Ohio) Agreement establishes a loosely federated Bosnia and ends the civil war in Bosnia (1992–1995)
1997	British Labour Party under Tony Blair wins the election 1998 Helmut Kohl defeated by Gerhard Schröder; Germany governed by a Social-Democratic/Green coalition
1999	Introduction of the Euro
	NATO admits Poland, Hungary, the Czech Republic
	War in Kosovo
2001	9/11 attacks on the World Trade Center in New York and the Pentagon in Washington, D.C., by members of Al-Qaeda
2002	U.S. invasion of Afghanistan
2003	Second Gulf War (U.S. invades Iraq and drives Saddam Hussein from power)
2004	EU enlarged by the inclusion of ten new members
	NATO adds seven new members

12
Charting a New Course: Europe in the 1990s and Beyond

THE FALL OF THE BERLIN WALL on November 9, 1989, symbolized for many the end of the Cold War. Pictures of happy East Berliners streaming past the Wall into West Berlin and being greeted by ecstatic West Berliners with champagne, flowers, and bananas flashed around the world. Within a year the German Democratic Republic no longer existed. At the end of 1991 the Soviet Union disappeared, replaced by fifteen republics. The Cold War was over; statesmen supposedly were putting the New World Order in place.

Some observers insisted that not only was the Cold War over but that the United States had won it. Ideas varied as to how the United States had triumphed. Some thought that President Ronald Reagan, by reviving the arms race, had forced the Soviet Union to bankrupt itself through its efforts to keep up. Another popular view, closer to the mark, is that the Soviet Union simply imploded, brought down by an aging, bloated, and uncom-petitive bureaucracy that resisted Gorbachev's attempts to reform the system to the bitter end. Triumphalism aside, it seems most likely that no one won the Cold War. While a great power rivalry between the two most powerful states at the end of World War II was inevitable, the decades of nuclear tensions and the billions of dollars spent on the arms race were unnecessary.

Cold War and Détente

In the 1960s, the idea of a Cold War seemed to be fading. The Cuban Missile Crisis in 1962 had been something of a wakeup call for both superpowers. Furthermore, the Berlin Wall (erected in 1961), while an ugly scar dividing Berlin, resolved the German Questions in a pragmatic if somewhat crude way. Willy Brandt's *Ostpolitik* (see Chapter 10 for more details) was a more elegant way of guaranteeing the postwar borders of the Soviet Union, Poland, and East Germany, and regularizing the status of East and West Berlin.

A measure of how détente worked could be seen in events in Vietnam. Although both the Soviet Union and the People's Republic of China (PRC)

249

worked to keep North Vietnam from being overwhelmed by the American support of South Vietnam, they were careful to limit support and avoided any direct confrontation with the United States. By the same token, the United States refrained from any actions that might cause either the Soviet Union or the PRC to intervene on a large scale. The Vietnam War was a "proxy war" for the Soviet Union and the PRC. While the United States had its proxy in South Vietnam, American involvement increased annually from 1964 and the Gulf of Tonkin Resolution, which granted the president the authority to wage war without a formal declaration of war, to 1968 and the Tet Offensive. Under President Richard Nixon (1913–1994), the United States tried to end the war on favorable terms. It only succeeded in signing a treaty with North Vietnam in 1973 that provided what some termed a "decent interval" before North Vietnam conquered South Vietnam. Running parallel with the American involvement in the Vietnam War were extensive and successful negotiations with both the Soviet Union and the PRC. It seemed through much of the 1970s that the great powers had found a way around the Cold War and had settled into something close to the great power rivalries that had characterized European history over many centuries.

The Strategic Arms Limitation Treaty (SALT) talks were the most promising development in the period of détente. The first set of negotiations, held between 1969 and 1973, was successful in banning work on defensive missile systems (antiballistic missiles) but was unable to place a limit on offensive systems. A second SALT agreement was negotiated between 1973 and 1979, and even signed, but it fell victim to the renewal of Cold War tensions in 1979.

The Helsinki Accords, based on a series of meetings from 1973 to 1975 of the thirty-five nations making up the Conference on Security and Cooperation in Europe (CSCE)—the United States, Canada, and all the European states except Albania, appeared to be a turning point in the Cold War. They dealt with three different areas (or "Baskets"). The first concerned peace and security, confirming postwar borders, and setting up Confidence and Security Building Measures (CSBMs). The second focused on social and economic affairs and proposed cultural exchanges, trade missions, and technology transfers. The third, emphasized by the West, took up the issue of human rights, specifically family reunification and the free flow of information and ideas. Subsequent meetings up to 1990 accomplished little other than name-calling. Disappointment with the realities of the Helsinki process was probably one factor in the Soviet Union's turn away from détente in the late 1970s.

Soviet adventurism in Afghanistan and elsewhere has already been mentioned (in Chapter 10). It was matched early in the Reagan presidency

(1981–1988) by a return to a primitive Cold War mentality. President Reagan characterized the Soviet Union as the "evil empire" and saw Nicaragua and El Salvador as outposts of the worldwide communist movement. The invasion of the tiny island of Grenada in 1983, ostensibly to prevent Cuban communists from building an airport that could accommodate military jets, would have been comical except for the fact that people were killed or wounded in the effort. Eventually, however, Reagan was charmed by Gorbachev and largely converted to the idea that the Cold War could be dismantled. Only Reagan's failure to understand Soviet anxieties about his pet project, the Strategic Defense Initiative (SDI), the so-called "Star Wars" effort to create a satellite-based missile defense system, prevented more rapid progress from being made. Largely thanks to Gorbachev's insights and efforts, the Cold War was rapidly winding down by 1989, a factor of incalculable importance both for the revolutions of that year and for the successful effort to unify Germany the following year.

German Unification

The German Democratic Republic, or East Germany (GDR), was the best positioned of all the former satellites, whether it remained independent or chose to unify with the Federal Republic, or West Germany (FRG). Many within the old Socialist Unity Party, which renamed itself the Party of Democratic Socialism (PDS) in December 1989, wanted to remain independent and to reform the political and economic systems of the GDR. Most of those active in the citizens' movement, members of the New Forum or Democracy Awakening, for example, also hoped to reform the old systems. By December, however, the majority of those who participated in the demonstrations in Leipzig, Berlin, Dresden, and other cities and towns of the GDR were beginning to think about the possibility of quickly gaining a western standard of living. Even after the Wall opened, East Germans continued to leave in large numbers for West Germany. The average East German wondered why he or she should be part of a new socialist experiment when the tried-and-true West German approach was readily available.

To his credit, Helmut Kohl understood early on that a possibility existed of bringing East and West Germany together in the very near future. He daringly decided to take the lead and to support a process of rapid unification early in 1990. With very little support from his west European colleagues and with Gorbachev and the Soviet Union still a question mark, this was a brave move. Kohl did have the backing of President George H. W. Bush (1924–) of the United States. He also felt the continued influx of East German refugees into West Germany would eventually work a hard-

A demonstration in the streets of Leipzig, November 7, 1989. The banner at right reads "Away with the Leading Role of the SED" (Communist Party). An earlier demonstration in Leipzig, on October 9, is often noted as the beginning of the Revolution of 1989 in East Germany. AP/Wide World.

ship on the West German economy. However, Kohl underestimated the difficulty of restructuring the East German economy and raising living standards to West German levels.

The first free elections in the GDR, in March 1990, were for the *Volkskammer* (the People's Chamber, the parliament of the GDR). The main issue was unification. West German politicians campaigned for their East German counterparts. The Christian Democrats (CDU) formed a coalition with several smaller parties and strongly supported the idea of rapid unification. They won a stunning victory over the Social Democrats, who had been lukewarm toward unification. The new government under Lothar de Maizière (1940–) plunged into negotiations for the introduction of the Deutschmark into East Germany in July. Kohl contributed a crucial element to the unification process through a meeting with Gorbachev. The meeting resulted in Germany agreeing to pay the Soviet Union a large sum and the Soviet Union not only giving its blessings to unification but also agreeing to a timetable for withdrawing its troops from the eastern part of Germany. Further negotiations between East and West Germans that summer led to unification in October and to the first free elections in all of Germany since November 1932. Kohl and the coalition of Christian Democrats and Free Democrats (FDP) easily beat the Social Democrats. In the east, only a few delegates from the PDS were elected. Almost no one from the citizen movements was elected. Although some Germans complained that the GDR had been "annexed," unification had been accomplished in less than a year from the beginning of the German Revolution of 1989. Germany began to pour billions of marks annually into the east to undo the damage done by the old regime and to bring the infrastructure up to West German standards.

The unification of Germany led also to full sovereignty. In addition to negotiations between East Germany and West Germany, there were the "2 + 4" talks involving the two Germanies and the four ex-Allies from World War II, the Soviet Union, Britain, France, and the United States. The major result was a treaty that formally put an end to any remaining rights held by the four powers in Germany.

The whole process changed Europe in profoundly important ways. In many respects European history since 1990 has been an attempt to deal with the various ramifications of German unification. The new Germany is larger and far stronger economically than any other European state. A Franco-German partnership in Europe now depends not on the relatively equal weight of the two countries but more on Germany's conscious efforts to maintain it. More than ever before, it seems important to Europeanize Germany in various ways. (See the latter part of the chapter for a discussion of some of these efforts.)

The Soviet Union Disappears

For many in the Soviet Union, the events of 1989 and 1990 appeared only to underline the decline of the Soviet Union as a world power. President Bush's "New World Order," as it took form in the crusade against Iraq, the first Gulf War in 1991, appeared to offer the Soviet Union only the role of junior partner. In the Soviet Union itself, Gorbachev had not succeeded in making perestroika work in the economy. In fact, the economy seemed stuck between two systems, communism and capitalism. The Soviet economy would probably have run into serious trouble even without perestroika, but Gorbachev's experiments gave people something to complain about.

While Gorbachev maneuvered politically, seemingly moving well to the right in 1990, Boris Yeltsin emerged as a rising political star. Elected president of the Russian Republic, Yeltsin (1931–) began immediately to enhance the power of the republics of the Soviet Union and to decrease the power of the central government. By the late summer of 1991, he and his fellow presidents of the republics of the Soviet Union appeared to have achieved success. A treaty setting up a federal arrangement that would have given the republics a good deal more authority was scheduled to be signed. Gorbachev had swung back to the left and looked ready in August to agree to the treaty.

Before the treaty could be signed, members of Gorbachev's own government staged a coup. They placed Gorbachev, on vacation in the Crimea, under house arrest. Yeltsin, in his capacity as president of the Russian Republic (which made up the major part of the Soviet Union), defied the coup from the Soviet White House, the building housing the parliament, in Moscow. The coup leaders lacked direction and nerve. The military refused to move against Yeltsin and his supporters. Television coverage worldwide by the ubiquitous CNN (Cable News Network) worked against the coup and for Yeltsin.

After the collapse of the coup, Gorbachev returned to power in Moscow, but his days were numbered. By the end of the year, the Soviet Union had been dissolved. Several republics, Estonia, Latvia, and Lithuania, went their own way. The remaining republics grouped together in the Commonwealth of Independent States (CIS). By far the most powerful was the Russian Republic under Boris Yeltsin. Other important republics were Belarus, Ukraine, Georgia, and Kazakhstan.

Seventy-four years after the October Revolution, the Soviet Union ceased to exist. In many important ways, however, the Russian Republic continues to play the same role in the world. While it has cooperated with the United States in the important task of disarmament, especially in the area of nuclear weapons, it regards itself as a major power with its own set of interests and objectives. To date, it has been relatively forbearing within the old Soviet Union, intervening on occasion in Georgian affairs and in the affairs of some of the Central Asian republics, and fighting a bloody war against the Chechens within Russia itself. It has been periodically upset by NATO's efforts to expand to the east, but it has also enjoyed playing a role in the G-7 (Group of Seven) meetings of the major industrial states.

Under Yeltsin, Russia made only limited progress toward a working democracy. President from 1991 to 1999, he soon tarnished the brave image he had established during the coup of 1991. In a bizarre turn of events, Yeltsin, in a quarrel with the Congress of People's Deputies in 1993, sent tanks to fire on the [Russian] White House in order to quash attempts by deputies to unseat him. Yeltsin led Russia into a disastrous war against Chechnya, a former republic of the Soviet Union located in southwestern Russia.

The elections of 1996 nonetheless resulted in a victory for Yeltsin. His most serious competition came from the leader of the Communist Party, Gennady Zyuganov (1944–), who forced Yeltsin into a run-off election. Vladimir Zhirinovsky (1946–), a rabid nationalist and anti-Semite, gained serious support from the extreme right. Some observers of the elections believed that holding elections and running a parliamentary system, despite obvious ups and downs, constituted an important step forward. Others pointed to the corruption of the system and the arbitrary use of power as indications that democracy had not yet taken root.

A kind of robber baron capitalism characterized the 1990s in Russia. It was most successful in Moscow and a few other major Russian cities. There was also the disturbing presence of a large, well-organized Russian mafia, which operated abroad as well as in Russia. Under Yeltsin, the economy shrank from a Gross Domestic Product (GDP) of $1.1 trillion to $193.2 billion. Insiders managed to grab valuable state holdings for pennies on the dollar. Finally, in 1998, Russia defaulted on its international debt and its currency (the ruble) collapsed.

On the last day of 1999, Yeltsin resigned. He picked a former KGB colonel, Vladimir Putin (1952–) to replace him as temporary president. In the 2000 elections, Putin was elected president. To date he has done surprisingly well. The economy has improved and politics have stabilized, now that the mercurial Yeltsin is no longer on the scene. Putin appears to be moving to break the power of the economic oligarchy. In March 2004, he won re-election as president for a second term with 71 percent of the vote. According to the constitution of the Russian Republic, he is not eligible to serve a third term.

The economy, although improved, is deeply troubled. It depends heavily on exports of commodities such as oil, natural gas, and timber. For many Russians, the market economy has little to offer. Often unpaid for months at a time, unable to deal with high prices and different ways of conducting business, it is no surprise that some yearn for the old days when the Soviet Union was a major power and life was predictable if also drab. Simply put, Russia is still not fully a part of the new European system. It retains the capacity to surprise and will likely remain Europe's wild card.

The Disintegration of Yugoslavia

The disappearance of the Soviet Union was a more or less natural process. By contrast, the disintegration of Yugoslavia was largely the work of two political leaders willing to put their own power above the welfare of the people of their countries. The better known of the two and the first to fan the fires of ethnic hatred was Slobodan Milosevic (1941–), the leader of

Serbia. The other was Franjo Tudjman (1922–1999), president of Croatia, someone not generally recognized for his part in the Yugoslav tragedy.

It was perhaps remarkable enough that the delicate, complicated governmental system of Yugoslavia survived the death in 1980 of its founder, Marshall Tito, by more than a decade. By 1990, however, Milosevic, in order to maintain power in Serbia and also to begin turning Yugoslavia into a greater Serbia, played the nationalism card, i.e., played on Serbian fears of other ethnic groups, first in Kosovo, an autonomous province of Serbia with an Albanian majority, and then in Vojvodina, another autonomous province of Serbia, in this case with a large Hungarian population. Croatia and Slovenia met these challenges to the federal structure of Yugoslavia with their own versions of emotional appeals to ethnic separatism.

In June 1991, Slovenia and Croatia declared independence. Germany contributed to the developing conflagration by recognizing the two states diplomatically, despite the fact that other members of the European Community (EC) wanted to withhold recognition in the hopes of keeping Yugoslavia intact. Serbia's response was to use the Yugoslav army against the two republics. Slovenia, favorably situated both in terms of geographic location and a homogenous population, was able to defend itself and escape the civil war. Croatia and Serbia, not for the first time in this century, went to war with one another. For many Serbs, memories of World War II and the activities of Croatian fascists in the *Ustasha* were still strong.

The war became even more complicated the following year when Bosnia declared its independence. Bosnia had once been a model of the possibilities for a harmonious existence of Serbs, Croatians, and Muslims. The population spoke the same language, Serbo-Croatian, although Serbs would use the Cyrillic alphabet to write it while Croatians would use the Roman alphabet. They differed, of course, in terms of religion, with the Serbs belonging to the Orthodox faith, Croats to the Catholic religion, and the Bosnian Muslims to Islam. Up to 1992, however, despite differences, there had been a great deal of intermarriage and mixed neighborhoods were common.

The Serbian siege of Bosnian-Muslim Sarajevo, which only a few years before had been the site of a Winter Olympics, became the centerpiece of the Yugoslav tragedy. "Ethnic cleansing," an euphemism which meant in reality anything from forcibly driving a particular group away from an area to systematic and repeated rape of women to the torture and killing of men, entered as a new term into the vocabulary of the world.

Efforts by the EC to negotiate a settlement or even to find a common position were for the most part unsuccessful. The United Nations sent a peacekeeping force, which was largely ineffectual to the extent that it did not actually work to the advantage of the Serbs. In 1994, however, Serbia distanced itself from the Bosnian Serbs because of the effects of economic sanctions against it. NATO began to weigh in with air strikes against the Bosnian Serbs. Finally, in 1995, the combatants reluctantly agreed to the Dayton (Ohio) Agreement calling for a loosely federated Bosnia. Troops from the United States and from other NATO nations arrived soon after to enforce the agreement.

The last act of the Yugoslav tragedy came in Kosovo. It was here, in 1987, that Milosevic had begun his nationalistic campaign. While civil war raged elsewhere in Yugoslavia, the Serbs stripped Kosovo of its autonomous status and worked to ensure Serbian control of every aspect of life in the province. A Kosovar (Albanian) resistance movement appeared. In 1991 a Kosovo parliament declared the independence of the province. Up to 1995, however, both the Kosovars and the Serbs avoided direct confrontation. In the meantime, the Kosovo Liberation Army (KLA) formed. The Dayton Agreement, which seemed to give Milosovec a free hand in Kosovo, galvanized the Kosovar resistance.

Ethnic Albanians fleeing Pec, in western Kosovo, ride in trailers towed by tractors towards the Kosovo-Montenegro border, 1999. AP/Wide World/David Brauchli.

In 1996 the KLA went on the offensive. In response, in 1998 Milosovec stepped up the level of military actions, authorizing the use of helicopter gunships and armored personnel carriers against civilian targets and destroying homes and villages. This, in turn, radicalized the Kosovars.

The international community faced a dilemma. Although the KLA had initially been seen as terrorists, Serbian reprisals had created a humanitarian crisis that appeared patterned after Serbian ethnic cleansing campaigns in Bosnia. The United States and western European countries threatened the Serbs with NATO air strikes and compelled them and the Kosovars to negotiate at Rambouillet, outside Paris, in February 1999. The Kosovars eventually agreed to a plan that would have brought NATO peacekeepers to Kosovo and forced Serbian troops to leave. Kosovo would have remained in the truncated Federal Republic of Yugoslavia as an autonomous province. The Serbs refused to sign.

NATO began bombing on March 24, 1999. Even before the bombs began to fall, the Serbs had embarked on a massive campaign of ethnic cleansing. Operation Horseshoe was designed to drive all the Kosovars from the province. By June 10, when NATO ended the bombing campaign, nearly 900,000 Kosovars, about half the Albanian population of Kosovo had fled the province. The others were on the run within the province.

Once NATO began the campaign, it had to continue to victory or lose all credibility. Milosovec also faced a difficult decision. On the one hand, Serbian troops could only be dislodged by ground troops, which NATO was reluctant to introduce. On the other, NATO had not called off the air strikes and Russia had failed to stop them. The situation in Serbia itself was rapidly deteriorating. On June 10 Milosovec agreed to withdraw troops from Kosovo in return for an end to the bombing. He also agreed to the introduction of a NATO peacekeeping force. In the aftermath of the war, Kosovo Serbs became the victims. Nearly 200,000 fled the province by October.

Milosovec himself became a casualty of the Kosovo war. In September 1999 he failed to gain reelection as president. When he tried to falsify the results of his election, his former allies deserted him. Nearly two years later, on June 29, 2001, the Serbian government turned him over to the International Criminal Tribunal in the Hague to be tried for war crimes and crimes against humanity. He is presently still on trial.

Despite massive efforts by NATO and international aid organizations in Bosnia and Kosovo, the outlook is not good. As one author describes it, "Bosnia and Kosovo are NATO protectorates, troubled outposts on the margins of Europe."[1] Croatia and Serbia have an uneasy peace. Whether

1 William I. Hitchcock, *The Struggle for Europe: The Turbulent History of a Divided Continent, 1945–2002*, p. 408.

ethnic rivalries, stirred up once again by the demagoguery of ambitious and unscrupulous politicians, can be dampened is an open question for the twenty-first century.

The European Union

Before the revolutions of 1989, many observers of the European scene had predicted the 1990s would be the decade of the European Community. The 1985 report of the Delors Commission (Jacques Delors [1925–], a leading official in the European Community, president in 1990) called for the removal of all physical, technical, and fiscal barriers to the free movement of capital, goods, and people. This would create a single European market. The Single European Act (SEA-1986) legislated the necessary steps for implementing the report. By the time SEA went into effect, January 1, 1993, German unification and other changes in eastern and central Europe placed the European Union (EU—the new title for the EC) in somewhat of a quandary. Should it deepen, that is, become more fully integrated by pursuing a common fiscal policy and even a common foreign policy, or should it widen by taking in not only some of the old European Free Trade Association (EFTA) states but also some of the new democracies in eastern and central Europe?

Rather typically, the EU has tried to do both. Meeting in Maastricht, the Netherlands, in December 1991, what then was still the EC put together a treaty (Treaty on Economic and Monetary Union or "Maastricht Treaty") calling for further radical changes, among them a single European currency and a common foreign policy. The idea of a common foreign policy floundered on the inability of the EC to meet the Yugoslav crisis effectively. The idea of a single European currency, the Euro, was meant in part to integrate Germany even more tightly into the European framework. Those states wishing to join the monetary union had to meet a number of fiscal criteria, among them low inflation, budget deficits no more than 3 percent of Gross Domestic Product (GDP), and a government debt less than 60 percent of GDP. Progress toward these and other goals slowed in 1992–1993 as the result of an economic slowdown. In large part, the slowdown reflected soaring interest rates caused by Germany borrowing heavily to fund the reconstruction of the former East Germany. Europe began to pull out of the recession in 1994. In December 1995 the new currency received a name, the Euro. In 1998 eleven of the fifteen members (Austria, Sweden, and Finland had joined in 1995) met the criteria for monetary union. Denmark, Britain, and Sweden had opted out earlier, and Greece failed to meet the criteria. In June 1998 the European Central Bank began operation. In 1999 the EU began using the Euro in business transactions. Finally, on January 1, 2002, the Euro became the sole currency of twelve EU states (Greece qualified for membership in 2001).

In 2004 the EU took in ten new members: Cyprus, the Czech Republic, Estonia, Hungary, Latvia, Lithuania, Malta, Poland, Slovakia, and Slovenia. It is expected that Bulgaria and Romania will join in 2007. Croatia is another candidate for membership. Finally, Turkey, seemingly a perpetual candidate, remains in limbo. Although it is a member of NATO, it has not been able to move very close to membership in the EU. While there are many obstacles in the way of membership for Turkey, the key issue may be that its population is Muslim.

As the EU nears the fiftieth anniversary of its founding in 2007, it can be viewed as the greatest European achievement of a century generally characterized by war, genocide, and revolution. Like any institution, the EU is flawed and in need of a series of reforms, yet it is, all in all, a remarkable accomplishment.

After the Warsaw Treaty Organization (WTO) dissolved in 1991, it was difficult to justify the continued existence of NATO. Efforts to expand NATO to take in some of the former members of the WTO met with stiff Russian resistance. The United States proposed a "Partnership for Peace" which would allow Russia some participation in NATO affairs and in other ways ease concerns. Poland, the Czech Republic, and Hungary joined NATO in 1999. In 2004 seven more countries joined NATO: Bulgaria, Estonia, Latvia, Lithuania, Romania, Slovakia, and Slovenia. Participating in NATO's Membership Action Plan (MAP) as candidates are Albania, Croatia, and the Republic of Macedonia.

NATO in the 1990s was heavily involved first in peacekeeping in Bosnia, then the bombing campaign in Kosovo and Serbia and the followup peacekeeping mission in Kosovo. Among other issues, NATO is discussing the possibility of "out of area" operations, that is, peacekeeping missions outside the boundaries of Europe. One area that has been suggested is Iraq.

The Conference on Security and Cooperation in Europe (CSCE), an organization formed to monitor the Helsinki Accords (1975), was viewed early in the 1990s as an organization that might replace both WTO and NATO. Renamed the Organization for Security and Cooperation in Europe, it has been little more than an observer of developments during the decade. Almost totally lacking in infrastructure and experience, it is not viewed as an adequate substitute for NATO. The latter, originally designed as a Western military alliance to "contain" the Soviet Union during the Cold War, has found a new role as a European peacekeeping force in the new system of international relations.

Table 12.1   European Economic Community*

1957	Treaty of Rome signed by original six member nations: Belgium, Federal Republic of Germany, France, Italy, Luxembourg, and the Netherlands
1967	EEC merged with the European Coal and Steel Community (1951) and EURATOM (1957) to become the European Community (EC)
1973	Denmark, Republic of Ireland, and United Kingdom joined the EC
1981	Greece joined
1986	Portugal and Spain joined
	Single European Act passed
1992	Treaty on the European Union (Maastricht Treaty) called for movement toward economic and monetary union and intergovernmental cooperation in some areas
1993	EU formally in existence
1995	Austria, Finland, and Sweden joined the EU
1999	Euro introduced for business transactions
2002	Euro became the sole currency of twelve of the fifteen members of the EU (Denmark, Sweden, and the United Kingdom opted out of the monetary union)
2004	Ten new members joined: Cyprus, the Czech Republic, Estonia, Hungary, Latvia, Lithuania, Malta, Poland, Slovakia, and Slovenia

* The European Economic Community became part of the European Community in 1967. In 1993 the official title changed to the European Union.

The Revival of Terrorism

On September 11, 2001 (9/11), terrorists sponsored by Al-Qaeda[2] flew two commercial airliners into the twin towers of New York's World Trade Center. Another hijacked airliner flew into the Pentagon and a fourth crashed in a field in Pennsylvania. These horrific attacks followed a decade of terrorist actions directed against the United States including, among

2 Al-Qaeda (Arabic for "the base") is an international terrorist network. It works to end western influence in Muslim countries and to create fundamentalist Islamic governments. It grew out of U.S.-sponsored efforts to recruit and train anti-Soviet *mujahedeen*, holy warriors, in the 1980s in Afghanistan.

others, the truck bombing of the World Trade Center in 1993, an attack on American troops in Saudi Arabia in 1996, attacks on American embassies in Africa in 1998, and the attack on the U.S.S. Cole in 2000.

The American government reacted to 9/11 by first demanding that the Taliban government in Afghanistan surrender Osama Bin Laden (1955?–), thought to be the mastermind behind 9/11. When the Taliban refused to do so, the United States and its allies, including Afghan groups already fighting the Taliban, invaded the country and destroyed the Taliban government. The invasion forces failed, however, to find Bin Laden.

In 2003 the United States, together with its chief ally, Britain, and several other smaller countries, decided to invade Iraq. In effect, this was a continuation of the First Gulf War ("Desert Storm," 1991). Critics wondered what the invasion of Iraq had to do with the war on terrorism. In particular, France, Germany, and the Russian Republic opposed the American effort. Although the invasion was a success militarily, no weapons of mass destruction (WMDs) were found. Close ties between Saddam Hussein (1937–) and Al-Qaeda could not be established. It was, however, established that Saddam Hussein had not lent support to the attacks on September 11, 2001.

The failure to agree on steps to be taken in the war on terrorism is only one of a series of disagreements between the United States and its European allies. The United States, particularly under the administration of George W. Bush (1946–), had opted in several cases to pursue a unilateral policy or to cooperate only with those countries that were willing to follow its lead. Thus, the United States refused to follow Europe in its decision to work toward fulfilling the Kyoto Treaty (1997) on global warming. In similar fashion, the United States declined to support the World Criminal Court and several other institutions designed to increase international cooperation. The one body the United States has strongly supported, the World Trade Organization (WTO), has been strongly criticized by many Europeans as an important factor in causing poverty in some parts of the world. It is no small irony that the United States and many of its old European friends find themselves disagreeing on a large number of issues just as the sixtieth anniversaries of so many great examples of wartime and postwar Atlantic cooperation take place.

Conclusion

With the growth of both the EU and NATO, Europe is now more homogenous than it has been in centuries. Although many complain that distinctive cultures are in danger of being destroyed, it has achieved great economic and cultural power and plays a significant role in world affairs.

Nationalism, ethnic rivalries, and right-wing extremism more generally continue to cause problems, but Europe has accomplished a great deal in dampening these threats. Individual European countries have taken the lead in dealing with environmental problems, with alternative energy possibilities, and with a variety of social problems. At the same time, Europe continues to look to the rest of the world, especially to former colonies but also to other developing areas. While its current relationship to the United States is mixed, it has a long tradition of cooperation and alliance on which to fall back. The relationship with the Russian Republic is also in need of improvement and there European countries have less to work with but perhaps even more reason to want to work out a better relationship. Europe closed out the twentieth century and began the new century on a positive note. No longer the center of world affairs, as it was in 1900, it is nevertheless far better off in nearly every respect. Its prospects in the twenty-first century are excellent.

Suggested Books and Films

William I. Hitchcock, *The Struggle in Europe: The Turbulent History of a Divided Continent, 1945–2002* (2003). First-rate discussion of postwar Europe.

Tim Judah, *The Serbs: History, Myth, and the Destruction of Yugoslavia* (2000). Excellent discussion of a complicated situation.

Misha Glenny, *The Fall of Yugoslavia: The Third Balkan War* (1996), 3rd rev. ed. A reliable guide to the tangled history of the former Yugoslavia.

Marshall I. Goldman, *Lost Opportunity: Why Economic Reforms in Russia Have Not Worked* (1994). An excellent book by America's leading expert on the Soviet economy.

Noel Malcolm, *Kosovo: A Short History* (1999). Good background.

David Remnick, *Resurrection: The Struggle for a New Russia* (1998). Yeltsin's Russia by an astute and well-informed journalist.

George Ross, *Jacques Delors and European Integration* (1995). A helpful discussion of a very important topic.

Lilia Shevtsova, *Putin's Russia* (2003). A careful examination of Russia in the twenty-first century.

"Blood and Belonging," 1993, Michael Ignatieff. A six-part video series dealing with nationalism and right-wing extremism in Yugoslavia, Germany, Ukraine, Northern Ireland, and two areas outside Europe. Also available in book form.

Appendix I:
Additional Sources

Most historians, by definition, work at some remove from the present. The historian of the twentieth century, however, must try to understand and assess not only the events of the last few years but also present-day situations. We cannot leave this important task to political scientists, sociologists and others with the excuse that "it isn't history yet."

The following are a few useful items among the wealth of material available.

Several books should be mentioned in addition to those cited in the "Suggested Books and Films" for Chapter 12.

First, a number of fine textbooks have been published on Europe in this century. Most are far longer than our book and hence more detailed. Among the very best is by Robert O. Paxton, *Europe in the Twentieth Century,* fourth edition (2004). See also two useful world history texts: David Reynolds, *One World Divisible: A Global History since 1945* (2000); and Michael H. Hunt, *The World Transformed: 1945 to the Present* (2004). A unique and very useful history of the twentieth century is *Something New Under the Sun: An Environmental History* (2000) by J. R. McNeill. Finally, see Timothy Marton Ash, *History of the Present: Essays, Sketches, and Dispatches from Europe in the 1990s* (2000), a collection of pieces by an astute observer of the European scene. Another fine text, this on Europe after World War II, is by J. Robert Wegs and Robert Ladrech, *Europe since 1945: A Concise History,* fourth edition (1996).

A number of reference books are available and will help to place the recent past and the present in a wider perspective.

Alan Bullock et al., eds. *The Norton Dictionary of Modern Thought,* third edition (1999).

265

Alan Bullock and R. B. Woodings, *Twentieth-Century Culture: A Biographical Companion* (1984).
Joel Krieger, ed., *The Oxford Companion to Politics of the World,* second edition, (2001).
Cathal J. Nolan, ed., *The Longman Guide to World Affairs* (1995).
Dan Smith, ed., *The State of the World Atlas* (1999).
Peter Teed, ed., *A Dictionary of Twentieth-Century History, 1914–1990* (1992).

Several yearbooks and annuals are useful sources.

The Annual Register: A Record of World Events (annual edition).
The Europa World Year Book (annual edition; now divided into volume 1, International Organizations and Countries A–J, and volume 2, Countries K–Z).
Facts on File (appears weekly; compiled in annual volumes).
Political Handbook of the World (annual edition).
The Statesman's Year-Book (annual edition).
State of the World (annual edition).

Special mention should be made of *Current History,* which has long published issues on European topics. See also *Current History*'s website. http://www.currenthistory.com.

A number of periodicals offer timely coverage of contemporary affairs. Among the best are:

Daedalus, occasional special issues on European topics [see, for example, "A New Europe for the Old," summer 1997].
The Economist (Britain), excellent coverage of European developments, especially of the European Union.
Foreign Affairs often includes articles by government officials and other newsmakers.
The New York Review of Books, thoughtful essays by some of the best historians and observers of the European scene.
The New York Times Magazine [Sunday edition], interesting and useful articles on European topics.
The New Yorker, wonderful reporting of European affairs by Jane Kramer and David Remnick, among others.

Websites

Websites for history, as for virtually any other subject, exist in the thousands. Here are a few of the best sites:

"Index of Resources for Historians" (University of Kansas: http://www.ukans.edu/history

"Horus" (University of California-Riverside): http://www.ucr.edu/h-gig

Three large sources for texts and documents contain much that will be useful in the study of Europe in the twentieth century.

"Internet Modern History Sourcebook" (Fordham University): http://www.fordham.edu/halsall/mod/modsbook.html

"EuroDocs: Primary Historical Documents for Western Europe" (Brigham Young University): http://library.byu.edu/~rdh/eurodocs

"Public Broadcasting System," http://www.pbs.org

"Texts and Documents: Europe" (Hanover College): http://history.hanover.edu/europe.htm#modern

Videotapes, DVDs, and CD-ROMs

Videotapes and, increasingly, DVDs, are good sources for the study of history. Numerous catalogs are available. Reference librarians at public and school libraries can usually locate relevant videotapes or DVDs. A large number of quite excellent CD-ROMs on historical subjects are also now available.

Appendix II:

THE TWENTIETH CENTURY produced a bewildering array of abbreviations and acronyms for the many political parties, committees, organizations, and institutions that have appeared over the years. No one can hope to remember all the relevant short forms used in European history in this century. The two alphabetical lists set out below should help, however, in quickly determining what a set of initials stands for or how the name of a particular institution is commonly abbreviated. In some cases, the initials will not correspond to the English version of the name. This is because the initials are taken from the name as it appears in the language of the country. For example, the German National Socialist Workers' Party is abbreviated NSDAP, which stands for *National*sozialistische *D*eutsche Arbeiter*p*artei.

Belgium, Netherlands, Luxembourg	BENELUX
British Union of Fascists	BUF
Cable News Network	CNN
Christian Democratic Party (Italy)	DC
Christian Democratic Union (West Germany; Germany)	CDU
Committee for the Defense of the Workers (Poland)	KOR
Committee on European Cooperation and Security (*See also* Conference on Security and Cooperation in Europe)	CECS
Commonwealth of Independent States (Former USSR)	CIS
Communist Information Bureau	COMINFORM
Communist International (Third International)	COMINTERN
Communist Party (Germany)	KPD
Communist Party (Italy)	PCI

Communist Party (Soviet Union)	CPSU
Conference on Security and Cooperation in Europe (*See also* the Organization for Security and Cooperation in Europe)	CSCE
Council for Mutual Economic Assistance	COMECON
East Germany (German Democratic Republic)	GDR
European Coal and Steel Community	ECSC
European Community (*See also* European Economic Community; European Union)	EC
European Defense Community	EDC
European Economic Community (*See also* European Community, European Union)	EEC
European Free Trade Association	EFTA
European Monetary System	EMS
European Recovery Program (Marshall Plan)	ERP
Federal Republic of Germany (West Germany)	FRG
Geheime Staatspolizei (Secret Police in Nazi Germany)	GESTAPO
German Democratic Republic (East Germany)	GDR
German National Socialist Workers' Party (Nazis)	NSDAP
German Social Democratic Party	SPD
Group of Seven (leading industrial democracies)	G-7
Gross Domestic Product	GDP
Independent Social Democratic Party of Germany	USPD
Kosovo Liberation Army	KLA
Kriegsrohstoffabteilung (War Raw Materials Administration)	KRA
League of Communists of Yugoslavia	LCY
Main Administration of Corrective Labor Camps (USSR)	GULAG
New Economic Policy	NEP
North Atlantic Treaty Organization	NATO
Organization for Economic Cooperation and Development	OECD
Organization of European Economic Cooperation	OEEC
Organization for Security and Cooperation in Europe	OSCE
Party of Democratic Socialism (formerly the Socialist Unity Party)	PDS
Polish Socialist Workers Party	RPPS
Popular Republican Movement (France)	MRP
Royal Air Force (United Kingdom)	RAF

Russian Social Democratic Labor Party (Bolsheviks; Mensheviks)	RSDLP
Schutzstaffel (Protective detachment— Nazi organization)	SS
Secret police (East Germany)	STASI
Single European Act	SEA
Socialist Unity Party (East Germany)	SED
Socialist German Student Federation	SDS
Socialist Party (France)	SFIO
Socialist Revolutionaries (Russia)	SR
Soviet Secret Police (1935–1953)	NKVD
Soviet Secret Police (1953–1992)	KGB
State Defense Committee (Soviet Union)	GKO
Strategic Arms Limitations Talks/Treaty	SALT
Strategic Defense Initiative ("Star Wars")	SDI
Sturmabteilung (Stormtroopers—Nazi organization)	SA
Trades Union Council (United Kingdom)	TUC
Warsaw Treaty Organization	WTO
West Germany (Federal Republic of Germany)	FRG
World Trade Organization	WTO

BENELUX	Belgium, Netherlands, Luxembourg
BUF	British Union of Fascists
CDU	Christian Democratic Union (West Germany; Germany)
CESC	Committee on European Security and Cooperation (*See also* Conference on Security and Cooperation in Europe)
CIS	Commonwealth of Independent States (Former USSR)
CNN	Cable News Network
COMECON	Council for Mutual Economic Assistance
COMINFORM	Communist Information Bureau
COMINTERN	Communist International (Third International)
CPSU	Communist Party (Soviet Union)
CSCE	Conference on Security and Cooperation in Europe
DC	Christian Democratic Party (Italy)
EC	European Community (*See also* European Economic Community; European Union)
ECSC	European Coal and Steel Community

EDC	European Defense Community
EEC	European Economic Community (*See also* European Community, European Union)
EFTA	European Free Trade Association
EMS	European Monetary System
ERP	European Recovery Program (Marshall Plan)
FRG	Federal Republic of Germany (West Germany)
G-7	Group of Seven (leading industrial democracies)
GDP	Gross Domestic Product
GDR	East Germany (German Democratic Republic)
GESTAPO	*Geheime Staatspolizei* (Secret Police in Nazi Germany)
GKO	State Defense Committee (Soviet Union)
GULAG	Main Administration of Corrective Labor Camps (USSR)
KGB	Soviet Secret Police (1953–1992)
KLA	Kosovo Liberation Army
KOR	Committee for the Defense of the Workers (Poland)
KPD	Communist Party (Germany)
KRA	*Kriegsrohstoffabteilung* (War Raw Materials Administration)
LCY	League of Communists of Yugoslavia
MRP	Popular Republican Movement (France)
NATO	North Atlantic Treaty Organization
NEP	New Economic Policy
NKVD	Soviet Secret Police (1935–1953)
NSDAP	German National Socialist Workers' Party (Nazis)
OECD	Organization for Economic Cooperation and Development
OEEC	Organization of European Economic Cooperation
OSCE	Organization for Security and Cooperation in Europe
PCI	Communist Party (Italy)
PDS	Party of Democratic Socialism (formerly the Socialist Unity Party)

RAF	Royal Air Force (United Kingdom)
RSDLP	Russian Social Democratic Labor Party (Bolsheviks; Mensheviks)
SA	*Sturmabteilung* (Stormtroopers—Nazi organization)
SALT	Strategic Arms Limitations Talks/Treaty
SDI	Strategic Defense Initiative ("Star Wars")
SDS	Socialist German Student Federation
SEA	Single European Act
SED	Socialist Unity Party (East Germany)
SFIO	Socialist Party (France)
SPD	German Social Democratic Party
SR	Socialist Revolutionaries (Russia)
SS	*Schutzstaffel* (Protective detachment—Nazi organization)
STASI	Secret police (East Germany)
TUC	Trades Union Council (United Kingdom)
USPD	Independent Social Democratic Party of Germany
WTO	Warsaw Treaty Organization
WTO	World Trade Organization

Index

Twentieth-Century Europe: A Brief History, Second Edition
Developmental editor: Andrew J. Davidson
Copy editor and production editor: Lucy Herz
Proofreader: Claudia Siler
Indexer: Carolyn Sherayko
Cartographer: Jane Domier
Printer: Versa Press